TRADITION AND CHANGE
IN
PSYCHOANALYSIS

Books by Roy Schafer

Aspects of Internalization

A New Language for Psychoanalysis

Language and Insight: The Sigmund Freud Memorial
Lectures, 1975–1976, University College, London

Narrative Actions in Psychoanalysis: Narratives of Space
and Narratives of Time

The Analytic Attitude

Retelling a Life: Narration and Dialogue in Psychoanalysis

(Editor) The Contemporary Kleinians of London

Tradition and Change in Psychoanalysis

Roy Schafer

INTERNATIONAL UNIVERSITIES PRESS, INC.
MADISON, CONNECTICUT

Library of Congress Cataloging-in-Publication Data

Schafer, Roy.
    Tradition and change in psychoanalysis / Roy Schafer.
       p.   cm.
    Includes bibliographical references and index.
    ISBN 0-8236-6632-8
    1. Psychoanalysis—Philosophy. I. Title.
RC506.S2923   1996
616.89'17—dc21   96-46630
                                                        CIP

Manufactured in the United States of America

For my grandchildren

Contents

Preface

During the final decades of the twentieth century, psychoanalysis has undergone revolutionary changes. In important respects, theory has changed. Also changed greatly are some aspects of practice. Sometimes change in one has been closely tied to change in the other, either one following on the heels of the other, and sometimes these changes have seemed to go hand-in-hand. In each instance, the extent to which these two types of change are correlated has been the subject of continuing debate. The more significant debate, however, has been over whether some of these changes represent further development of basic psychoanalytic principles or abandonment of them. Equally significant is the debate over whether these basic principles were wrongly conceived in the realm of theory and either too narrowly or too vaguely conceived in the realm of technique. Whatever the case may be in each of these respects, the relation of change to tradition has remained a central concern in psychoanalysis. One finds that concern in publications, panel discussions at meetings, study groups, and the reflections of individual scholars and practitioners.

The essays gathered in this book represent my continuing participation in these debates. The reader will find in these pages spirited dissent from traditional views of the nature of *some* of Freud's contributions. With regard to the psychology of women and gender relations,

ix

the prevailing ideas of morality, and the place of values in analytic theory and practice, and the repudiation of the conceptual and technical contributions of Kleinian analysis to the entire discipline, I dissent from the position taken by many members of the ego psychological Freudian trend in psychoanalysis. Also, I raise questions about the conceptualization and analysis of emotion and other concepts.

Going beyond challenge, I offer what I regard as constructive suggestions regarding the possibility of alternatives. My guideline has been the idea of proposing something better, not necessarily opposed. For I have maintained a deep respect for contributions to the discipline made under the banner of tradition, and I have tried to show that respect in these same essays by sorting out what I see as strongest in these contributions, which is quite a lot, from what has come to seem to me and many others unduly confining, confusing, and self-contradictory. As a result, I have come to seem to many colleagues a maverick and to others too loyal or at least lacking the courage of my convictions.

For my part, I would put my position differently. As analysts do in clinical practice, I rely on the principle that there is bound to be continuity within change. Change is best approached as a matter of transformation. Consequently, we should think of ourselves as engaged in the study of transformations in theory and practice rather than radical discontinuities. For this reason, there cannot be manifestly different transformations that have destroyed completely traces of their common ancestry. Therefore, I believe that there is more than one psychoanalysis in this world, though the lines of their common descent are traceable. Appearances and claims notwithstanding, there have been no absolute breaks with the past.

In postmodern terms, one could say that those who proclaim radical emancipation from tradition and radical distinctions from other contemporary developments can still only conceive the new and argue for it by drawing on one common discourse. This is the discourse of the tradition that allegedly is being left behind. One must be drawing on it without being altogether locked up in it. Otherwise, no change could ever take place and no differences at all could develop. On this principle, change may be viewed as a retelling of the past, often with profound consequences that do not, however, obliterate the past. Here, the parallel to clinical psychoanalysis is so obvious that I need not dwell on it.

In this book I have assembled in one place and lightly edited a number of papers I have published since the appearance in 1992 of my previous book, *Retelling a Life*. Many of these papers have appeared in journals and edited books that are not widely read by psychoanalytic readers or not widely known among them. In these papers I develop a basic set of themes in a variety of contexts. I regard them as a family of essays that belong together in one place—call it a family reunion. I believe that when all are assembled in one place, they add to the force of each of them considered singly. I can only hope that in the end the reader will agree.

Acknowledgments

For her encouragement and her help in thinking through and editing each of this book's essays I am deeply grateful to my wife, Dr. Rita Frankiel. I owe a special debt to Dr. William Grossman for his interest and advice and also for the inspiration I draw from him as a model of high seriousness in approaching the numerous problems and opportunities in the realm of psychoanalytic discourse. My thanks to Mrs. Barbara B. Frank, especially, and also to Mrs. Victoria Wright for their capable secretarial help. Dr. Margaret Emery, Editor-in-chief of International Universities Press, ably guided this book toward publication.

Credits

The author gratefully acknowledges the following publishers for their kind permission to reprint the following papers.

Chapter 1 was originally published in the *International Journal of Psycho-Analysis* 76 (1995): 223–235. Copyright © 1995 Institute of Psycho-Analysis, London. Reprinted by permission.

Chapter 2 was originally published in the *International Journal of Psycho-Analysis* 74 (1993): 1023–1030. Copyright © 1993 Institute of Psycho-Analysis, London. Reprinted by permission.

Chapter 3 was originally published in *Psychiatry and the Humanities* 14 (1984): 1–21. Copyright © 1984 Johns Hopkins University Press. Reprinted by permission.

Chapter 4 was originally published in *Contemporary Freud—Turning Points and Critical Issues*, eds. J. S. Sandler, E. J. Person, and P. Fonagy. New Haven, CT: Yale University Press, 1993, pp. 75–95. Copyright © Yale University Press. Reprinted by permission.

Chapter 9 was originally published in the *Psychoanalytic Quarterly* 64 (1995): 496–516. Copyright © 1995 The Psychoanalytic Quarterly, Inc. Reprinted by permission.

Chapter 11 was originally published in the *Psychoanalytic Quarterly* 65 (1996): 236–253. Copyright © 1996 The Psychoanalytic Quarterly, Inc. Reprinted by permission.

Chapter 12 was originally published in *Psychoanalysis and Contemporary Thought* 17 (1994): 251–286. Copyright © 1994 International Universities Press, Inc. Reprinted by permission.

Part I

Changing Directions

In the five essays that make up Part I, I initiate my examination of tradition and change in psychoanalysis. Without extensive discussion conducted from one consistently maintained point of view, it is not possible to distinguish sharply the old that is old, the old that is still new, and the new. Psychoanalysis has never been characterized by uniform progress on all fronts. One of the great contributions of Heinz Hartmann, some of it worked out in collaboration with Ernst Kris and Rudolph M. Loewenstein, was his identifying the lack of coordination among Freud's theoretical propositions and his bravely attempting to remedy that problematic aspect of Freud's extraordinary legacy (Schafer, 1970). Hartmann saw that our self-understanding as analysts suffers and our work with patients is hampered when that coordination is lacking. Putting the matter broadly I would say that Hartmann shattered the smug illusion maintained by many others in his time that psychoanalysis can exist outside cultural, scientific, and professional history. And the fact is that since Hartmann's time psychoanalysis has continued to undergo change even while it retains its complex identity. It is especially from these efforts of Hartmann and his collaborators that there developed modern, systematic ego psychology.

It is fitting, therefore, to begin my examination with Hartmann's legacy and to trace his changing role during the recent decades of psychoanalytic history. In chapter 2 I then go on to describe what I accept as contemporary, significant, and beneficial changes in the epistemological and methodological underpinnings of psychoanalysis; there I also begin to illustrate some of the clinical consequences of these changes. After laying that groundwork I begin to summarize some of the main changes that have been taking place in the psychoanalytic psychology of women, first in chapter 3, which is devoted to an analysis of discourse on this important subject and then, in two chapters on two of Freud's classic approaches to this topic: his remarks on transference love (1915a) and his clinical report on Elisabeth von R. in the *Studies on Hysteria* (1893–1895). In these three chapters I try to sort out biased discourse from other discourse that appears to be free of patriarchal and authoritarian leanings and therefore more properly designated psychoanalytic (see in this regard, Grossman and Kaplan [1988]). There too I tie my discussion to practice by illustrating how Freud's remarks and clinical material might be approached today.

The biases I single out appear to me to have been lodged in the cultural and professional mores prevailing during Freud's early productive years. In this regard, I offer a critique of Freud as not so much an individual as a representative figure of his era who was, however, introducing revolutionary change at the same time. Throughout Part I and also in Part III where I return to some of these themes, my discussion has been guided by the premise that there can be no value-free exploration and exposition of psychoanalytic assumptions, concepts, methods, and apparently purely objective, empirical reports—my own included. I believe this premise is useful in studying any subject matter. My reasoning on this matter pervades these first five chapters and all the others that follow.

I also premise the inevitable presence of pluralistic tendencies in psychoanalysis. I believe that it is pointless either to condemn or to recommend these pluralistic tendencies, for they have always been part of the history of psychoanalysis. This we can see at the very start in the divergent views Breuer and Freud presented of the same material in the *Studies on Hysteria* (1893–1895). I do, however, advocate close study of these pluralistic tendencies and their consequences in promoting competing schools of thought as well as many versions of eclecticism. As before (1983, 1992) I try in this book to contribute to this study, which I have called comparative analysis (1984).

1

In the Wake of Heinz Hartmann

This will be an investigation of continuity within change during the recent history of psychoanalysis. Very much like clinical psychoanalysis, an investigation of this sort is aimed to show how the conflictual past lives on in the present in the form of fragmentation, inconsistency, self-contradiction, and undeveloped germs of ideas, as well as in transformations and changes of function. Many of these are unforeseen and some are even unwanted, but, however that may be, they are all amenable to characterization as continuous growth in at least some of their aspects.

The specific change within continuity on which I shall focus is the continuing relevance of Heinz Hartmann's thought to these major currents of contemporary change in psychoanalysis that seem to diverge greatly from all that he apparently stood for. It is, I think, important to single out Hartmann because, despite his once dominant position within the United States, over the past twenty-five years there seems to have occurred a great falling off of attention to his work. Even the attitude of

This chapter was originally presented as the 1993 Heinz Hartmann Award Lecture, and was delivered at the New York Psychoanalytic Society and Institute, November 9, 1993.

I want to thank Dr. William Grossman for his helpful criticisms and clarifications while I was preparing this essay.

some or perhaps many mainstream analysts toward his influence has changed, so that I have heard it said among them, and without dissent, that his work has had an "unfortunate" impact on psychoanalysis.

One might want to ascribe some of this change of evaluation to the tendency that I believe to be prevalent, especially on the European continent, perhaps most of all in France, to debunk adaptational theory in general and ego psychology in particular, and, with them, Hartmann as the chief villain (see, for example, the interchange between André Green [1991, 1992] and me [1992b,c]). The increasing interest of United States analysts in British and continental contributions to psychoanalysis may already have been based in part on this debunking attitude; perhaps it even required it for moral support in undertaking these new developments.

It will serve as a useful introduction to our topic to reflect on this negative attitude toward Hartmann's contributions. The problem is that it rests on reading "adaptation" to mean "conformity" or "superficial adjustment," and reading "ego psychology" to mean a "psychology of consciousness"; also, viewing all such theorizing as sterile, abstruse formalism. But this reading is a poor one, for what is overlooked are a number of important aspects of the work of Hartmann (1939, 1960, 1964), his noted colleagues, Kris (1975) and Loewenstein (1982), their joint work (1964), and the work of many others who have followed them. This reading even misrepresents Freud, and it does so through splitting and denial, for there can be no doubt that Freud was deeply invested during his last years in developing structural theory in general and ego theory in particular (see, for example, his *New Introductory Lectures* [1933], his paper on termination [1937a], and his "Outline" [1940]). Freud did not see this investment as requiring a departure from continuing interest in drives and unconscious mental processes as well as interest in daily clinical work, nor did those who followed him, Hartmann and his colleagues among them.

In all spheres of ego psychological interest, nothing is required to be said that diminishes the traditional analytic emphasis on drives and drive derivatives, the pleasure principle, unconscious fantasy, unconscious conflict, primitive morality, infantile danger situations, or transference. Instead, one aims to develop further the context for each of these dynamic concepts. The theory is designed to encompass the total mind and not just its damaged aspects and its primitive, id or primary process aspects. Moreover, by theorizing the mature, the rational, the stable, and the modulated, the ego psychologists have established that primitive and damaged must be defined by the otherness of the nonprimitive and the "normal." In this, they have been participating actively in developing contemporary modes of thought about human identity and existence. Thus, not only is their ego psychology a matter of necessary theoretical working through, it contributes as well to working through in clinical practice. Clinical values have not been neglected. Although these values were more evident in the great clinical papers of Kris and Loewenstein, they were, I believe, ever present in Hartmann's mind as he forged ahead.

Especially to be emphasized is the critics' glaring neglect of Hartmann's (1939) fundamental point that adaptation includes "fitting in" as only one possibility. This approach emphasizes equally making efforts to change one's situation or leaving that situation for others. Here there is no unreflective emphasis on adjustment through conformity. Plenty of room is left for adaptive nonconformity. Furthermore, there is little to support the view that some distinctively American superficializing tendency was at work in the ego psychology that developed around Hartmann. Hartmann, Kris, Loewenstein, Robert Waelder, Edith Jacobson, Annie Reich, Kurt Eissler, and others were mature European analysts before they came to the United States, and it is wild analysis to attribute to them exclusively, as has been done, the desperate conformity of frightened refugees. Critical readings do vary, of course, but some go too far astray to be of value, although they deserve the interest of intellectual historians. There is always a point beyond which, by current consensus, certain readings may be designated as unsound. Dismissive readings of Hartmann are unsound.

These brief remarks on misreading have been aimed at clearing away some of the fog that has obscured Hartmann's contributions. Hartmann does, of course, continue to command much mainstream respect, a fact that may be attributed to the continuing benefits he bestowed on psychoanalytic discussion through the stewardly role he played so brilliantly and with so much discipline. For many analysts his ideas still define a center for coherent theoretical discourse. It must also be recognized, however, that his ground-breaking ideas on the self and its object relatedness from the beginning contributed greatly to subsequent theoretical and clinical change.

In my 1970 study of Hartmann's monumental contribution, I pointed out that, in addition to a stewardly or conservative side, he also had a radical side, and it is principally to this radical side that I attribute the *manifest* waning of his influence. I say "manifest" because, as I shall try to show, that influence lives on as latent content in seemingly alien contemporary trends. This latent continuity within manifest discontinuity may be discerned specifically in contemporary emphases on dialogue and intersubjectivity; emphases that are not intrinsically alien to adaptational thought. But I shall also try to show that newer and valuable attempts at independent systematic psychoanalytic thought must be regarded as incomplete insofar as they do not take into account the other side of Hartmann's contributions: his structural, ego-centered formulations. These new and significant possibilities for conceptualization in clinical work do not in themselves constitute a balanced or rounded theory or a cluster of complementary theories (about which, more later). On my reading of him, Hartmann would have agreed with this point. At least, he would have been interested in and responsive to these recent trends, even if skeptical, and as usual alert to whatever is *inexact* in them (to use a term he favored).

I want next to review briefly how Hartmann appeared to me in my earlier studies of his work (1968, 1970, 1976). I argued then that the key to his thought was his having taken as his foundation the field-theoretical biological concept of adaptation. In 1939, field theory was already very much in the air. The specific concept of adaptation had aroused much interest in biology and had already been developed extensively during the earlier decades of the century. Taking adaptation as his foundational concept, Hartmann (sometimes with coworkers) critiqued, refined, and extended Freud's major concepts and propositions. He argued the necessity of viewing the mental apparatus as always already existing in the biological field of organism and environment, though at first perhaps not yet differentiated, just as, to begin with, and as Freud (1937a) had already suggested, the ego and the id exist as potentials that are not yet differentiated. This adaptational field is characterized by mutual preadaptedness and ongoing adaptiveness. Although distinguishable for purposes of discussion, organism and environment make up a unity, for each implies the other.

In making this move, Hartmann was responding in part to the lack of thorough systematization in Freud's contributions. In particular,

Freud's development of dynamic propositions had far outstripped that pertaining to structure and psychoeconomics. Therefore, much of Hartmann's thinking was devoted to detailing the ego's complex relations to the id, superego, and external reality, and also the theory of transformations of drive energy into energy needed by the ego to do its various jobs, and then, later on, needed by the superego, too.

The structural and psychoeconomic emphases came together in Hartmann's theorizing of the ego as the organ of adaptation and of its ego functions characterized by their greater or lesser autonomy from drives. It is not always recognized that any theory of developed minds that rests on drive theory requires concepts of relative autonomy and neutralization of drive energies. Hartmann went on to differentiate the reality principle into its broad adaptive sense and its narrow familiar sense of delay, thought, and reality testing. Additionally, he gave a coherent account of the formation of psychic structure during the course of development, and he traced the vicissitudes and uses of aggressive energy as well as libidinal energy in all of these transformations. Sublimation, rational action, and reality relations also had to be rethought, as a result of which there was stimulated what Kris called a "new consideration of the environment" and a "new environmentalism" (Kris, 1975). What was new about this consideration was its being given a place within traditional metapsychology, for trends away from the Freudian tradition, such as the interpersonal, had already been developing environmental emphases of another sort. It was Hartmann's work, often mediated by Kris, that was to play an important role as time went on in legitimizing, among other things, the direct psychoanalytic study of child development within the dynamic field constituted by parents and child, but most of all by mother and child.

These theoretical and empirical moves were inevitable consequences of Hartmann's having recognized that all of psychoanalytic theory had to be situated in the context of modern adaptational biology. Other consequences of this move are too important to be left unmentioned here. Most of all, the psychology and metapsychology of ego functions had to be greatly extended. Therefore, perceiving, remembering, acquiring language and engaging in communication, creating and experiencing aesthetic pleasure, arriving at interpretation and insight, and much more, all had to be formulated in structural and energic terms; all this also had to be formulated in terms of the *intra*systemic problems of organization that were consequences of change and development. It was in these explorations that Kris and Loewenstein made some of their most notable contributions.

Inevitably, the requisite theorizing became quite complex at times. Some colleagues were willing to follow Hartmann only so far in this direction. They would begin to speak of his having become "too abstract" or "too theoretical" (whatever these words mean) and in any case too remote from practice. Nevertheless, these critics continued to extol the close ties of theory to practice. In so doing, they were indicating that they preferred an incomplete, fuzzy, or in some respects even self-contradictory theory to Hartmann's disciplined, thorough, elegant, and demanding working through of the basic theoretical ideas already laid down by Freud. Notwithstanding their hesitation, however, in their practices these analysts did adopt many aspects of the ego psychology worked out by Hartmann and his close coworkers. One can see this in the ever finer phenomenology of ego functioning characterizing psychoanalytic presentations: representations of ego functioning both stable and in flux, both infantile and mature, and adaptive as well as defensive and wish-fulfilling. It was as if within psychoanalysis a recognition had developed that paralleled what the architect Mies van der Rohe once said: "God is in the details."

It was no longer enough to be attentive to the universal unconscious dynamics or the id, the compromise formations expressing impulse versus defense, and the embodiment of these factors in character. The fine details of reality relations, self and object representations, ideals, affect signals, and countertransference became more prominent. Far from being superficial, as the critics of this ego psychological development seemed to imply, this was the way clinical analysts learned to work through basic conflicts effectively.

This development was sparked by Hartmann's having taken it upon himself to bring to bear on psychoanalytic theorizing a broader intellectual outlook than Freud had used. Certainly, psychoanalysis was a radically new development, but just as certainly it had come into being within the long tradition of humanistic and scientific thought, so that, sooner or later, to do itself justice it would have to situate itself securely within that long tradition. Inevitably, the time comes when disinterested scholarship situates all works of greatness or genius within history. For the lone worker cannot conquer a tradition; he or she can only modify it in significantly new ways. Self-origination is a fantasy.

In making his own demonstration of continuity within change, Hartmann showed that he would not allow his obviously unshakable allegiance to Freud's psychoanalysis to limit his perspective. He was sophisticated enough to maintain the position of a detached meta-theorist demonstrating that, in order rationally to formulate, integrate, and amplify the concepts and propositions of any new discipline, one must be standing somewhere, one must have a vantage-point, a broad set of assumptions, and an organized methodology as well as an over-arching perspective, all rooted in the history of ideas. Disciplines have genealogies, so do concepts. Adaptation has its genealogy, too, much of it in Freud, as we can see particularly in his major paper of 1911, "Formulations on the Two Principles of Mental Functioning." But concepts also have their problematic consequences, and it is to these consequences of Hartmann's contributions that I shall turn next.

Earlier I mentioned Hartmann's conservative bent. I believe it was this bent that held his theoretical powers in check even as he was moving forward. For, as I shall argue, he did not fully develop his biologically conceived, preadapted and mutually adaptive schema of the organism in its environment. That schema must lead to the development of a version of psychoanalysis featuring dialogue and intersubjectivity. Hartmann never went that far in his writings. Either he could not see this theoretical consequence or he deliberately drew back from it. However that may be, any cursory review of contemporary psychoanalytic publications will show that dialogue and intersubjectivity have been moving to the center of psychoanalytic interest. These two organizing ideas come in different versions, but one way or another they pervade current thinking.

To put it briefly, "dialogue" conveys the idea that in the course of psychoanalysis the understandings and the changes that take place can only come about through an evolving dialogue between analyst and analysand; in other words, the definition and reshaping of the self and other only take place in verbal and nonverbal dialogue. And "intersubjectivity" conveys the embeddedness of each person's cognitive and emotional position and his or her dialogic orientation in so-called real or imagined relations with others.

Thus, in this shift of orientation, theory must constantly deal with more than the self and the other, it must focus on the self *in* the other, *by* the other, *for* the other, and likewise the other in relation to the self. In this view, language is not viewed as a tool of thought, but as constitutive of thought itself. Although seeds of this development can be found scattered throughout Freud's writings and the writings of Hartmann and his coworkers, they became far more important, mostly later on, in the work of such quite varied thinkers as Sullivan, Melanie Klein, Fairbairn, Winnicott, Erikson, Kohut, Loewald, Leo Stone, and those who in recent years have followed in their wake, among them, Gill, Greenberg, Mitchell, Hoffman, Lichtenberg, Stolorow, and Poland.

Before getting into these new trends in a concrete way, it will be necessary, even if at times difficult, to pause over a number of epistemological and methodological implications of these trends; otherwise it will be difficult to grasp what these trends are all about.

The first proposition to consider is that it makes no sense to speak of identity without affirming otherness, even if only implicitly. In saying, "It is this," one is simultaneously affirming, "It is not that." Thus, a "this" *and* a "that" must be assumed before one can advance propositions that make any sense at all. Identity depends on difference: that is one way in which this matter has been put and studied, particularly since the time of the linguist de Saussure. Consequently, in the realm of psychology, discussion of any one individual necessarily implies the existence of other individuals. Just how these others matter and the degree to which they matter at any given time will be both variable and debatable, and, expectably, these very questions have become lodged in the center of psychoanalytic controversy. Nevertheless, each and every point of view necessarily confronts the idea that self and other, or ego and object, always imply one another. There can be no independent psychology of characteristics of either member of these pairs. Hartmann's conceptualization of adaptation requires this changed perspective.

If, however, we look closely at the Freud–Hartmann conception of the psychoanalytic method, on which everything depends, we can see that, at bottom, it is not primarily field-theoretical in the required way. Instead, it features an independent psychology of the self and the other. It presents as an ideal and as a necessary assumption for clinical and theoretical discourse an autonomous, separate, objective observer observing an analysand. That's where psychoanalysis starts and ends. The analysand is presented as a specimen object to be studied in and of itself and not as an influential party to an evolving, jointly shaped dialogue, verbal and nonverbal. The analysand is not presented as one person who is both defining and being defined by another. Clearly, certain intersubjective processes, such as unconscious communication in relation to the transference, are acknowledged, but essentially they are not made central to the general theory. Rather they remain subject matter for the detached observer, specifically the analyst.

That Hartmann was being held back he made evident when, in his 1960 monograph *Psychoanalysis and Moral Values*, he referred to the practice of psychoanalysis as a technology. The word *technology* was not meant to convey that the analyst should lack all feeling or "humanness"; it was meant to underscore the value of the analyst's also maintaining the posture of an utterly detached observer. "Technology" cancels out the analyst's role in defining and shaping the phenomena being observed while also being influenced by them. But this point of view goes against the field-theoretical conception of adaptational processes, which must move in both directions, even if, with respect to conventional consensus on fact and reason, those movements are of different kinds and degrees, as they are in clinical analysis.

I have already characterized Hartmann's unreadiness to move beyond Freud and explore these implications of his foundational assumption as a manifestation of his conservative, stewardly tendencies. These tendencies were buttressed by two factors: the positivism that was dominant in the social and biological sciences during his development and was still influential during his prime—though much less so now—and the fact that, as always, psychoanalysis was under philosophical, scientistic, and journalistic attack as a moribund, mumbo-jumbo religion.

The second prefatory philosophical proposition counterbalances the first. It holds that the dialogic and intersubjective systematizing of psychoanalytic theory cannot be carried through to a point of completeness. For that attempt at complete systematization must take for granted that the speaker or writer on its behalf is an objective observer who may be relied upon to give a once-and-for-all definitive account of the analysand, the analyst, and the analytic process. In other words, the systematization necessarily presupposes a privileged protagonist who is qualified to argue the superiority of the dialogic and intersubjectivist position. Thus, there is a hidden return to, and dependence on, the rejected positivism, and by the same token, a new vulnerability to a critique developed from the standpoint of perspectivism, and so on ad infinitum. This is so because this presumably privileged protagonist, too, must be standing in some definite place, must be grounded somewhere with fixed and absolute assumptions and referential criteria. And that ground cannot be characterized as secure against any and all critiques, for assumptions can always be challenged.

In his sophistication, Hartmann was not unaware of this problem. He attempted to come to terms with it by positing the relatively autonomous ego functions that make possible rational action and judgment, stable object relations, affects reduced to their signal functions, and dispassionate judgment—what in general could be called neutrality and objectivity. In this way he tried to develop a basis for believing in the reasonably objective observer who is a nonparticipant in the observational field of clinical practice, and who, accordingly, can take an absolute stand on what is going on in that field. But even this approach rests on arguable foundations, for, among other things, there can be no absolute, unarguable criteria of autonomy that are independent of method and the observer's assumptions.

What I have been describing in the preceding paragraphs is an inevitable paradox. On the one hand is the fiction of the analyst standing outside of the field of observation. This fiction is necessary for presenting a rounded and balanced theory of mind and of the analytic process and the changes it can induce. Dynamic explanations alone cannot provide that theory. Even a full account of how dynamic changes come about and are stabilized requires an independent observer standing outside the field. This is the observer who speaks confidently of change in psychic energy, rationality, autonomous functions, stable structures, and so on, and who then organizes all these variables into a picture of the whole mind. Importantly, it is also the analyst who, ethically, takes responsibility for assessing the analysand's overall condition and response to treatment and who is consistently concerned with the analysand's welfare. On the other hand, there is the inevitable recognition and acceptance of perspectivism as the only epistemological stance that makes sense, accompanied by a rejection of positivistic argument.

Confronting this paradox, one must, I believe, come to the following conclusion: no one approach can do a complete clinical and theoretical approach all by itself. It is in the nature of each and every systematic approach that it sets limits on what is available to it. Each approach equips us with instruments of thought that bring both light and darkness to its subject matter. Its epistemological and methodological grounding can never be of the sort that precludes alternatives or skepticism.

Thus it is that we confront a chronic and inevitable conflict between the objectivist on the one hand and intersubjectivist and dialogical participant on the other. This conflict has generated more or less influence over psychoanalytic theorizing from its very beginning, as we can infer from the long-standing debate over whether Freud was a humanist or a strict or too strict scientist. Hartmann's theorizing contains this tension within it, in that, on the one hand, it calls for intersubjective elaborations when its details are worked through, and on the other, it demands an observer and theorizer standing at a further distance from the phenomena and talking about a mental apparatus as an essence existing "out there" in nature. Consequently, this theoretical situation must be regarded as one of ongoing tension rather than one that is amenable to resolution.

As I understand the postmodern view of systematic thinking, this conclusion is all that one can aspire to. System building always generates its own inner vulnerabilities and tensions.

I move on now to consider some of the main features of the thinking of those analysts oriented toward dialogue and intersubjectivity. They attend more extensively and intensively than ever to what they regard as inevitable and useful transference–countertransference interactions, using for this purpose the broad conceptions of these two variables. They view many of these interactions as fostered by the details of the analytic situation itself. They see both parties to the analytic relationship as continuously communicating unconsciously as well as consciously, and each of them as continuously reactive to consciously and unconsciously registered stimuli emanating from the other. Theirs is a constructivist position; that is, they hold that, inevitably, these communicative actions and reactions express the personally characteristic ways in which each party constructs the meaning and significance of its situations and relationships. Thus, they attempt to avoid the position of the outsider saying what is real or true. Analysis is to be discussed consistently in terms of psychic reality.

They argue, and I have myself argued the same point (1976, 1983, 1992a), that each person has a hand in creating that which he or she seems only to encounter; that persons, situations, events are neither pure reality nor pure subjectivity or fantasy; that psychoanalysis simultaneously creates and discovers in one and the same act. Thus, in the analytic situation, both analyst and analysand are continuously constructing their individually experienced situations. And yet, each of them does so while also remaining a more or less conventional observer. As a conventional observer, one adheres to a noteworthy extent to the conventions of what it is to be realistic or objective. It is only on this basis that the two parties involved can genuinely communicate with one another and claim to be discovering or uncovering core conflicts and their consequences. Psychic reality is not synonymous with primary process thinking. This adherence to convention, so far as it goes, always allows correction or revision, and we know that these changes are made continuously during analysis.

According to this perspective, "objective" simply refers to one's adhering in a reasonable way to social conventions; in the analyst's case, however, it also refers to her or his adhering to a systematic point of view that has demonstrated its value as a way of perceiving reality—to analytic conventions of some sort. Consequently, with regard to the psychoanalytic process, one must assume that, on some level and to some degree, both the analyst and the analysand are sufficiently integrated to be capable of conventional reality testing, consistency and coherence, and agreements on points of controversy; for only then can psychoanalysis take place, even if only intermittently. Being a communicative form of treatment, psychoanalysis depends on shared and socialized understanding and practices, however nonverbalized these may be.

If, now, we shift back to the ego psychological perspective explicitly developed by Hartmann, working in the wake of Freud, we are in a position to emphasize the following balancing consideration. In psychoanalysis, it is specifically ego psychology that tries to give an account of the development of this complex admixture of constructivism, conventionality, and systematic thought, and of what is required to maintain and extend it. Those who reject Freud's and Hartmann's ego psychology or, even more broadly, its structural theory, are simply ignoring this area of complete conceptualization and explanation. They claim too much for intersubjectivity alone.

Because both parties to the analysis continuously encounter, create, define, and explain the phenomena of the psychoanalytic field, each of them confronts considerable and unavoidable ambiguity in establishing what has been found or encountered and what has been created or coauthored. One consequence of this ambiguity is that the intersubjective analyst's guiding assumption is that it is necessary constantly to be on the lookout for merely attempted or actually achieved *enactments* in the analytic relationship; these may be neurotically colored or psychotically colored. It is in this intersubjective sense that, for example, a Kleinian analyst might come finally to interpret an analysand's regressive shift as manifesting a reaction to the analyst's unconsciously participating in a sadomasochistic enactment. Perhaps the analyst participated in the seemingly innocent form of making appropriate interpretations when it could be seen that his or her doing so was being experienced as condemnation and as thereby confirming a paranoid–schizoid stance in the analysand's internal world of object relations. In a superficially similar but basically different way, owing to a radically different position on internalized object relations, a self psychologist might view that same regressive shift as communicating something about empathic failure on the analyst's part, an empathic failure which may go unrecognized until he or she reflects on the recent history of interaction and does so not from a presumably "objective" point of view but from how it seems in the inner reality of both participants.

As another example of the dialogic and intersubjectivist way of working, consider a gesture that the analyst may consciously intend as encouragement or as support, not that that is a characteristic analytic intervention. The analysand may experience that gesture as the analyst's being unempathic, showing lack of confidence, acting omnipotent; upon reflection, the analyst may realize that the gesture did express unconscious needs to take the part of an uncomprehending, threatening, or insecure figure in the transference. It is just here that this newer approach would not view the countertransferential enactment simply as a disruptive factor in the treatment; instead, it would scrutinize it as a potentially rich and primary source of material for subsequent intervention, for it may get to be understood as a reflection of the analyst's response to the analysand's transference. For example, the analysand might be trying to provoke enactment of that kind as a repetitive demonstration of his or her masochism. The dialogic and intersubjectivist approach tries to make analytic gold out of enactments, and it claims that it is often successful in doing so.

Much of what I have been describing here has come to be subsumed under the heading of analysis in the here-and-now. And before going any further, I must emphasize my recognition that traditional ego psychological Freudian analysts are no strangers to this kind of analysis. Indeed, they may rightfully claim credit for pioneering and perfecting much of it. They might subsume their contributions under different headings, such as the analysis of transference, resistance, character, acting out and acting in—in general, as further analysis of the ego. Like Freud, however, the traditional analyst has viewed these here-and-now phenomena primarily as "new editions" of the old; accordingly, the analyst's principal job is thought to be to go on from this to reconstruct explicitly the analysand's pathogenic past, and in this way especially to bring about structural change through emotionally experienced insight. In other words, for these analysts the present is still, in large part, of special interest as an objectively defined source of material for reconstructing the analysand's past and the history of his or her development of stable characteristics, both adaptive and pathological, and making all this conscious. Furthermore, when the traditional analyst "acts in" with the analysand, that is to be regarded as indicating an unfortunate lapse away from objectivity and into countertransference; hence, it is a lapse that would best be corrected as soon as possible and avoided in the future. One would not ordinarily view it primarily as an inevitable and potentially instructive aspect of clinical psychoanalysis.

On their part and in one way or another, the intersubjectivists conceptualize the past differently and interpret it differently. Viewing the countertransference in feeling or action as an essential part of the analytic process, they tend to approach reconstructions of the past also and equally as part of the work of defining the present. The past becomes a resource for understanding complex interactions in the here-and-now. It clarifies a working definition of the present that is to be still further understood by continuing recourse to the past. Therefore, with respect to time or life history, these analysts freely reverse the explanatory and technical priorities. For them, reconstruction continues to be useful, though not of such exclusive importance or predominant interest. And the tone of the process becomes more provisional, because more limited to what can emerge from this two-party dialogue about how, in the here-and-now, past and present mutually define one another. History and present experience remain always in flux.

Some analysts might take the shifts I have been discussing as confirming earlier fears of the consequences of Hartmann's innovative ideas: too much reality and not enough unconscious fantasy. I do not find convincing evidence that these fears were ever justified to any significant extent. There have always been analysts trying to superficialize psychoanalysis, and some have rationalized their efforts as falling in line with Hartmann's thought; for this it is wrong to blame Hartmann. Do we blame Freud for the superficiality of other analysts who claim to speak in his name? Within a contemporary perspective, the fears of Hartmann's influence seem to me rather to express a fear of change, controversy, or breadth of vision—and in some instances—fear of tarnishing an idealized image of Freud.

It is not the case, however, that no new problems have arisen with the advent of dialogue and intersubjectivity as hot topics. In my earlier discussion, I already alluded to one of them, specifically that those who adopt an absolutist position on intersubjectivity are making claims about knowing, facticity, or reality testing that they cannot totally support in practice. Here I would point especially to those self psychologists and interpersonalists who claim that the analyst is not, and should never try to be, the ultimate authority in the clinical dialogue on what is real, true, and correct, or else fantastic, false, or distorted; in other words, to those who claim there can only be encounters of two subjective realities in what is implicitly a completely solipsistic universe. This claim contains a paradox. For it is the analyst who keeps the record and the frame of the analytic work; it is the analyst who steadily tries to affirm and integrate and safeguard the treatment and the analysand. Furthermore, it is the analyst who gives the final account of the analysis to colleagues, or generalizes from it, and thereby helps create and sustain what we have agreed to call the reality of psychoanalysis. Another problem that faces each proponent of totally egalitarian intersubjectivity is the necessity always to argue the value of his or her tradition relative to other such traditions; for example, self psychology is not interpersonal psychology and neither of them is Winnicottian, even though they all share an intersubjective emphasis.

Problems, however, should not give rise to pessimism. In these inherently unstable, debatable, provisional, but constructively critical ways, different approaches, different attempts at systematization, even different interpretations do get to be developed. They may be developed on ever higher planes of understanding and application. Nevertheless, it requires of us that, to be intellectually responsible, we analysts must sacrifice that sense of absolute and permanent certainty we long for in our work to give us much needed emotional support. Now, that claim of certainty is considered arbitrary. Certainty is possible only briefly within an ever changing systematic point of view. Even relative stability and reasonability are arguable claims rather than dead certainties. On this basis, the field develops further.

I would emphasize a bigger problem about post-Hartmann trends: the increasing trend toward eclecticism among those who accept the dialogic and intersubjective orientations and recognize the pluralistic nature of the contemporary analytic world. Specifically, a growing number of these analysts seem to find it agreeable and effective to use various assortments of propositions in their work, often while remaining more or less unconcerned with questions of theoretical origins, consistency, or potential for integration. Those who do strive for theoretical integration are, I think, too easily satisfied with their products. Many, however, are less ambitious and simply pick and choose from among the various impressive developments within psychoanalysis. Whatever seems to fit is worth trying. They do not regard this practice as being necessarily careless or inexact, as Hartmann certainly would have done, for, as they believe, if all systematic presentations are provisional in their very nature, none should have binding and exclusionary power.

Thus, instead of taking as an ideal rigorous and absolute fidelity to one system of thought, there are many now who take that fidelity as a bowing down before authoritarian power, thereby reinforcing an emphasis in psychoanalysis of which, as they see it, we have already had more than enough. In this way, eclecticism now gets to be equated with egalitarianism, liberal individualism, and as always, progress. In the process, the systemic fidelity that Hartmann exemplified is devalued, and the field is left wide open to the influence of unconscious valuations and unintegrated preferences.

Obviously, this kind of eclecticism implies a perspective on theory itself that differs from that of both Hartmann and Freud. Again, there are potentially positive consequences to consider. For example, the eclectic analysts' tendency to focus more on local issues and expertise and less on impersonal generalizations or universals is not out of joint with modern times. This localistic perspective has been noted and accepted in various other disciplines, including physics and other natural sciences. A fundamental change in orientation has taken place as regards the need for thoroughgoing systematization. Even so, local theorizing or small-system building is still systematic; it is not the same as mushing together concepts with incompatible implications for theory and practice. That looser eclecticism cannot generate integrated self presentations, and so it does not lend itself to comparative assessments, that is, assessments of better or worse fits in theory and consequences in practice. Then, there is no way to establish agreed upon standards or meanings of any utility. The final theoretical and clinical consequence for psychoanalysis is nihilistic.

Another high price paid for these haphazardly eclectic versions of the dialogic and intersubjective has long been familiar. The price is that the fruits of various systematizing efforts are being picked and enjoyed without due respect for the fact that they have ripened in the context of rigorously developed and maintained theoretical perspectives. We must wonder then how they will fare once they have been picked and also where the choice fruits of the future will come from.

Further on behalf of eclecticism: it is possible to acknowledge the potential value of its serving to free up imagination, expose new possibilities, and increase technical facility. Additionally, I believe that many psychoanalytic ideas are not as embedded in specific schools of thought as one thinks or as one is *supposed* to think; that is to say, not all the propositions of each of the existing systems of psychoanalysis are both unique to that system and inextricably bound to all its other propositions. One example of what I mean is the way in which Annie Reich's (1973) pioneering and brilliant papers on self-esteem regulation highlighted the profound and lasting influence of early ties to the real and imagined mother. Clinically, her contributions could have fitted easily into one or another object-relational system of thought. She, however, tried to fit them into the ego psychological framework of the 1950s. Accordingly, she kept invoking developmentally later oedipal and phallic issues in what I regard as an abrupt, almost mechanical way. In the end, as I read her, she forged a synthesis that included a major revision of ego and superego theory, and that, in certain respects, helped pave the way toward Heinz Kohut's self psychology.

With examples of this sort in mind, I would argue that the danger of nihilistic consequences of eclecticism, while not negligible, can be exaggerated. We know that at first many changes are feared as nihilistic. Even Hartmann's propositions were feared on this basis. We cannot exclude the possibility that from new mixtures of thought may come significant and useful developments.

It may, however, also be expected that this eclecticist trend will lead to some atrophy of critical thought in psychoanalysis. What may take the place of critical thought are ever more naively individualistic, ultimately narcissistically romantic versions of psychoanalysis. Then, those psychoanalysts invested in this change may lose their perspective on their individual analyses and on each other's work, not to speak of their effectively giving up hope of occupying an esteemed place in the long tradition of humanistic and scientific thought.

I believe that I have been describing one piece of a cultural revolution in psychoanalysis. It is no longer possible to claim that there is only one monolithic Freudian theory or that there should be one. There is no single theory that reigns supreme and specifies exclusively what psychoanalysis is or even how the name *psychoanalysis* is to be used. Instead of one, there are now a number, each vying for dominance, and many individual analysts have been forsaking strict fidelity to any one of them.

I view these new orientations within psychoanalysis as local manifestations of a general change in the modern or postmodern world of ideas and critical thought. In this postmodern world there is, at bottom, a rejection of the idea of the grand metanarrative that will take account of all possible questions and problems within a discipline and will also lay out the paths for future work. On my reading, Hartmann still believed in the grand metanarrative; that is what his work on metapsychology was about. That is what the idea of psychoanalysis as a general psychology was about. But metanarratives have now become the foci of critiques directed at their inherent self-contradictions and ultimate ungroundedness, there being no uncontestable view of a single reality or nature.

Consequently, universal propositions are now approached with suspicion as to their implicitly sponsoring or reinforcing prevailing distributions of power and values. Within this general postmodern development, one finds sponsored versions of absolute and limited relativism, pluralism, contextualist hermeneutics, and deconstructionism, each with its own set of relations to power and values, as we see in the various backlashes to them as well as the intense internal rivalries they generate. I would also mention here the searching challenges posed by contemporary feminist critiques (see, for example, Schafer, 1994a). The result today is a widespread development or one or another kind of what we may call *skeptical provisionalism*.

Leading thinkers in many disciplines are prepared to sponsor ideas provisionally. Once the belief in unquestionable foundations is given up, it is only skeptical provisionalism that makes sense. According to that provisionalism, critique is always possible, wide-ranging challenges are inevitable, and, far from being an evil, this state of affairs is fertile ground for the cultivation of both what is at hand and what is always being newly created or newly understood.

If this is a valid picture of the contemporary and future world of analytic thought and practice, we must also accept that it is a world in which theory has lost the grandeur, majesty, or mythic proportions that it had for Freud and for Hartmann after him. There is, however, compensation for that loss, for the world is now one in which we all become fully active participants. We may see ourselves as constructivists, shaping whatever it is that we do observe and in turn being shaped by that very process. Thus, as analysts in this new world, we have ever more reason to think of ourselves as protagonists in the drama of human minds-in-relation and not just as curious and awestruck witnesses of single minds in isolation.

This is the new drama, the one from which we seemed to be excluded by mechanistic and objectivist perspectives and the values they expressed. Not only excluded, but left feeling guilty *or* ashamed that consciously we wished it to be otherwise, and that in practice we never did accept that exclusion fully. Therefore, however controversial a conclusion it may seem to those analysts who still honor their established construction of Hartmann in his prime, I would assert finally that it is that very Hartmann who may be seen as having played a great part in paving the way toward modern transformations of psychoanalysis that ushered in the era of dialogue and intersubjectivity; of pluralism, uncertainty, and undecidability; and of a new set of internal contradictions, limitations, and tensions. That is why I present it here as the era that can only be fully understood as following in the wake of Heinz Hartmann.

2

The Conceptualization
of Clinical Facts

Freud said of infantile psychosexuality that it is all there if only one knows how to look. In this essay I shall be concerned with what is involved in knowing how to look, different ways of looking, and the consequences of looking one way or another. In order to develop my argument, I shall have to review much that is familiar. A clinical example will serve to ground this discussion in practice.

I begin with a look at corporeality. The experience of corporeality is never unmediated. To enter into experience, as opposed to remaining in an inchoate state of sensation, corporeality must be thought, which is to say that it must be symbolized, however primitively (e.g., Fiumara, 1992).

Symbolization is a constructive process in that it selects, organizes, and makes salient. The symbolization that provides the requisite mediation for corporeality must be regarded as a process of construction. However conventionalized its outcome may be, that is, however natural

This paper was presented at the *International Journal of Psycho-Analysis* 75th Anniversary Celebration Conference, London, October 14–16, 1994.

or inevitable corporeality may seem to be before we reflect on it, the body is always open to alternative or enriched symbolizations. In principle, it could have been symbolized differently to begin with, and it remains permanently open to change. For this reason, there is no one fixed corporeality to be seen when one looks. That is why we find the construction of corporeality varying across developmental levels in the life span, across genders, across subcultures within a general culture, and across general cultures. This construction also varies over the course of history in every respect, even though it may vary more in some epochs and in some respects than in others. Variation through history has been shown, for example, in the construction of the anatomical genital differences between the sexes (Laquer, 1990).

Constructions always imply contexts of narration and dialogue, no matter whether these are spoken, written, or just imagined (Schafer, 1992). Each construction tells something to someone for some reason. Communication is involved even when one tells something to oneself, as the common saying has it, for this saying implies a subjective narration of dialogue between multiple selves.

My introduction has centered on corporeality because the body seems to present itself to us as a brute, unmediated fact, something we just know or feel, something on which our existence seems to depend, and also because traditional psychoanalysis has centered its theory on corporeality as the starting fact of ego development (Freud, 1923a). Corporeality serves well to illustrate my position on the conceptualization of clinical facts. My position is that there are no unconceptualized clinical facts. All facts have already been symbolized and are always already there to be thought about further. Therefore, the idea of conceptualizing *clinical* facts makes sense only as a way to refer to *re*symbolizing or reconceptualizing and *re*telling facts for clinical reasons. In psychoanalysis, these clinical reasons will, of course, vary with the clinician's individualized version of his or her preferred school of thought (Schafer, 1992).

The details of clinical situations, though themselves already and necessarily symbolized as facts, are not yet *clinical* facts. They become clinical facts only after they have been defined within a clinical context. The context provides definition by facilitating linkage to other already established or accepted clinical facts. The thematic organization of all these facts defines a clinical situation or a moment in the clinical process, such as the enactment of unconsciously maintained transference fantasies. For example, a male analysand wears a shirt and tie to his session for the first time ever. This change is merely a detail. It becomes a clinical fact once it is contextualized, for instance, as announcing to the analyst an increased concern for appearances in response to previous interpretations of disturbed bodily narcissism. That increased concern might be repressive, compliant, self-fulfilling, or some combination of all three, so that the clinical act has not yet been fully conceptualized; it may change in complexity, sense, and significance.

Further conceptualizations or reconceptualizations can be carried quite far. They may move through a series of transformations to higher levels of abstraction. They may shift to other dynamic aspects of some compromise formation. In the case of comparative analytic studies, they may redefine findings in the terms of other schools of thought, a process that inevitably is inexact, owing to its both subtracting and adding meaning.

My clinical example, to which I will now turn, requires a brief methodological and epistemological preface. The example had to be substantial enough to allow a productive discussion of the clinical facts it would yield, though also brief enough for a time-limited presentation. To be substantial, it had to provide contexts for the details to be conceptualized. The constituents of these contexts had to include preceding, ongoing, and subsequent dialogue so that not only the clinical sense but the clinical weight of the conceptualizations could be decided. Differential weighting of facts is an essential aspect of their construction. All contexts and all constructed facts had to be approached tentatively or accepted only provisionally, so that they would remain open to revision or reconstruction as new details emerged and new narrative lines were required. This is to say that facticity must remain in flux. This my example will show. No other account can do justice to the evolution of an analytic process. Facts presented as permanently fixed should be viewed with suspicion. I shall return to these points later on.

CLINICAL EXAMPLE

Mr. T, a single man of 35, came complaining of a readiness to sink into heavy depressive moods, a recent falling off of sexual interest, and unsatisfactory relationships with women. Of the obsessive type, he was controlled, emotionally dry, and rationalistic. He described himself as having been relatively withdrawn as a child; at table burying his nose in a book and at camp remaining friendless. He said that for many years and up to the time of his father's death some years earlier, he had been strongly attached to his father. He felt that his mother had carried out her maternal responsibilities conscientiously, but with little feeling; however, during analysis we clarified that she must have done so with variable emotional availability. On his part, he had always held back feeling when with her, felt nothing at all, or been rejecting.

During the preceding fifteen months, the time he had been in analysis, he had frequently and spontaneously documented how analysis was helping him at work and in his social life; however, his obsessional rigidity in the sessions had decreased only by minute increments. And yet, these increments had added up to appreciable, even if still limited, changes.

The first session to be reported here began with his saying that, the previous weekend, he had felt less of his newly experienced desire for his latest woman friend, Anne. Not for the first time, he told me he felt awkward talking to me about sexual activity, and, indeed, previously he had done so very little. He was surprised by the decrease in his desire, because, during the preceding week, he had found that whenever he thought of her, even if he was not thinking of her in a sexual way, he would become aroused. This, he said, was not as it had been when he began analysis with me. He then ruminated obsessively over this loss of desire.

As I often did with this man, in order not to frighten him into blocking or a flood of rationalizations, I began working away from the transference. I said that this difficulty could almost have been expected. Why? Because he was getting to feel much more involved with Anne and therefore, as he knew, afraid of getting overinvolved, too excited, and out of control. I pointed out that he would have already felt some alarm over his ready arousals the week before. After agreeing that that "made sense," he spent some time trying to develop a direct rational attack on the question of what he could be afraid of.

It was his usual style to attempt such frontal approaches to problems. In the past, I had taken up with him more than once that his doing so was a sign of his anxiety about the lack of structure he experienced in relation to associating freely. Now, in a preliminary move toward the transference, I reminded him that he had said that that lack of structure opened up possibilities of his saying things he would regret; however, it was still not clear what he feared he would say. He then analogized both free associating and his feelings about Anne with skiing downhill. He said the right way to ski is to throw yourself down the hill rather than, what feels natural, to tilt back away from it; and once he had overcome his anxiety and skied the correct way, and despite his having taken some tumbles, he had always had the satisfaction of making it down to the bottom.

Dropping this analogy, he simply continued his rationalistic quest for the explanation of his recent falling off of desire. First, he tried to do some further reconstruction of a significant change in the feeling between him and his mother when he was a young child; this was a topic we had spent some time on in the past. Then, he speculated that he might have been angry with Anne, since he knew from previous analytic work that there can be a frustrating aspect to his holding back his feelings, as he had done with his mother; perhaps he had intended to frustrate Anne. Earlier in the work, he had confessed that once he had noted a flash of sadistic satisfaction in not coming through emotionally for his mother. At that earlier point, he had gone on to confess that there was one time that he had had that same sadistic feeling with me; it was when he informed me that, during the next month, owing to a particularly difficult work schedule, he would miss a bunch of sessions.

Next, he turned away from his speculations on frustrating intent and reiterated intellectualistically his fear of dependency and exploitation if he were to develop an emotional commitment. This was another idea we had taken up a number of times before, especially in connection with his once having maintained a long-standing attachment to a frustrating, sometimes dismissive, and sometimes even verbally abusive woman. In the past, the analysis had seemed to show that he had persisted with her just because her unlovingness protected him against the danger of emotional commitment. In this session, however, each of these intellectualistic searches soon gave way to blocking—a common outcome.

Then, approaching the transference head on, I commented that I thought he was doing the same thing with me that he had done with Anne. Specifically, he was trying to keep a strict control over the session because it seemed to him potentially overloaded with emotion. Once again he was clinging to his frontal approach through reviews of memories and previous discussions plus continued rational speculation. I added that by his pushing ahead here with his quest to reason it all out by himself, he was leaving me out of it, in that way avoiding a situation with me in which he would feel he was becoming too involved or dependent. (I realized later that I could also have pointed out that he was frustrating me, too.)

He agreed with me on the points of control and detachment and went on to talk about how much he used to confide in his father. This was another familiar topic and another favorite way of switching manifest content away from him and me. He reviewed the insight we had jointly developed in the past, largely through the analysis of transference, that confiding in his father had been problematic, because he had often had a vague feeling that he was doing it more for his father's sake than his own. Characteristically, he now made no mention of my part in developing that insight. Previously, we had gone on to recognize signs that his father, on whom he seemed to rely so heavily, might have seemed to him dependent on him, that is, needing him to be the attached son with many confidences to share, even to the exclusion of intimacy with his mother; also, that his father rather may have needed him to act always in a compliant and dependent manner. All of which he had kept repressing when his father was alive, and all of which he had denied was a factor in his dealings with me.

In the sessions immediately following the one I have just reported, there was ample opportunity for me to return to the interpretation of earlier days that he was experiencing me, too, as a dependent and fragile father figure who needed that kind of reassurance from him. Accordingly, and as with his father, he had been using shows of compliance and gratitude to cover his resentment, rebelliousness, and sadistic pleasure in withholding. He said he could see my point, but his obsessive rigidity continued pretty much as before.

I had no reason to doubt that, behaviorally, his conduct was freer when he was away from me. The analyst is often the last to see these changes. Now, however, it dawned on me that he had been emphasizing these positive changes not so much to keep me posted or to seek my approval as to reassure me, in my assumed insecurity, by emphasizing how helpful I was to him. His struggling hard, even if unsuccessfully, to associate freely now seemed to be a simulation of confiding in me without restraint. Also, it now seemed that whenever he emphasized that he had just told me something that he had not even told his father, he was simulating his being a good son to me.

But before I could relay to him any of my new understanding, he explained that whenever he talked about his father's problems or limitations, even when he did so only speculatively and with many qualifications, he ended up after the session in a depressed mood. He implied some resentment of my putting him in that situation.

With only one minute left in this session, I limited my response to pointing out that this acknowledgment of pain and resentment helped make sense of his having told me recently that sometimes, and apparently for no reason, he could see that he did not want to come to his sessions.

Two weeks later he reported a dream. "I was in an apartment and there was a party going on next door. The party began to break through the wall of my apartment, and I just wanted them to get out of there." The analysis of this dream in its context of recent material and all that took place during the work on the dream itself culminated in the following interpretation: What was crashing in and threatening him was Anne, his joyous excitement about her, which felt like coming alive, and a sense of emotional separation from his mostly silent, glum, inexpressive parents. Defensively and resentfully he was attributing all of this commotion to my pressuring him too much with my expressive language and my interpretations of his defenses against emotion, especially his positive feelings towards Anne and me. He was beginning to recognize that he felt safer in a downcast, lifeless mood, and that he could unconsciously induce these moods to spoil "the fun," as when he approached a date glumly or felt reluctant to come to his sessions.

I want next to review some of the high points in the preceding clinical account. My eye will be fixed less on any final formulation of the case and more on the question of conceptualizing clinical facts. First, Mr. T reported his unexpectedly experiencing a falling off of sexual desire for Anne. This report remained simply an utterance, a detail, and not a clinical fact until, by contextualizing it, I made it part of the psychoanalytic process. For this, the report had to be resymbolized and further narrativized along some analytic storyline. Was it to be retold as an abject confession, a challenge in the transference, a layering of both, or what?

To start this retelling, in my own mind I supposed simply that he was enacting some ambivalently held desire for emotional and sexual involvement with Anne. The general context I used was his having come for analysis saying he hoped to develop a capacity for that kind of involvement, and the specific context was my having spent some time analyzing with him his anxieties and ambivalence in relation to getting involved with both Anne and me.

Further conceptualization of this ambivalence was made possible by way of recontextualizing it and enriching its narration. Here, there were choices to be made, for more than one extended account could be developed. For example, and speaking only schematically, thinking as a standard ego psychological Freudian, I could have developed further the clinical fact that he was frightened by the strength of his impulses. Slowly, the ground could be prepared to mention more specifically that his defenses against a bisexual oedipal transference with attendant castration anxiety were not stable. The *broad* context of this retelling would have been organized around the knowledge that, in his early life, Mr. T had developed a markedly negative oedipal orientation. The *immediate* context would have been, on the one hand, his having unconsciously begun to identify Anne with his mother, as a result of which he was unable to sustain his passion for her. On the other hand, his having tried unconsciously to quell his castration anxiety in the homosexual part of his transference by displacing sexual feelings for me onto Anne. In a complex compromise formation, he was trying to be sexual with Anne out of love for me, while, out of antagonism to me he was making sure to fail in the attempt.

Although my intervention was influenced by these ideas, it was conceived rather more in my understanding of the Kleinian mode. On the basis of defensive splitting and displacement, Mr. T was enacting with Anne his transference to me. I brought this up when I pointed out his controllingness and his isolating himself from me. I was implying, though not yet stating outright, that he was also using projective identification to locate his desire for change in me; on this basis he was withholding from me in a sadistic, anal-retentive manner. All of which would involve repetition of pushing away his mother in his inner world, and doing so out of disappointment in her and mistrust of her. The context for this extension included the history of his general withdrawal from a mother he experienced as an erratic, often mechanical caretaker. There would also be mistrust of himself on account of his pent-up rage and destructive greediness as well as a sense of taboo about getting close to her or to me as her representative in the transference. Not to be neglected in the midst of all this is blocked incorporation of his mother's goodness—hers, Anne's, and mine.

Here, let me introduce a supplementary clinical detail that was also part of the context of these conceptualizations. Characteristically, Mr. T routinely qualified or amended or had first to disagree with whatever I said, only later to agree with it bit by bit; always, it seemed, he did so to make it look as if it was an idea he had developed himself. I viewed this as parallel to his behavior with Anne and his mother, specifically, blocking incorporation of goodness, and in my case blocking the experience that I was giving him helpful interventions. By leaving me out of it, he was keeping me out of him. For him, it was only "the analysis" that was helpful; it was nothing that I had specifically done. In this way he was combining sadistic provocation and defense. In related ways, he was dealing with Anne similarly. In my next intervention, I began to approach the conceptualization of these facts.

I move on now to the moment when I bypassed the splitting and displacement implied by his speaking only of Anne and went directly to his enactment within the transference. First, I mentioned the control of excitement and involvement in relation to Anne; then, Mr. T's doing the same with me; and then, a limited reference to his leaving me out of the quest for analytic understanding. These direct comments on the transference bring us to a significant point in conceptualizing this session analytically.

How might we conceptualize that significant point? As I mentioned, different analysts will answer every such question more or less differently. Therefore, my next thesis on the conceptualization of clinical facts must be this: in the same way that an analysand's initial utterances are not yet clinical facts, an analyst's utterances are not yet clinical facts. They remain mere details until it is established just what they are to be seen *as*, and our establishing that will depend on analytic retellings that transform the details into complex, psychoanalytically significant actions. In the terms of dialogue, the mere record of my utterances does not convey what I communicated; it indicates what I consciously intended, and it leaves it open whether he heard any of them as such, and also what he had done with those that he had heard.

At this point, I must discuss yet another aspect of conceptualizing clinical facts. Before we can transform an intervention into a clinical fact, we must track its vicissitudes in the material that follows it, noting how it is elaborated by the analysand and what its other consequences are. Thus, its facticity is determined by its future. Its facticity has a temporal aspect. As new facts are added to the context, clinical fact becomes more or less convincing, stable, clear, and bounded or enlarged or else more uncertain. It was to provide grounds for making this point that I included the material from subsequent analytic sessions that I shall soon discuss.

This plasticity of clinical facts must never be forgotten. If present clinical facts can be conceptualized adequately only by taking into account later as well as earlier conceptualizations of clinical facts, then we are operating in a circular fashion—the hermeneutic circle, it has been called—and I maintain that correct application of the analytic method limits us to conceptualizing facts only tentatively or provisionally. They are facts for the time being. They are facts of a certain kind for the time being. They matter for the time being. They are true for the time being. They are facts in psychic reality, which, for us, is as real as any other, but our ideas about that psychic reality change as the analysis moves ahead.

Well, now, what was Mr. T's response to my intervention? Manifestly, he spoke of his father's dependence on him for confidences. It seemed then to be a clinical fact that he was just continuing on with his sadistically controlling approach to me, associating as though determined to leave me out of it by ignoring my intervention. True enough, but not the only truth. Additionally, I believe that he was telling me in a displaced way that, like his father, I was being burdensome by pressuring him for confidences, for wanting the two of us to stay close together and collaborate in maintaining the fiction that the relationship was simply one in which he was dependent on me for help. Heard in this way, he was staying right on the point. But we can say it was the point of it all only if we know what to look for, as Freud said, and as I add, if we only look in one way rather than another.

Now it was necessary to conceptualize in quite another way what I had just said to him. Moreover, now it seemed clearer than ever to me that he had constructed and experienced the entire analytic process and setting as a repetition of the situation with his parents: parading his father and crowding out his mother, though his mother had always to be kept in the picture as the one he would constantly push out of it; and, in his solitary rationalizing, replaying the childhood scene of sitting at the table with his nose buried in a book, in this manner reacting against coercion toward dependent closeness. The clinical facts were changing! Their contexts were changing! The plasticity of the facts of the transference was plain to see.

On the basis of these considerations, the further conceptualization of these facts may move in each of the two directions I mentioned earlier. Retold in one way, he had been vengefully and defensively castrating me as the rivalrous father who, through fostering dependence and closeness, was always pushing him into a negative oedipal, castrated attachment; perhaps as well, in spurning me, he was spurning the advances of an oedipal mother who is both untrustworthy and seductive; he might even have been negating the perception of the primal scene represented in the past in the screen memory of the scene at the dinner table, in the present by his not accepting my interventions.

The other way to retell the clinical facts is the one I thought more useful for this man at this time. I thought that he was showing me that he was locked into a position somewhere between the paranoid-schizoid and the primitive depressive. Terrified of dealing openly with his ambivalent love for his objects, feeling guilty over his rageful wish for separation and emancipation, and dreading the loss that that separation would entail, he was rightly busying himself, on the one hand, with sealing off his tumultuous, sadistically colored, and needful feelings within himself and, on the other, with seeking only well-disguised, indirect outlets for these feelings.

I believed that this retelling was both facilitated and supported by the analysis of his subsequent dream of the lively but unwelcome party breaking through his wall. That dream expressed his feeling that he was being invaded and coerced by me; also that he was experiencing his overcontrolled and overcontrolling way of life as a safe "psychic retreat" (Steiner, 1993) or a near-death (Joseph, 1988). Whatever it cost him in social isolation, sexual deprivation, and heavy depressive mood, he felt it was worth the gain in psychic equilibrium and limitation of psychic pain. At this point, we are well beyond his fragmentary details and are considering quite a complex array of clinical facts and making some consequential choices as well.

Now to summarize briefly: in our daily work, we and our analysands play active roles in constructing the clinical facts that we seem only to encounter "out there in the world." The clinically unconceptualized details of the analytic encounter are undefined, unconstructed utterances, movements, and silences. Through dialogue and through slowly building and revising clinical contexts and shaping them narratively, we transform these details into the clinical facts of psychic reality. Over time, these are facts of increasing complexity and possibly changing importance. Facticity depends on the conceptual options we choose, and it remains constantly in flux. We are permanently occupied with keeping our conceptualizations open and making the most of our unsteady state.

3

On Gendered Discourse and Discourse on Gender

The bulk of postmodern discourse on gender has been developed by feminist scholars. Although their discussions are far from unified or harmonious, in my reading they center on, or at least imply, a set of interrelated themes. At the risk of appearing to be trying to impose closure on what gives every evidence of being a wide open, constantly evolving field of study and controversy, I begin with a summary of these themes. I do so because I believe that postmodern feminist studies bring to light much that present-day psychoanalysts should be aware of, and also because this course should establish a helpful context in which analysts may consider gendered discourse. In particular, I go on to emphasize certain implicit, unexamined, and disruptive preconceptions about gender that we analysts are always in danger of imposing on our material. Some of these preconceptions will be more evident in omissions than in the analyst's words, for discourse is made up of silence as well as speech. Following this lengthy introduction, I apply my summary to the analysis

This chapter was originally presented in Washington, D.C. as the Fifteenth Edith Weigert Lecture, sponsored by the Forum on Psychiatry and the Humanities, Washington School of Psychiatry, April 24, 1992.

of two jokes and a quotation from Freud. Finally, I apply the ideas I have been developing to two clinical problems that occur frequently in contemporary psychoanalytic practice.

I

Gender should not be approached as an immutable, irreducible fact of nature. Instead, it should be approached as a construction; more exactly, it is a never-ending process of constructing ideas about male and female characteristics and differences. This constructionist process is likely to be regulated by, as well as expressive of, those discourses on gender that are most powerfully represented in one's cultural setting at one or another historical moment. As a discourse-controlled process of construction, gender is an unstable mix of socially conformist beliefs and practices and individually varied, often hidden or marginalized forms of both submission to and rebellion against normative pressures.

Traditionally, we have employed a binary, or dichotomous, approach to discourse on gender: male and female. In poststructuralist critical theory, however, binary classifications have come under critical attack for their implying both absolute differences and a hierarchy of value, as in good-bad, high-low, white-black, and in this case male-female. The hierarchy of value is implied in the usual practice of implicitly putting the first term above the other in value. Thus, the binary approach to discourse on gender guides and licenses universalized and discriminatory conceptions of the sexes, and discourse itself becomes gendered. These biased conceptions presuppose that we both seek and find fixed essences in men and women rather than processes of gender development that remain in flux and are better approached as matters of degree and kind than of essence and value.

Additionally, the binary format obscures rather than highlights the relational aspects of gender. These relational aspects are both descriptive and prescriptive. Descriptively, the characterization of neither gender stands on its own feet, for the ways in which both sexes are characterized are interdependent; it does not do to set them apart. "Male" defines "female" and vice versa. Prescriptively, the implicit hierarchy of gender conveys directives for conforming to those patterns of interaction between the sexes that will support the traditional discourse of fixed essences and total, absolute, and hierarchical difference.

The binary conception of gender is also politically conservative in that it is based ultimately on taken-for-granted ideas about genital reproductive anatomy. At least it is rationalized in the terms of the anatomical difference between the sexes. Briefly, either one has a penis or a womb or one does not, and that is what gender is all about. But that reasoning cannot comfortably accommodate biological variations within the anatomical realm, such as the various kinds of degrees of hermaphroditism. Nor can it comfortably accommodate subjective identities that do not correspond precisely to anatomy.

Another conservative consequence of this genital–reproductive focus is its reinforcing of the phallocratic values of our society. Only males can and should rule the world. It reinforces these values by implying that being female absolutely requires heterosexuality and childbearing in the context of a traditional nuclear family. By assigning females to this stereotyped role, one places them closer to untheorized ideas of nature. As creatures of nature, females are simpler, more emotive or "hysterical," more inconstant and elusive, and their "destiny" is known in advance. In contrast, men are located higher in the order of things. They are beings who have emerged from nature to occupy a stable, complex, godlike position at the center of power, reason, language, and ordered change. They are plainly visible, whereas women are hidden in mystery or behind artifice. That's why *male* comes first in the verbal coupling; women, being less definable, are what's left over. At bottom, however, and just like women, men are captives of the dichotomy, for the sharp division implies that they, too, are expected to conform to heterosexual reproductive models. Thus, Freud (1905a) concluded that being sexually polymorphous beyond early childhood is "perverse" and thereby advanced a prescription that normal sexuality should be classified in simple binary terms.

Contrary to conventional understanding, however, conceptions of gender and sexual practices have not been identical all through history, and they more or less vary from one culture to another. There are even discursive variations in how the biological body is represented (e.g., Laquer, 1990; Lewontin, 1991). Once we adopt this historical, cultural, and discursive perspective, we are left with no good reason to argue "the truth of gender." Nothing is to be gained by defining gender in static, polarized, ahistorical ways. Consequently, the fruitful way to go seems to be to study the genealogies of conventional meaning and value in the realm of gender; that is to say, more is to be gained from studying in specific instances how "gender" has come to signify whatever it does signify and the consequences of that signification in the relevant areas of life: sexual practices, social roles, rules of decorum, occupational rewards, and so forth.

One last introductory word on gendered discourse: although the clinical work of psychoanalysis is assumed to be unconfined by conventional gendered discourse, everything that comes up in analysis being potentially open to analytic question, that work cannot avoid gender conservatism entirely. The reason for this lag is that to some extent the work of clinical interpretation cannot dispense with the terms of conventional discourse. Also, because the conventional conceptions of gender have ramified so extensively throughout our language, we must necessarily use problem-laden language to conduct analyses. This limitation includes analysis of the problems involved in the construction of gender, such as selective preferences for only certain metaphors and colloquialisms. This inherent tension of language—its inevitably enacting the very thing that it seeks to objectify and correct or change—has itself been much emphasized in postmodern thought, for example, in deconstructionist critical theory; consequently, discursive inconsistency need not invalidate an entire argument.

Here I conclude my summary of postmodern, largely feminist themes. Each of its prepositions is open to modification, articulation, elaboration, supplementation, and challenge. That openness itself testifies to the constructivist nature of gendered discourse. Indeed, the implications extend far beyond discourse on gender to all that we claim as our knowledge of reality and our way of getting to know reality, and what I have summarized itself draws on the work of many leading thinkers who have been developing philosophical orientations for purposes other than developing feminist critiques. Within all of these contemporary philosophical orientations, the chief working principle is that concepts are epistemological instruments. They are instruments for creating knowledge of the world of a certain sort. They are necessary master narratives that imply a limited set of story lines for specific instances. In other words, the world can be known only in the versions of it we narrate, and what we narrate is controlled by conventions of conceptualization. Each epistemological instrument, such as one or another master narrative

(Schafer, 1992), is limit setting, sometimes violently so. But the limits do not seem to be eternally fixed. Discursive systems are never totally closed to change; the stories change.

My summary itself is best regarded as an epistemological instrument; as such, it cannot lay claim to a forever privileged position. It lays out just one way to go about the job of studying the discursive construction of gender; however, it can lay some claim to being a relatively coherent, active, and thought-provoking narrative of gender, and so it should help reduce the power of established sex-role stereotyping and its unhappy consequences in social and clinical practices and intellectual inquiry.[1]

II

This has been a heavy beginning. For some leavening I turn next to the two jokes and the quotation from Freud that I mentioned earlier. Not a whole lot of leavening, however, as my anatomizing of these jokes and the quotation will be a serious attempt to demonstrate how to detect some of the presuppositions of conventional gendered discourse and how to assess the consequences of these presuppositions. As I see it, the three instances I take up are not essentially different from a set of examples of clinical analysis, for that, too, may be described as a search for, and an assessment of, the presuppositions that enable the narratives that analysands develop.

The First Joke

In one of her writings Muriel Rukeyser retells and revises the popular version of the myth of Oedipus and the Sphinx:

---

[1] In preparing this summary and in developing the argument of this essay, I have drawn especially on, and have been much helped by, the writing on gender and general feminist issues of Ellman (1968), Felman (1981), Culler (1982), de Lauretis (1984), Moi (1985), Jacobus (1986), Scott (1988), Flax (1990), and Butler (1990). These authors tend to refer to one another's work frequently and also to the work of other significant figures in this realm, such as de Beauvoir, Irigaray, Wittig, Nancy K. Miller, and Gallop, all of whose writings appear, along with many others, in such useful anthologies as those put together by Abel (1982), Belsey and Moore (1989), de Lauretis (1986), Miller (1986), Moi (1987), and Showalter (1985).

Long afterward, Oedipus, old and blinded, walked the roads. He
smelled a familiar smell. It was the Sphinx. Oedipus said, "I want to
ask one question. Why didn't I recognize my mother?" "You gave
the wrong answer," said the Sphinx. "But that was what made everything possible," said Oedipus. "No," she said, "when I asked, What
walks on four legs in the morning, two at noon and three in the
evening, you answered, Man. You didn't say anything about women."
"When you say Man," said Oedipus, "you include women, too. Everyone knows that." She said, "That's what you think" [1978, p. 498].

A joke it is, but at bottom not really a laughing matter and that not
only because of the tragic destiny of Oedipus; for the story addresses
seriously the way in which the male gender has been universalized and
elevated in the hierarchy of beings. We surely have used *man* and *man-
kind* and similar words to refer to all human beings, just as we have used
the pronoun *he* to refer in the singular form to persons of both sexes.
Descriptively, *woman, womankind,* and the pronoun *she* have been put
in a class of lower value, and, prescriptively, it is implied that that is as
it should be in that woman make less of a difference in the world.[2] After
all, as Oedipus would put it, "Everybody knows" that God is a he—that
he is God the father and, as such, stands for the supreme omnipotent
and omniscient male. And anyway, it is said, this common elevation of
the he is merely an editorial convention; not to worry. No such luck,
says the Sphinx.

Some feminists have argued that one major consequence of this universalization and hierarchization of maleness is the stripping away of
women's identifying gender. In one argument the linguistic practice
leaves women genderless, absent from gendered discourse or, at best,
pushed to its margins and admitted into language only on an ad hoc basis.
Language is for *him*, not for *her*. In another argument, one that moves
in the opposite direction, the linguistic universalization of the male has
so elevated him that it has removed him from gendered discourse altogether, leaving the female as the only gendered being and implying that
gender is creaturelike. Thus, whichever direction we move in, we begin
to detect in our male-centered conventions a built-in derangement of the

---

[2]Even today male and female editors alike often object to an author's persistent
use of *one* as an alternative to the all-purpose *he*. And many readers and writers still object
to *he or she*, the alternation of *he* and *she*, and the use of *she* as an all-purpose pronoun.

"natural," that is, the presupposed and symmetrical order of things. The binary mode of thought that is supposed to reflect and insure order is creating disorder.

Further on Rukeyser's joke: it reminds us that in Greek mythology the Sphinx is a woman, and it highlights her as an empowered and potentially dangerous woman relative to the power-hungry male adventurer, the boy seeking manhood. Implicitly, she has made Oedipus pay for his masculinist answer, "Man." The joke implies that *Man* should be recognized to be merely a relational term. Taken in itself, the answer doesn't have a leg to stand on, and to fall back on the "Everyone knows" position—to rely on nothing more than powerful conventions in gendered discourse—is to enforce and reinforce a host of objectionable power-oriented, phallocratic assumptions. Postmodern feminists argue that the usages I have been discussing should be given up and replaced by individualized propositions and local formulations; that is, discourse that is specific to persons, practices, contexts, and methods of knowledge: which woman or women, in which cultural context, studied by which means (sociological, psychoanalytic, autobiographical, etc.), ascertained to be doing what, and so forth.[3]

The Second Joke

On the surface this joke seems to raise issues of a sort quite different from Rukeyser's; as I shall try to show, however, this appearance is mostly misleading. Two male friends meet and greet one another cordially. "How's it going?" "Fine, and you?" "Pretty good." The first man then asks, "How's your wife?" to which the second man replies, "Compared to whom?"

"Compared to whom?" is a clever response, one that unexpectedly shifts the context from friendly concern or social decorum to the bawdy. On first hearing, many enlightened people, I among them, have found the joke quite funny. Upon reflection, however, those of us concerned with gender issues in general and with men's conventional degradation of women in particular, as I am, are likely to feel some shame that we

---

[3]This argument accepts the methodological recommendation of "thick description" emphasized by the noted anthropologist Clifford Geertz (1973) and illustrated in historical studies in an especially fine way by Joan Scott (1988).

laughed. For in the world of white male supremacy there can be no mistaking the wisecracker's phallocratic commitments. Here phallocratic refers to conventional male power and authority, both attributed to his phallic identity. In this joke, the man dismisses conventional marital concern and decorum as well as respect for women's feelings by flaunting his role as philanderer and by using the occasion to engage in the kind of heterosexual braggadocio that indifferently reduces women to interchangeable objects.

Reflecting further, we may realize that the wisecrack may be damaging in other respects. Assuming that the question is intended personally and is not just a social nicety, we would take the wisecrack to be transforming a moment of actual or potential intimacy between male friends into a locker-room type of encounter. It would be creating distance from the questioner by adopting a competitive, "mine is bigger than yours" attitude. By assuming this more powerful and distant position, the respondent implicitly pressures the questioner to be just "one of the boys" instead of continuing to distribute his gender interests equally and trying to get emotionally closer. In other words, the questioner would do better to get back into line—the phallocratic line, the power line. Thus does the need of many men to assert supremacy over other men as well as over women disrupt relations between men.

In this view the wisecracker's response may be characterized as narcissistic rather than as interpersonally related. It is aggressively power-oriented rather than welcoming and egalitarian. It boasts of superior sexual appeal, potency, and connoisseurship and makes a positive value of consciencelessness. Additionally, we may suspect that the alacrity with which the respondent lays claim to a kind of masculine omnipotence betrays an insecure sense of masculinity, if not of overall personal impressiveness. And, as I indicated earlier, we may suspect that some of this insecurity is homophobic in that it could be spurning a male friend's caring approach by superimposing macho "hardness" on friendly "softness." All this at the same time as the wisecracker excludes tender personal concern from his relationship with his wife by reducing her to the status of one sexual object among others. It is an unpleasant, unfriendly joke, and, yet, at first hearing many do laugh.

In connection with the prevailing masculinist emphasis in our gendered discourse, we must note that ordinarily the joke would not succeed nearly as well if it were told about two female friends or about a man and woman. Although some social change has already taken place in this respect, especially among the young, for the most part our superficially conventional society continues to put a premium on female modesty, passivity, and monogamy; it decrees that, to be ladylike, a woman should not engage in men's kind of lockerroom bragging. In our cultural context people in general would be much less likely to laugh if the joke were to tell of one woman responding to another woman's question about her husband with a "Compared to whom?" wisecrack. One would be more likely immediately to assume an attitude that is questioning or even diagnostic. The spontaneous response might well be to wonder why the wisecracking wife was so predatory or even so open about it or so coarse or contemptuous or so intent on striking a pose of that kind. To begin with, the question would be, "What's her problem?"

I submit that these conventional responses, although different in form from laughing at the male–male story, would manifest the same phallocratic orientation in that the responding woman would be defined normatively as showing a lack or a fault or at the least a negation of values, that is, degrading herself by displaying a "failing" for all to see.

As I mentioned, there are now breaches in those conventions. For example, a feminist might ask, "Compared to whom?" in order to parody macho conversation or to make an ironic reverse allusion to men's philandering and the double standard. An entertainer of the Mae West variety relies heavily on this kind of parody and irony: enacting a feminist critique of the masculinist conception of gender relations, and relying on the role of the outsider—in her case, the pariah—she applies her wit to exposé and indictment.

And, finally, if the joke's cast of characters were to be a man and a woman, the man as respondent would conventionally be thought to be trying to embarrass the woman or to be propositioning her, or both, and the woman as respondent to a question about her husband would be thought of as being sexually inviting or at least teasing.

We may say that the second joke exposes the play of power in gendered discourse. The joke implicitly universalizes women by condescendingly putting them all in the class of sex objects and allowing them individuality only as better or worse sex objects, as judged by men. The joke also brings out the relational aspect of gender, the masculine being described and prescribed as the relatively more narcissistic, hostile, power-focused, and homophobic of the genders and the female as the repository of more primitive, creaturelike features. In general, the joke is a directive on how to behave in gendered settings and how to think about male and female social roles. Looked at in the present context, our laughing shows the pervasive, insidiously influential operation of our tendencies to retain these conventions of gendered discourse.

My discussion thus far has relied on a general principle of psychoanalytic understanding (as will all the discussions to follow). This principle concerns the importance of interpreting in context. In terms of gender relations, the principle specifies that with each change of local context—male-male, female-female, female-male, or feminist send-up— there occurs a change in the meaning of gendered rhetoric, such as we encounter in responses like "Compared to whom?" and "That's what you think." And with that change there occurs a change in the emotional and cognitive positions of males and females as well as a change in the distribution of power between them. Briefly, the principle states that what the concept of gender will be taken to refer to is context dependent. It should be added that whatever is said or done in a gendered context also modifies that context, if only by reinforcing it. Mae West shrewdly modified conventional contexts all the time. If, therefore, the choice of meaning to be ascribed to gender is not impervious to time, place, person, and rhetorical gesture, we can only gain in understanding by considering it an ongoing and context-dependent process rather than a static and universal attribute.

FREUD'S QUESTION

Freud asked, "What does a woman want?" (Jones, 1955, Vol. 2, p. 421) and, instead of immediately coming up with an answer, he has had a lot to answer for ever since. Postmodern thought is especially sensitive to the epistemological power of the kinds of questions that are asked, and it does not accept sharp distinctions between epistemological power and political power. In this context we may say that, unlike Oedipus, who *answered* in a biased way, Freud was *asking* in a biased way. Freud's question has become a shot heard round the feminist world. It has been responded to by the development of searching critiques of Freud's orientation to women, and to men too. Leading feminist theorists (e.g., Felman, 1981; Jacobus, 1986) have critiqued Freud's question. To develop that critique further I draw on those previous discussions, on general trends in the feminist literature, and on my 1974 article, "Problems in Freud's Psychology of Women."

Freud's question capsulizes a firm, traditional patriarchal orientation. In relation to theory his seemingly curious question tends to limit the possibility of a wide-ranging investigation and discussion. How is this so? The rhetoric of Freud's question is that of the empirical scientist feeling frustrated over his not yet having answered *his* research questions. It assigns a privileged position to the *male* investigator as the one who can ask the question; we may note in this regard Freud's 1933 discussion of femininity in which he states that women cannot resolve this problem, or answer his question, because they *are* the problem. To his mind the question is one for men to answer as well as to ask. Women are to remain silent on the subject of their "true" nature.

That this methodological prescription does not express cautious empiricism on Freud's part is evident once we note how far Freud privileged the male investigator in relation to men. He never even wondered how a man—to begin with, he himself—could hope ever to work out the psychology of men when men are the problem. "What does a man want?" For Freud that is a question that a man can both ask and answer; indeed, he believed he had already done just that. A man need never remain silent. After all, as Freud said (in one of his switches to nonanalytic discourse), men are more lucid, rational, and capable of impartial moral judgment than women (1920b, 1925; see also Grossman and Kaplan 1988). The total history of psychoanalysis undermines Freud's confident position, for it shows that, in significant respects, Freud's answers to the question about men were both limited and contestable. Today's analysts have more questions to ask about men, and they have available to them more complex, varied, and individualized answers to these questions. It is old-fashioned to limit one's approach to men's psychology to that of Freud alone.

Further on Freud's question, "What does a woman want?": It is arbitrary in its universalizing of the idea of "woman." Freud was not asking, "What does *this* woman want?" He was not asking, "What does she want under *these* conditions or *those* conditions?" Nor was he asking, "Have women *always* been this way? If not, how and why have they changed, and what are the consequences?" And so on. Freud's all-inclusive one-shot question presents women as interchangeable and fixed entities, as members of the species "woman," every member of which is predestined to "want" the same thing at bottom and to want it consistently enough to justify being classified at once. We can see that Freud's question follows the same line of thought as the "Compared to whom?" joke does.

True, Freud was never quite satisfied with the adequacy of the general answers that, over time, he had proposed: specifically, a woman wants a penis; she wants a child by the father, preferably a boy, as compensation for her penisless state; she wants assurance of the stability of being loved by the other; she wants narcissistically satisfying idealization by desirous and prostrate males. Later, and it seems largely in response to prodding by female analysts, Freud added that she wants revenge on mother for her seductions and deprivations beyond those in the oedipal sphere that he had already analyzed. It is not clear why Freud made a special point of being dissatisfied with his account of the psychology of women, for in the end his was not that simplistic an account. It is clear, however, that in his general theorizing he never questioned his presupposition that one could explain women totalistically—and, for that matter, men too. In his individual case discussions, however, and despite the biased generalizations he used, he did try to develop particularized portraits of women (see, e.g., 1905a, 1920b).

An additional restriction on knowledge imposed by Freud's generalized question is its presupposing that fundamentally a woman's desires must be different from a man's. His question does not convey what his own work prepared the way for: that sense of bisexual resemblance of the sexes, that unconscious androgyny they share, some of it by virtue of cross-projections and cross-identifications.

Yet another restriction stems from the implication that women can be defined by their wants. On my reading, Freud consistently implied that men should be defined by their typical conflicts. Of course, their conflicts include their wants, but they are not exhausted by them; there are always the questions of the anxieties and guilt feelings associated with these conflicts and the characteristics of the defensive and adaptive psychic structures men develop to manage both these conflicts and the painful affects associated with them. Shouldn't the question about women have therefore read, What are women's typical conflicts and painful affects, and what kinds of structures do they develop to manage them? Freud's actual question seems to assign women to a position closer to untheorized "nature" and "the passions," and thereby to render women as being more simple and creaturelike than men. He said that he did not think they developed all that much psychic structure; he thought they had less reason to. This condescending conception is entirely consistent with his usual patriarchal outlook on women.

Finally, it is arguable that the question's rhetoric implies some exasperation over the alleged inconstancy of women. The question may have a tinge of, What do women want of me (or of men)? There are other ways to state the problem; for example, "There are aspects of women's psychology that I have failed to work out to my satisfaction, and I wish I knew how to proceed further," or "I seem to have relatively more countertransference problems in my work with female analysands." It is relevant to note in this context the abrupt, rejecting, and injurious way in which Freud ended his treatment of Dora (1905a) and the so-called homosexual young woman (1920b). Consequently, we may well ask whether, in these cases, the right question was, "What did she want?" and whether the right or adequate answers, the ones he provided in these cases, were "Defiance" and "Revenge." And we may be justified in forming the impression that Freud did not take well to those women, or perhaps particularly those *young* women, who challenged his patriarchal authority, among other things by preferring women to men and not readily entering into an idealizing, sexual–oedipal transference to him. And so the question, "What does a woman want?" may be more petulant and autocratic than curious.

III

The two common clinical analytic problems that I have chosen to examine are, first, the common practice of female analysands privileging female analysts and, second, difficulties in the way of analyzing women for whom "the biological clock is ticking."

Privileging the Female Analyst

Today it is common in the United States and perhaps elsewhere that women who are prospective analysands seek out female analysts *because they are female.* I shall try to show that many phallocentric preconceptions enter into this preference, which, by the way, is shared by some analytic consultants. I emphasize in advance that my discussion does not support any general conclusions in favor of female analysands being treated by male analysts. Not only does one error never justify another; in this instance, it would be the same error being committed in a different cause. Again, it is individualized judgments that are called for.

The privileging of female analysts is based on a number of highly contestable preconceptions. Foremost among these preconceptions is the idea of commonality of subjective experience among women. It is thought that the female therapist will understand more quickly, empathize more sensitively, and interpret more effectively when the analysand is a woman. Having been exposed to the same inimical influences on girls and women in our phallocratic society, and having similar if not identical bodily experiences and concerns over the course of her development, the female analyst will be more identified with her analysand and so should be closer to being an "ideal" therapist for her than a man could ever hope to be.

In its totalistic form this is not a strong argument. First of all, one could argue that the kind of identification in question will involve significant, disruptive countertransference potentials. Since the female analyst has experienced the same problematic societal and bodily impingements, and since subjective experience should be regarded as constructed rather than passively observed, her identification may well involve the same anxieties, self-esteem problems, and difficult moods as those plaguing her female analysand. Thus, she might well have impaired vision for, and too greatly reduced distance from, just those problems that consciously matter the most to many women or that will come to matter the most in the thick of their analyses. And, to the rejoinder that the female analyst's own analysis will have helped her eliminate or greatly reduce her problems with being a woman, one could ask, "Treated by whom?" By a man—as is often the case? By this logic one would have to conclude either that female analysts have been left in too unanalyzed and conflicted a condition or that male analysts can analyze women effectively.

Even in those cases in which the female analyst has been treated by another woman, the same question arises, though displaced back one therapeutic generation; for, looking backward, it takes only a couple of generations to identify an almost totally male world of analysts. Further-more, the evidence suggests that, with only a few partial exceptions, the women who practiced analysis in the early part of this century did not depart significantly from Freud's masculinist approach to gender differences.[4]

I turn now to a second general difficulty with the privileging of female analysts. Freud's view of gender development is that it is an-drogynous at its core, specific gender choices being resultants of fields of force occurring in the setting of ambivalence, loss, repression, and oblique returns of the repressed that signal, more or less, ambiguity of gender identity in psychic reality.[5] Analysts of both sexes should, there-fore, have a common core of unconscious fantasy and trial identi-fications to draw on in their work. Female analysts encounter paternal transferences too (e.g., Goldberger and Evans, 1985).

Further, male and female therapists commonly manifest features conventionally ascribed to members of the opposite sex. Looked at from the outside, their analytic work easily lends itself to a mixture of con-ventional masculine and feminine descriptions: caring, nurturant, em-pathic, forceful, active, passive, empowered, creature of nature, pillar of rationality, and so forth. With the help of their own analyses, analysts of both sexes are expected to have access to their own androgynous con-structions of subjective experience in order to be ready to fill the bill as analysts in how they act as well as in how they empathize with and in-terpret their analysands' paternal and maternal transferences and their own gender-mixed countertransferences.

---

[4]Karen Horney (1967) is regarded as a special case by many feminists, and in-deed she did attack some of Freud's phallocentric basic assumptions. In my view, however, she retained the male-modeled and misleading universalizing tendencies that impaired Freud's work. Melanie Klein is sometimes cited as another notable excep-tion (Segal, 1964); however, I read her foundational work as a compromise between, on the one hand, retaining Freud's flawed, overgeneralized propositions concerning gender and, on the other, subordinating them to other dynamic variables that did some-what shift the emphasis away from Freud's steady focus on gendered sexuality. It would lead too far afield to pursue these issues here. In any case, Klein and Horney, between them, could not have analyzed great numbers of future female analysts and therapists.

[5]It has frequently been noted that Freud himself did not adhere rigorously to the line of thought laid down by his theoretical emphasis on primary bisexuality and mixed gender identification in both sexes; all I can say in the present context is that his prac-tice did not live up to his theory. It is, however, toward Freud's theory, not his prac-tice, that feminist thinkers have directed most of their critiques.

It must also be assumed that female analysands who present only "female" problems in analysis are not being fully analyzed. Similarly, female analysts who deal only with maternal transferences and feminine identifications and ignore androgynous, paternal, and homosexual transferences, in which they and their analysands partly figure as male or male-equivalent, are also not carrying out complete analysis; in addition to defensive counteridentification, these analysts may have their own homophobic problems. Because analysis deals largely with psychic reality, one should never take it for granted that the analysand's biological femaleness limits her analysis to one specific, exclusive, and fundamental narrative of gender.

Women do vary among themselves in the strength and content of their masculine identifications and in their degrees of conflictedness in this area. These factors cannot be assessed except in relation to the strength and content of feminine identifications and conflicts over them. Particularly important in this regard is identification with the version in psychic reality of the mother with whom, from one's earliest days, one has built one's idea of being a woman; however, a counterpoised identification with the father will never be ignored if the analyst's approach to gender definition and subjective experience is conceived in the relational terms rather than binary terms.

And what of men in this context? Some male analysts would seem to have strong and well-integrated identifications with conventional maternal figures. It is certainly possible that, with these significant latent female identity components, such a male analyst may be in a less conflicted functional position as a "maternal" analyst than a woman with tons of "female" subjective experience, all of it conflicted. Should these men, too, be automatically ruled out by female analysands?

I turn to one last argument against privileging the female therapist. Analysands present varied cultural backgrounds. Sometimes analysands are much older than their analysts, sometimes unlike them in being married or single, with children or without, with chronic illness or severe experiences of object loss, and so on. Further, female analysts, of whom there are ever increasing numbers, do not regularly or frequently back off from analyzing men. There is no evidence that any of these differences regularly precludes effective analytic work. Indeed, it sometimes seems that the "outsider" has the advantage of observing and interpreting phenomena that do not touch her or him personally in any acute way and so can do the job with fewer disruptive counter-transferences.[6]

I believe that my arguments in this context have been consistent with some of the feminist critiques of the binary approach to gender. What must be added now is that, when properly carried out, psychoanalysis helps free many attributes of being a person from conventional binary classifications, such as the ones that Freud used when he equated *female* with feminine-passive-submissive-masochistic and *male* with what he took to be their opposites. In our society the majority of women who are studied in analysis seem to be unconsciously haunted and confused by the idea that intellectuality, activity, assertiveness, leadership, power, nonconformity, and many other characteristics or ways of living are "masculine." Usually, they do not want to be masculine or to be thought to be that, and so they shrink back from being all they can be or else they suffer unnecessarily. (Schafer, 1984) Additionally, our culture seems to strengthen the link in unconscious psychic reality between these masculinized attributes and possession of the penis, and so to intensify envy of men (so-called penis envy) and to stand in the way of a woman's feeling and acting feminine or womanly in whatever way and to whatever extent she prefers to do so without disruptive ambivalence.

Upon reflection, even the primary genital-reproductive emphasis in the description of gender differences—that apparently most fundamental and undeniable component of the binary classification of gender, the anatomical difference—can be viewed as an expression of a choice of what to emphasize. In this view it is a choice that prejudges or precommits one to a certain outlook on social relations, and in particular the childbearing role or destiny of women. It is a value-laden choice. It is a perceptual–cognitive difference, a rhetorical difference, a historically rooted power difference that sets up prevailing hierarchies of biological "facts" (Laquer, 1990).

---

[6]Those feminists identified with the "different voice" approach (e.g., Gilligan, 1986) may reject this statement as the kind that only a man would make; there are, however, many other feminists who reject the different voice argument as misguidedly conservative in its manifesting all the faults of the universalizing, essentializing, binary mode of thought that, as they see it, has helped to keep women over the course of history in an inferior position in this gender-hierarchized society. For present purposes I must note only that the matter is not settled. The different voice proponents do not have the last word; they speak only for one position among others.

Cultural and political power being what they are, and interpretation and insight not possessing the omnipotence one might wish, total emancipation from sex stereotyping is difficult to achieve through analysis. But analysis can do some of the job; it often has. Modern feminist critiques point out, however, that much rethinking of gender issues remains to be done by psychoanalysts.

The Ticking of the Biological Clock

Often enough these days the analysand is an unwed childless woman in her middle to late thirties who hears the "biological clock" ticking away and feels unable to establish satisfactory and stable relationships with the kind of man who is available for marriage and the responsible fathering of a baby. Feeling that her time for satisfying motherhood is running out, this woman introduces at the very beginning a transference–countertransference gender problem, for, as she emphasizes, she has turned to psychoanalysis, often after prolonged, ineffectual attempts at psychotherapy of various kinds, to help her realize her goal. Implied is the "natural" necessity and the urgent desirability to confirm or consolidate her "female identity" by bearing and rearing a child in an ongoing heterosexual relationship. Inevitably, it is implied that, in large part, it will be the analyst's burden to bring her to fruition. In an attempt to avoid serious misunderstanding, the analyst is obliged at the very beginning, when recommending analysis, to convey in some way that she or he can extend no such promise or guarantee and to explain that what analysis may accomplish is helping her reduce those disruptive conflicts that have stood in the way of her reaching the goals she has set for herself.

Frequently, it soon becomes clear that the initial clarification of what analysis is about has only served to drive the analysand's demands underground. Her readily and sincerely accepting the analyst's explanations of psychoanalysis proves to have remained pretty much on the level of conscious and preconscious understanding of the complex nature of identity formation, love relationships, and the life cycle. And so the demands resurface directly or are expressed indirectly. The analysand may complain that all this analysis is interesting and even helpful, but still she has no man, no love, no heterosexual gratification, and no maternal prospects; or she may substitute detailed accounts of encounters with men, past and present, for free association, as though attempting to convert the treatment into premarital counseling; and so forth. Whatever the manifestations, the biological clock will be heard ticking in the analytic sessions.

Well aware of and empathizing with the analysand's distress on this score, and knowing about men's narcissistic exploitation of overeager women and the like, the analyst will nevertheless be alert to the possibilities of constructing interpretations concerning: the analysand's intense ambivalence over female identity; homosexual inclinations or intense fears of them; denied but powerful rage against men combined with much envy and competitiveness; deep-seated needs for omnipotent control; pervasive underlying depression with severe problems of self-esteem and self-assertion; major doubts about one's potential to be a good enough spouse and mother; reservations about motherhood owing to the disruptions, burdens, and risks it entails; and a host of unresolved problems with her own mother. These are common human problems, even in those who are well married and with children, but it is fairly likely that they are more severe in the woman we are considering. The problems are not unique to women. With few appropriate changes being made, the same list of problems applies to the average man in analysis too.

The analyst soon discovers that, among other things, the female analysand is using the ticking clock as a defense against analytic insight. It will be recognized that the analysand wants to mother a child in a heterosexual context *as an alternative* to looking into and resolving chronic personal problems that have made for a frustrating and painful life no matter what her occupational and other social achievements. Indeed, she may well be hoping that having a child will somehow cure all these other difficulties and resolve all her doubts. At this point a delicate phase of the analytic relationship will be reached, for interpretive approaches to this defensive use of the biological clock may readily be seen by the analysand as rigid, unempathic, withholding, blind, indifferent, even cruel, and certainly sexist.

In time the analyst will have grounds to interpret that the analysand expects, symbolically if not literally, that the analyst will be the father of the desired child or the empowering and restorative mother who holds the power to fulfill or thwart the analysand's own maternal aspirations, or, in an androgynous way, both. The fantasy of the male analyst as father or cofather of the child is common in analytic work with women who want to get pregnant and do, and who deliver a baby during analysis, and that fantasy even comes up frequently in the analysis of women who already have children and bring up child-rearing problems during analysis. In the case of maternal transference to a male or female analyst, the analysand may imagine the analyst to be the mother who might finally relent and no longer hinder the daughter's wholeness, separation, and oedipally colored gratifications.

I want next to indicate briefly the way the ticking clock is linked to my introductory remarks on the concept of gender. First, it is a powerful convention in our society that motherhood does confirm a woman's natural female identity. We idealize motherhood; we even sanctify it, as may be observed in the blissful and exalted way in which we tend to react to a woman's announcing that she is pregnant and to her swelling belly. We tend to forget how many women are deeply unprepared for womanhood as well as motherhood, just as many men are unprepared for manhood and fatherhood. We tend to forget the androgynous unconscious, the preoedipal fixations, the consciously repudiated but still influential identifications with sadistic and withholding mothers, the woman's rage at the baby who violates her body image, saps her vitality, and disrupts her career, and so on. In short, we do as the female analysand of my example does: we defend in the name of motherhood, and thereby, from a societal point of view, we reinforce all the phallocentric, totalistic, binary-oriented reductions of women to the creaturehood of reproductive roles.

Upon analysis the countertransference will be found to express conventional emotional positions. For example, the analyst might unconsciously link the analysand to her or his own mother and thereby to familiar familial contexts, such as destructiveness toward real and imagined siblings, rivalry with the actual or potential father, and reparative aims in relation to the mother of psychic reality whom one has damaged in one way or another. The analyst is then in danger of feeling that she or he is the bad child who is not helping the mother to be a happy and fulfilled mother, and so a "good" mother, and may, in consequence, gradually shift into an attitude more appropriate to an eager midwife.

However solid our feminist convictions may be, in psychic reality we analysts remain more or less vulnerable to those countertransferences that will fit in with the analysand's defensively deployed demands and keep us feeling pressed, inadequate, guilty, or on the defensive. Insofar as we begin to collude with defensive use of the biological clock, we limit our effectiveness as analysts and reduce the woman's opportunity to accomplish enough working through of her general problems to enhance her chances of living a satisfying life, with or without motherhood.

The analyst's ideal is to fortify the operation of the analysand's reality principle. Then, the ultimate satisfaction of the pleasure principle will be achieved through the delays and the detours of thought as it tests inner and outer realities and assists one's coming to terms with oneself *analytically.* On this reality-principled basis the desire for motherhood will be reduced in ambivalence, and the desperate belief that one is "a mother or nothing" will lose much of its force. Obviously, not every childless woman who is significantly helped by analysis will become a mother, and there may be many circumstantial reasons for this. Whatever the reasons, these analysands will have some mourning to do for the child they have never had or, so to say, lost. Nevertheless, they will also know that they are sexual women, worthwhile grown-ups, with realistic opportunities for pleasure, pride, and love relationships available to them and with access to alternate routes to the gratification of at least some of their caretaking needs.

IV

In conclusion, I have tried to provide an orientation to postmodern, principally feminist thought about discourse on gender and gendered discourse and to show how this orientation helps us understand sex-biased use of language, story, joke, and the investigation and treatment of psychological problems. The psychoanalytic method and the postmodern approach to discourse abide by similar principles with respect to the recognition and interpretation of convention, rhetoric, belief, power, and gender. In every case we are examining the operation of epistemological instruments: scrutinizing (deconstructing) how knowledge and belief are constructed, revised, and rejected and how values are thereby enforced and reinforced.

I have applied my remarks in a critique of widespread assumptions concerning the female analyst's special competence to deal with female analysands and in some reflections on the analysis of women preoccupied with becoming mothers before their time of fertility has run out. I have assumed that, in this respect, we psychoanalysts are not radically different from all members of our culture: having been steeped in the traditional biases of gendered discourse, we, female as well as male, must remain especially alert to how this discourse always threatens to induce countertransferences that control and limit the way we work. We must be aware of our tendency to believe that our ideas of gender refer simply to prelinguistic essences or fixed classifications in nature and that language merely describes these "facts of nature" in the only objective way possible. On this self-critical basis, however, we may hope to move existing controversies concerning the conceptualization of gender onto a higher plane, a plane on which we may generate new and ever more fruitful dialogues concerning discourse on gender. By these means we may also achieve greater consistency in maintaining a truly analytic attitude in our clinical work with members of both sexes and those who resist binary classification altogether.

4

Five Readings of Freud's "Observations on Transference-Love"

Like so many other of Freud's works of genius, "Observations on Transference-Love" (1915a) is wide in scope, deep in understanding, and forceful in the way it challenges conventional modes of thought. But it is a short piece, and the price of its brevity is that it deals with each of its major topics in only an introductory or cursory fashion. It is also a relatively early work. Consequently, the essay calls for clarification, amplification, coordination of its various propositions, interpretation of implied or latent content, and methodological and epistemological reconsideration. And in responding to this call, we should express our own views and concerns as contemporary psychoanalysts now that more than seventy-five years have passed since the essay was written; we should not simply try to establish exactly what Freud "had in mind," for Freud's topic is now and will always be of great concern to all analysts.

I wish to express my gratitude to Dr. William I. Grossman for his penetrating, thorough, and helpful critique of an earlier version of this essay.

The five perspectives on or readings of "Observations on Transference-Love" will supplement one another, each bringing out different aspects of Freud's text. In certain respects my readings emphasize the major contributions of the essay; in other respects, its limitations and its controversial aspects. The essay's difficulties derive either from its having been written during the relatively early years of the development of psychoanalysis or from Freud's philosophical, social, and personal commitments, values, and biases.

THE DEMOLITION
OF CONVENTIONAL BOUNDARIES

Even today most people draw sharp lines between the normal and abnormal, between childhood and adulthood, and between psychoanalysis and "real life." By "most people" I refer not only to the general public and many analysands undergoing treatment but also to many people who work in the helping professions. Dichotomous thinking has wide appeal; it satisfies a need for simplicity and a sense of clear structure. We can see in many places that dichotomous thinking appealed greatly to Freud too (for example, Pain-Pleasure, Pleasure Principle-Reality Principle, Life Instinct-Death Instinct).

It is, however, an outstanding feature of Freud's writings that, at bottom, they continuously challenge conventional beliefs. Rejecting simplistic conventional dichotomies, Freud is steadily identifying and articulating transitional phenomena, transformations, and the dynamics of change: tracing the retention of the old in the new without denying the new; demonstrating the benefits of thinking in terms of differences of degree rather than of kind; seeing people as occupying mixed, internally contradictory or conflicting positions. In his dream book (1900), for example, we encounter him arguing for the continuity of mental life in sleep and waking; in the *Three Essays* (1905b), undermining any hard and fast distinction between perversion and normal sexuality; in various papers on sexuality, such as "On Transformations of Instinct as Exemplified in Anal Erotism" (1917b), approaching psychosexual development as a series of transformations rather than sharply delineated phases and portraying the interpenetration of these phases in a most subtle fashion. And there is no need any longer to dwell on Freud's

not accepting an absolute normal–abnormal distinction but rather insisting that the same fundamental issues shape the lives of normals and
neurotics.[1]

Many of those who reject Freud's work do so because they mistake his search for continuity within transformations over time as simple-
minded reductionism. Typically they cite statements torn out of the total
context of Freud's writings and the mode of thought they stand for. In
using these citations as warrants for their rejection, they miss the point
of Freud's inspired breaks with those conventions of his time that gov-
erned the construction of psychological knowledge.

The breaking of various conventional conceptual boundaries can
be discerned in "Observations on Transference-Love." I select for special emphasis one piece of demolition that, on my reading, Freud accomplished more impressively and explicitly in this essay than anywhere
else. Viewed narrowly, it is the demolition of the boundary between transference love and "real love"; viewed broadly, the demolition of the
boundary between the analytic relationship and "real-life" relationships.

In this essay, Freud seems content for some time to develop his
technical thesis that transference love must be handled as something
unreal, that is, as an irrational, unconsciously motivated repetition of
repressed desire and conflict that takes the form of resistance. Only well
into the argument (p. 168) does he pause and, with his ever-restless and
self-questioning genius, challenge his own insistence on transference
love's *un*reality. It is as though he has just recognized that he had become so involved in technical concerns with differences that he had lost
his cherished perspective on continuities in mental life. His perspective
regained, he goes on to assert that the difference between normal love
and transference love is not so great after all; at most, this difference is
a matter of degree, and while it remains useful technically to bear in mind
and interpret transference love's exaggerated nature and unrealistic features, doing so should not limit the recognition that normal love, too,
has many of the same unrealistic aspects. Normal love, like transference
love, has its infantile prototypes; it, too, is repetitive, idealizing, and

---

[1]Elsewhere (1970) I have taken up ways in which Freud never did free himself
entirely from dichotomous thinking. There, I tried to show that it was Heinz Hartmann
in particular who developed more fully and systematically the freer aspect of Freud's
analytic thinking. It would be unreasonable for us to expect Freud to have done the
whole job singlehandedly.

replete with conflictual transferences; it, too, is a complex mix and not simply a new and pure experience.

In developing this position on love, Freud is actually asserting three fundamental continuities simultaneously: that between the infantile and the adult, that between the normal and the neurotic (the rational-realistic and the irrational-unrealistic), and that between psychoanalysis and real life. It is the last of these that we can read as a major step forward in psychoanalytic understanding of the total personality and its develop-ment in the context of human relatedness; the other important continu-ities I just mentioned had already figured for some time in Freud's thought about development, psychopathology, and the treatment process.

Although we could piece together clues in Freud's previous writ-ings to show that he had already reached these interpretive conclusions concerning love as transference and transference as love, and although we could also argue that he had already conveyed this understanding in other writings, in pursuing that course we would, I think, be mistaking tacit knowledge and fragmentary insight for express conviction in a developed and integrated context. Further, we would be overlooking Freud's own sense of fresh awareness in "Observations on Transference-Love" and his pointed emphasis on and implicitly pleased interest in this further contribution to his theories of both love and the psychoana-lytic process.

Notwithstanding these various merits, it could be argued that Freud's essay taken as a whole is an indecisive and incomplete document. He presented transference love as both unreal and "genuine" and suggested that, technically, it should be treated simply as unreal, even if it is basi-cally genuine. For technical purposes, transference love is to be regarded as repetition, merely a "new edition" of an old text of love. And yet, because of its continuity with genuine love, our analytic approach could or should allow for new attachment; that is, for the analysand's relating to the analyst as a "new object."

Much later, Loewald (1960) argued just this point when he dis-cussed the theory of the therapeutic action of psychoanalysis. Loewald focused attention on the new and higher levels of organization made possible by analysis and on the possibility of new modes of experience of self and others in relation that attests to the implied structural changes. This new mode of relatedness and of the experience of self and others is no longer kept excessively rigid or fluid, overwhelming or indifferent by primitive suspicion, depression, ambivalence, and the like. In this context, one may encounter "new" objects and so experience "new" love.

On this point, however, Freud remained conspicuously silent. Out of respect for his perspicacity, I would like to think that he decided not to take on the difficulties of theorizing about the "new" in the same essay in which he was warning the presumably young, inexperienced, or even unanalyzed analyst not to be misled and certainly not to be carried away by the analysand's declaration of newfound love. Freud was surely right to be steadily concerned that any significant relaxation of the properly detached analytic attitude might easily lead one to slide into an ethically and therapeutically compromised role in the course of doing analysis. Today more than ever, we are aware of how often therapists do lapse into having affairs with their analysands or at least approaching them sexually. Very much in the eye of the alert public, these scandals are no longer considered occasional and isolated. In the far more frequent case, the analyst who gets carried away emotionally but refrains from sexual overtures or responses is still in no position to interpret the analysand's conflictual love helpfully.

We cannot, however, be sure of this pragmatic explanation of Freud's silence on "real" love in the therapeutic relationship. Consequently, we must allow for an alternative, namely, that in 1915 Freud may well have been both *personally* and *theoretically unprepared* to think further about the implications of the real aspects of transference love for technique and the theory of the analytic process. I shall return to Freud's personal unpreparedness when I consider his discussions of technique and countertransference and when I comment on his patriarchal orientation. Concerning his theoretical unpreparedness, it may be inferred from Freud's zeal in developing his central theses that he sensed that taking up the real elements in transference love would or could compromise his thoroughgoing emphasis on the determining of the present by the past. This determinism is seen in the compulsion to repeat, in transference and acting out, and in other signs of the inextinguishable infantile unconscious. His first order of business, in addition to economy of explanation, was demonstrating the unconscious continuity of human lives over time.

An additional limiting factor in this connection may be derived from a consideration of historical context. In 1915, Freud had not yet developed his ego psychology, which, as Hartmann (1939, 1964) was to argue later on, does allow a theoretical place for the new and the autonomous and can do so without rejecting Freud's theoretically precious premises of determinism and continuity.

MANAGING THE EROTIC TRANSFERENCE

Freud repeatedly experienced himself as forcibly confronted by the erotically charged romantic feelings and demands of his female analysands. Some women manifested these feelings and demands quite plainly while others seemed to show only subtle signs of them and were instead engaged urgently, though often unconsciously, in combating or defending against them. Characteristically, and to the lasting benefit of all of us, analysand and analyst alike, Freud set about working out what could be learned from these emotional developments. What could these phenomena reveal about the depths of his analysands' mental lives and the sources of their neuroses?

Freud came to view the female analysand's outpouring of romantic and passionate feelings and demands in two ways. On the one hand, it was a resistance insofar as it enacted her pressure on the analyst to change the analytic relationship into a love affair. By inducing a shift away from the psychical sphere toward the physical, she could substitute neurotic action for therapeutic remembering. With the same stroke, Freud explained, she could "bring down" the analyst from his position of authority in the relationship and prove to herself that the treatment is dangerous and warrants determined resistance. On the other hand, Freud regarded the resistance-serving erotization of the therapeutic relationship as a gateway to the analysand's repressed infantile libidinal desires and conflicts. Once analyzed, that resistant maneuver could reveal her unconsciously maintained "preconditions for loving" and "all the detailed characteristics of her state of being in love" (p. 166). In this view, transference love is like dreams: on the one hand, a complex set of disguises; on the other, a royal road to the therapeutically essential memories of childhood. These are the memories by which Freud could hope to demonstrate to the analysand the origins and driving forces of her neurosis and at the same time demonstrate to the world the truth of his theories.

We can see that Freud viewed the erotic transference as a way of blocking analysis that is motivated unconsciously by all that is essential to the analytic cure. On this understanding, the analysis of transference love as opposition is invaluable. Here lies much of the sense of Freud's remark, "The only really serious difficulties . . . lie in the management of the transference" (p. 159). Freud emphasized that the carrying out of this delicate task depends on the analyst's remembering that this transference love is created by the analytic situation itself. It is a product of the observational field and method, not a simple, direct response of one person to another; in other words, there is no reason to expect the analyst to carry a special transference valence.

We shall soon come to consider the implications of Freud's apparent failure to consider the possibility that, in both form and content, analysands unconsciously collaborate with the analyst through transference love; specifically, they employ it as a communication in the form of a showing rather than a conscious remembering and verbal telling. His focus remained on opposition and the overcoming of inaccessibility.

Today we encounter a special, situationally provoked defensive use of transference love: women who, on the basis of a smattering of analytic knowledge, enter analysis with the conviction that they are supposed to fall in love with their male analyst; if they do not, this only proves to them that they are bad, rebellious, or otherwise unfit analysands. In these cases, the analyst must first find opportunities to interpret their conflicts over being "good" and "bad" and their fears of spontaneity in what are for them the as yet uncharted waters of psychoanalysis. In 1915, however, Freud had to be concerned instead with those ill-prepared analysts who encouraged analysands to fall in love with them or at least thought it necessary to alert them to that eventuality (p. 161).

In this essay, Freud tries to lay the groundwork for consistent reliance on interpretation in overcoming the resistance expressed in the erotic transference. In some places, however, Freud seems to rely on rational argument and pressure as well. For example (p. 167), he seems ready to argue with the analysand about the unreality of her love, asserting that she would be compliant rather than oppositional if she truly loved the analyst. In statements of this sort, and despite his pointing out how important it is that the analyst be patient, Freud comes across partly as a rationalist technician, working rather closer to the intellectually persuasive than the emotional end of the continuum (Schafer, 1992, chap. 14). Although we can appreciate the fact that Freud is portraying an extreme version of an erotic transference and is appropriately concerned to protect the treatment from an untimely and mutually painful ending, upon reflection we can also realize that that very fact serves better the argument *against* resorting to or relying too heavily on intellectual explanation and exhortation. Furthermore, Freud himself emphasized early in his essay that, in this overheated context, rational explanations fall on deaf ears. To Freud's emphasis we might now add that, if anything, those explanations and exhortations usually only add fuel to the fire, in part by seeming to the analysand to confirm her transference fantasies that the analyst *is* attached to her.

In this oscillation on the question of the uses of reason and pressure, Freud may have been exposing some personal discomfort with respect to transference love that I shall soon be discussing. First, however, we must return to the subject of Freud's theoretical readiness for conceptualizing real love in the transference. Freud wrote "Observations on Transference-Love" almost ten years before he presented his ego psychology in developed form. In 1915, he still believed that it was the lifting of repression and the recovery of memories in early childhood—"making the unconscious conscious"—that is the essential curative factor in the therapeutic process. That belief was based theoretically on his topographic conception of the mind. It does, however, necessarily slant technique in a direction that is simultaneously pressuring and rationalistic; it fosters an adversarial slant on resistance and too great reliance on conscious understanding as the route to mastery.

In contrast, Freud's later structural formulations emphasized the need to modify defenses, reduce superego pressures, and in general strengthen the ego: "Where id was, there shall ego be" (1923a). By then Freud had realized that the total personality is involved in neurotic problems. Consequently, he induced a considerable shift of emphasis in the direction of recognizing that insight based on emotional experiencing as essential in bringing about deep and lasting change in the mind as a whole. This new role of emotional experience extends beyond the emotions of transference love itself; it is the kind of experience that is possible only in a prepared structural context, developed through analytic interpretations of repetitions within life history. This shift from topography to structure underlies many of the advances in psychoanalytic technique that have been made subsequent to 1915. (Especially to be noted about this shift is the analyst's constant and heightened concern with preparing the ground for transference interpretations rather than just seeming to read the unconscious straightaway.)

When considering Freud's ideas in historical context, we must also be alert to what seem to be intimations of the future, for Freud was, in a sense, always catching up with himself. Already in such papers as "Formulations on the Two Principles of Mental Functioning" (1911), "On Narcissism" (1914b), and "Mourning and Melancholia" (1917a), he gives the appearance of straining toward that formal theory of the ego that could lead to a decisive break with rationalistic pressuring and a shift toward consistent interpretation.

Meanwhile, the inconsistency or vacillation persisted, and we must be impressed by how large a part of "Observations on Transference-Love" is devoted to cautioning the young, inexperienced, or unanalyzed analyst against the temptation to yield to the analysand's entreaties. For Freud, however, more was involved than reinforcing the doctor's sense of ethical responsibility. He was not only urging the analyst not to forfeit any of his public dignity and therapeutic authority by responding in kind but developing his general theory, in this instance emphasizing the point that romantic or sexual gratification could have no therapeutic value because the analysand's neurosis, rooted as it is in the highly conflictual infantile past, renders her incapable of genuine gratification in the here-and-now (p. 165).

I have already suggested, however, that one cannot rest easy with the belief that Freud was simply intent on remaining realistic and practical as he went on developing his clinical insights and their theoretical context. I believe that he was also manifesting some unresolved countertransference of his own. It is, for example, noteworthy that, despite his having argued in an earlier essay (1914a, p. 150) that repetition and acting out can be understood as forms of remembering, in this essay he emphasizes almost exclusively the here-and-now function of transference love as a resistance; that is, its blocking of remembering by insistence on repeating. Although, as I mentioned earlier, Freud realized that this resistance could be analyzed down to its infantile roots, the split-off aspect of this realization conveys no recognition that the analysand might also be collaborating by communicating, via enactments, something of value. Elsewhere (1992, chap. 14), I have attempted to show that Freud's continued concentration on the oppositional aspects of resistance in all its forms can be considered as a manifestation of an adversarial countertransference. To deal effectively with the question of Freud's countertransference, specifically to transference love, we must next look at his explicit discussion of countertransference in "Observations on Transference-Love": what he says, how he says it, and what he neglects to say.

It will, however, help pave the way to pause here to consider enactment as communication. One finds special emphasis on this point in the writings of leading modern Kleinians, such as Betty Joseph (1989). But there the argument is not adequately developed, for it does not follow that whatever is interpretable, as an enactment may be, is intended as a communication. The analyst can learn from observing noncommunicative behavior, too, and that point is not ignored by Joseph. The issues involved are too complex to go into here, but I must at least say that, when the analyst is keeping a steady focus on transference–countertransference dynamics, constantly seeking to define the object-related, interactive aspects of the events of the analytic session, it is heuristically useful to regard the analysand as always experiencing simply being, as well as using words, as a means of relating to another, hence of getting something across to someone else. I further believe that most analysands respond well to an atmosphere in which *how* they are as well as *what* they say is taken to be an active part of relating to the analyst in an informative way.

COUNTERTRANSFERENCE

In a footnote to "Observations on Transference-Love" (pp. 160–161n.), James Strachey comments that this is one of the very few essays in which Freud referred explicitly to countertransference. It seems self-evident why this is so. In 1915 Freud was working with a theory framed almost entirely in terms of the driving force of libido. Although he took account of the ego instincts, as he then called them; although he had already developed his ideas about the secondary process, reality testing, and the reality principle; and although he was consistently cognizant of aggression and guilt in human relations, he still had no general and systematized theory of aggression and restraining psychic structure. In 1915, conflict was pretty much a matter of repression versus the libidinal drives; and, of course, the very roots of Freud's theory are embedded in the idea that the flesh is weak and repression is never accomplished once and for all. Additionally, with Freud's development of his ideas on narcissism already under way (1914b), we can understand his taking up specifically the narcissistic aspects of the analyst's erotic countertransference; that is, the analyst's temptation to accept and enjoy being idealized by the aroused analysand.

From the standpoint of today's analyst, however, Freud's approach to countertransference, while groundbreaking, is clearly rudimentary. Numerous countertransferential factors that now figure prominently in our thinking are not even mentioned, nor are there signs that Freud appreciated the usefulness of countertransference for the analyst's interpretive work. It seems that, in part, it was Freud's positivistic scientific ideal of total objectivity, founded on personal detachment, that led him to advocate that one should try to expunge all countertransference by personal analysis, self-analysis, and a sound grasp of his theories of development, psychopathology, and the therapeutic process. Already at this point we can infer the presence of some characterological countertransference, for it is inherent in Freud's general theory that all human relationships are more or less colored by infantile transferences (his principle of continuity over time). Yet Freud seems to want to exempt the analyst from this fundamental proposition. Again, as in dealing with transference love, we encounter some split-off rationalistic bias in Freud's simply negative attitude toward countertransference—one might say a countertransference to countertransference.

It may be objected that it is unwarranted to think of countertransference in this connection, that it might be quite enough to refer to characterological tendencies that can become sources of countertransference in specific relationships. I believe that this objection stems from preference for the traditional conceptions of both character and countertransference; these conceptions are narrower and more split off from each other than those I regard as more useful. The first difference to consider here is that traditionally countertransference has been looked on with disfavor, whereas in the broader usage pioneered by Kleinian object-relations theorists countertransference is a routinely expectable phenomenon, in which the influence of unconscious inner-world dynamics can always be discerned by psychoanalytic means. Consequently, to attribute countertransference to Freud seems not at all to charge him with a fault but rather to face him squarely as, in principle, no different from anyone else engaged in analytic work.

A second difference to consider pertains to character. Traditionally, although lacking a uniform definition, *character* is a term used to refer somehow to an array of stable and interrelated traits or modes of action (broadly defined); it is an array that can be analyzed as compromise formations made up of id, ego, and superego tendencies. In contrast, from the object relations standpoint, character would refer to the patterning of preferred, customary, real, and fantasied relations with others; these patternings could still be analyzed as expressing enduring aspects of inner-world dynamics.

Taking these two differences into account, one may go on to think of generalized or characterological countertransferences. This way of thinking was adopted long ago and usefully developed, though not precisely in these terms, by Annie Reich (1951). In her articulation of types of countertransference, she intended to emphasize how characterological countertransference inevitably pervades the work of every analyst owing to her or his distinctive life history of conflict, compromise formation, sublimation, and consequent modes of relating to others.

On this basis, I surmise that in Freud's case we are witnessing a characterological countertransference with regard to countertransference itself. He viewed countertransference in a manner that reflects the idealization of reason buttressed by some moralistic leanings; this view eventuates in putting more emphasis on the scope of rational control than can be supported by psychoanalytic experience. Such an emphasis may itself indicate that overestimation of rationality is rooted in unconscious conflict. That is why at this point we hear echoes of what I took up earlier as consequences of Freud's topographic orientation, such as his pressuring suggestions that consciousness can be effective in combating resistances.

Although many contemporary analysts continue to take Freud's problematically narrow and negative position on countertransference, it seems correct to say that the trend in contemporary psychoanalysis is for analysts to approach countertransference more broadly and positively. In one respect, they use countertransference as a way to monitor the analysand's unconsciously enacted communications. Here they are actually following Freud's advice to analysts in another of his papers on technique (1912a, pp. 115–116): Bend your unconscious toward the analysand's on the understanding that it is a finer instrument for receiving information about the analysand than focused, conscious attention. The contemporary extension of Freud's advice goes further, however; now analysts also attend to their own emotional reactions to an analysand as containing useful information about the analysand. Freud did not develop his recommendations along this line, and I believe that we have to thank especially the Kleinian object-relations school of analysis for having done so (Heimann, 1950; Racker, 1968; Segal, 1986; Joseph, 1989).

Today, countertransference is viewed as a significant element in another way as well. This view also resembles Freud's without being identical to it. Analysts tend currently to be constantly alert to the possibility that they may be provoking the analysand's immediate feelings. They do not regard themselves as exempt from enacting their own conflictual desires in the way they conduct each analysis. With regard to transference love specifically, male analysts will be alert to how they might be fanning the flames of the female analysand's desires. They already know many of the reasons why they might do so—to avoid problems of aggression; to engage in guilty reparative efforts by romanticizing the relationship; to seek to charm or dominate a woman in order to bolster their own flagging self-esteem; to ward off recognition that they are dealing with an analysand who at that time is emotionally "dead"; or to ward off recognition of the analysand's maternal transference by heating up the heterosexual, apparently paternal transference. It seems to me that male analysts frequently resort to countertransference on this last mentioned provocation. As I shall argue soon, it may be that Freud did too.

I have already indicated, however, that Freud did not approach this complex conception of countertransference in his writings. He was committed to developing and forcefully advocating his idea of the analyst as a scientific healer and an ethical man objectively observing a specimen of irrationality and inductively coming to purely rational conclusions, albeit with the help of his own unconscious mental processes. During the analysis, the observer's personal feelings other than respect and responsibility are to be kept "in check," if not eliminated, for they corrupt the treatment. Freud's personal and theoretical rationalist constraints and overestimation of conscious reason pushed the more or less fluid experiential aspects of analytic work into the margins or off the page altogether.

In addition to its narrow and negative view of countertransference, the rudimentary nature of Freud's approach is also evident in his neglect of the role of aggression in the analyst's erotized *counter*transference. Today, we would be alert to parallels in the countertransference to the constitution of the analysand's transference, and in particular to parallel hostility; for we are careful now not to neglect the insight that the analysand's seductive efforts also, and perhaps primarily, express the hostility of negative transference: hostility in the guise of "intractable" love and desire. In this respect, we seem to concur with Freud's alertness to hostility in transference love, as when he pointed out how it may be used in an effort to undermine the analyst's professional authority. But Freud was viewing this hostility as part of a strategy designed to block access to infantile libidinal memories; that is, it is the "fight" aspect of the analysand's sexual repressions.

We, on the other hand, might view transference love as being pushed forward in order to block access to negative transference; alternatively, we might suspect the female analysand is making desperately forced efforts to feel something, anything, as a cover or "cure" for feeling herself to be dead or an emptied-out victim. Finally, not to go on too long about it, we might emphasize the analysand's willingness in therapy, as in the rest of her life, to offer romantic and sexual feelings to a man in order to be held and soothed, in which case we could be focusing on a defensively deaggressivized, unconscious maternal transference. We are likely to see transference love as a fluid combination and layering of more than one of these factors, and perhaps others. In any case, we would be constantly attending to the vicissitudes of both aggression and relations with the mother as well as those of sexuality.

We can believe that Freud was being influenced by his sensitivity to the criticisms of psychoanalysis by the public and other professionals for its scandalous openness about sexual matters. We can accept that he was sensitive as well to similar objections raised by family members of his analysands, those critics who were always in a position to undermine the continuation of Freud's treatments and his scientific explorations. Also, a footnote reference (p. 159) suggests that Freud still had an acute memory of Josef Breuer's countertransferential flight from Anna O and its disruptive effect on their scientific collaboration. To all this we might add the surmise that Freud was smarting from the relatively recent scandal surrounding Carl Jung's affair with his analysand Sabina Spiel-rein and its continuing reverberations.

By placing this paper in historical and personal context as well as in the context of Freud's dedication to making psychoanalysis a pure empirical science and an effective scientific therapy, we can understand his paternalistically narrow approach to countertransference, the warning and admonishing tone and content of this essay, and so on. But making sense of the direction and limits of his discussion does not invalidate our inference concerning the operation of characterological countertransference in Freud's thinking. Indeed, it goes some way toward understanding the role of Freud's own countertransferences. Just because he was concerned with struggles and worries about the public, his professional standing, the conduct of his followers, and his need to make a rational science out of what he was doing as an analyst, he was relating to his analysand with culturally well-established attitudes that were in keeping with his own characterological countertransferences and the extratherapeutic aims they entailed. How else could it be? For present purposes, cultural and historical contexts explain away nothing; actually, they alert us to and fill in our understanding of repetitive conflictual behavior.

We have additional reason to infer the controlling influence of countertransference on Sigmund Freud's thinking about counter-transference. Freud's own writings show that, for internal reasons, he felt it necessary to be dismissive of mothers and to remain preoccupied with fathers, and so to dwell throughout his writings on paternal transference in male and female analysands alike. A number of analysts who have examined Freud's major clinical case studies have shown that maternal and preoedipal transference and countertransference are not well-developed ideas in his writings (Blum, 1980; Silverman, 1980; Bernheimer and Kahane, 1985; Mahony, 1986; Frankiel, 1992). In his view these were oedipal transferences, and in the case of women were primarily positive in nature. But we know now that the male analyst must always be prepared to recognize that he is also serving as a female, probably maternal, figure in the transference. Freud, however, when pressed finally by female colleagues to take more account of maternal transference, could only say that he left it to them, as women, to explore that issue (1931, pp. 226–227). Similarly, in *The Ego and the Id* (1923a), after portraying the Oedipus complex of boy and girl alike as bisexual, Freud went on to present a predominantly patriarchal conception of the super-ego as the heir of that complex.

Today we see how difficult it would have been for Freud to have remained, as he did, primarily on the oedipal level if he had opened his work wider to include signs of maternal transference, for we understand much of that transference to be preoedipal in nature. We may, therefore, surmise that a patriarchal bias was one of Sigmund Freud's counter-transferences. It is to this specific countertransferential factor that we now turn. It will be useful, I think, to single out this patriarchal factor, because it has come to occupy a prominent place in certain telling femi-nist critiques of Freud's work (Bernheimer and Kahane, 1985).

FREUD'S PATRIARCHAL ORIENTATION

Freud gave serious and frank consideration to female psychology at a time when the culturally normative position was one of shame disguised as modesty or tact. It was a time and a setting when a hush-hush atti-tude and false dignity were expected. In his insightful way, he made fundamental contributions to the psychoanalytic psychology of female development and psychopathology. Many of these contributions, such as those pertaining to the female Oedipus complex and bisexual factors in the personality, have stood the test of time, even though today we would present a more complex picture of these matters and of women in general. And yet it seems that, with all his dedication and insight and all his creativity and courage, Freud did not recognize and shake off a patriarchal bias in his thinking about women. Here I am using the term *patriarchal* to refer to a mixture of consciously benevolent paternalism, consistent authoritarianism, and pervasive condescension.

I addressed a number of aspects of this bias in some detail in my 1974 paper entitled "Problems in Freud's Psychology of Women." I shall not here offer a full summary of that discussion. Suffice it to say that I questioned Freud's conclusions that the morality and judgment of women are second rate; I argued against the limitations imposed by his assump-tion that women's full development depends on their being given a baby, especially a son, by a father-substitute, as compensation for their "cas-trated" state and as balm for what Freud hastily and narrowly termed their "penis envy." On linguistic as well as psychological grounds, I characterized as sexist his equating passive, submissive, and masochistic behavior with femininity; and I emphasized his relative disregard of preoedipal development and the centrality therein of the girl's tie to her mother. Before my 1974 essay and certainly since then, many feminist writers, including some who value psychoanalysis, have criticized Freud's orientation to women as patriarchal, masculinist, sexist, and phallocentric—words with overlapping but not identical connotations.

In "Observations on Transference-Love," it is particularly his patriarchal tone and imagery, as well as his limitation of analytic attention, that stimulate critical comment. Freud's tone and imagery are shockingly condescending in several places. He refers to the "comical" aspect of the woman's transference love for the male analyst (p. 159). He is dismissive toward those women who, apparently driven by transference love, do not respond to his interventions, referring to these analysands as, "in the [unnamed] poet's words," women who understand only "the logic of soup, with dumplings for arguments" (p. 167) and throwing up his rhetorical hands in wonder that a woman can be so consumed by elemental passion that her need for love is "intractable." (Here he was clearly no longer thinking as an analyst but rather defensively, I would suggest, and, in effect, no longer referring to women as people.) He makes the simplistic assumption (intended to be relayed to the analysand) that, if it was true love, she would become "docile" and seek to get well in order to "acquire value in the doctor's eyes" (p. 167). He writes that "when a woman sues for love" the analyst has "a distressing part . . . to play," especially if that woman is refined rather than crudely sensual, Freud seeming here to exempt this bit of gallantry from countertransference analysis (p. 170). Perhaps even when he introduces the metaphor of a dog race with the prize of "a garland of sausages," a race that would be disrupted if a sausage (the analyst's desirous countertransference) were thrown onto the track (p. 169). Freud's resort to this condescending rhetoric complied with the patriarchal norm of his times, but, as I have already pointed out, it must also be approached as manifesting countertransference within the psychoanalytic process.

Equally important in this connection is the question of Freud's selecting for his discussion of transference love a female analysand who is in great romantic distress or unreasoning passionate arousal. Is it really enough for Freud to explain that he is selecting only one instance of a problem with a broad scope? Why select just this one, and why discuss it in just this way? And is it enough that he emphasizes the realistic problems I alluded to in the previous sections of my essay? I think not. Where, I ask, is there in his writings any equivalent discussion of the male analysand's transference love of the male analyst? Where did Freud sort out that potentially disruptive homosexual love in the interest of furthering objective psychoanalytic work? However similar the issues sometimes may be in male and female transference love, are they not sometimes radically different? Why did Freud deal so consistently and relatively narrowly with male transference in terms of rebelliousness toward the father's authority? Why did he not give careful consideration to lesser, simpler forms of female erotic transference to a male analyst and other forms of love that, whatever their infantile psychosexual origins, can play large parts in the analytic process? And why, finally, pay so little attention to erotically colored maternal transference?

On the basis of these considerations and questions, and others presented elsewhere (1994a, here chap. 3), I propose that Freud's patriarchal orientation predisposed him to select for discussion of transference love the aroused, importunate, excessive, but somehow attractive woman and to portray her as the sole initiator of all the significant, simply sexual currents of the analytic relationship. Consequently, he could feel consciously comfortable in his patriarchal orientation and spend much time in this essay issuing reminders, warnings, and exhortations, meanwhile neglecting to provide detailed and balanced coverage of transference love in all its forms and with all its functions. Even had he not covered these issues comprehensively, he could have done what he did so often in other contexts: raised searching questions and pointed out persisting ambiguities and the need for further study.

POSITIVISM, PERSPECTIVISM, AND NARRATION

In the preceding sections of this essay I have presented supplementary observations and various critiques garnered from the subsequent history of the topics touched on in "Observations on Transference-Love." My presentation demonstrates plainly that Freud's essay provides only one limited version of only one facet of the analytic relationship. Since 1915, numerous authors, including Freud himself, have presented modified, extended, or alternative versions of transference love and its mental and situational contexts. As psychoanalysis changes, transference love keeps being retold, as it should be, for new developments in psychoanalysis call for new versions of familiar narratives (Schafer, 1983, 1992). The emphasis shifts even with variations of perspective within ego psychological Freudian analysis; certainly it shifts between schools of psychoanalysis. Psychoanalysts live now in an age of multiple perspectives, and as yet they have failed to agree on some common ground; it may even be fruitless to search for any such ground (Schafer, 1990).

We have already noted how the telling of transference love changed once analysts broke away from Freud's narrowing approach. If we now take up another example, that of the Kleinian object-relational version of Freudian analysis, some significant further aspects of perspectivism and narration may become accessible. I present here only a schematic version. I suggest that, in the Kleinian narrative, the analyst must try to locate the manifestations of transference love within the framework of the paranoid–schizoid and depressive positions (Segal, 1986). Thus, in one instance, the analyst could approach that love as an attempt to forestall persecution by propitiation of a figure into whom the woman has projected her own rageful self and which she then has defensively idealized as a source of protective love. In another instance, the analyst might approach the erotic transference as the expression of sadomasochistic sexual excitement based on unconscious fantasies that the analytic relationship is an enactment of sadomasochistic practices. Or perhaps the Kleinian analyst would see a particular woman's transference love primarily as manifesting a reparative move, stemming from within the depressive position; that is, as an attempt to cure the object through love (Feldman, 1990). We might recall in this connection that Freud saw transference love as the analysand's seeking to cure *herself* through love; reparation of the love-object did not figure prominently in his narratives.

Note that none of these Kleinian versions denies the sexual charge and the romantic fantasy involved in transference love. What they do is situate these factors in the two positions or dynamic configurations that are fundamental to their approach to interpretation: the paranoid-schizoid and the depressive. They do so in order to provide their own developmental contexts and an appropriate array of interpretive storylines to work with. In Freud's perspective, the essential context is the

inevitable infantile phases of libidinal development, especially the oedipal phase and, most particularly, the positive oedipal phase. In the
Kleinian perspective, the analysis would emphasize the vicissitudes of
aggression rather more than libido.

In these two perspectives we see contrasting but not unrelated hierarchies of variables. Associated with each hierarchy are typical narratives and individual storylines such as those I used in giving specific
examples in the preceding paragraphs. We cannot avoid seeing the shortcomings of Freud's efforts to establish a science that yields only one
definitive account of its constituent subject matter, such as the matter
of transference love. For in the event, the practices of psychoanalysts
show psychoanalysis to be an interpretive, hermeneutic enterprise that
is made manifest in a variety of preferred narratives, some of them significantly different from Freud's. Those preferred narratives enter into
method and thereby into the eliciting and shaping of clinical phenomena that will then be interpreted in keeping with these very narratives.
This is the hermeneutic circle, and it provides knowledge that is not
available to the traditional positivistic approach.

The hermeneutic view of psychoanalytic understanding is just that:
a view or a perspective, not a new technical prescription; that is, it describes what analysts do. In this view, Freud's positivistic perspective
seems to hold up unmodified only when we arbitrarily rule all other
perspectives out of court and when we also go so far as to ignore or
minimize the considerable variations even among Freud's close adher-
ents. Indeed, in every section of my essay there are arguments implying
a poor fit between Freud's creation and his favoring of the positivistic
conception of this creation.

It should be noted, however, that Freud did not always advocate a
straightforward positivist conception of psychoanalysis. This we can see,
for example, in some of his methodological discussions (e.g., 1909a,
pp. 104–105; 1915b, p. 117) and in his clinical examples. There, he did
not maintain his "official" scientific position; he did recognize, at least
implicitly, the necessarily hermeneutic aspects of this discipline he was
creating.

Nevertheless, it is with his usual formal propositions that we must
be concerned, for it was by means of these propositions that Freud was
trying to establish the conventions for how to constitute and so be able
to talk about those subjective experiences that he deemed crucial to the

psychoanalytic process. Seen in this light, these conventions are epistemological directives to the analyst as to how to process the ambiguous
associative material: how to decide what will count as evidence and
insight. But if more than one interpretive method and outcome is, as we
see, always possible, then the epistemological propositions must be
challenged and the presuppositions on which they are based revised.

I contend, therefore, that Freud was not presenting unmediated reports of detached observations. Instead, he could only have been retelling lives, past and present, as they emerged, mediated by linguistic and
epistemological assumptions, in his clinical dialogue with his analysands.
And these were dialogues much of which had been shaped by his preferred master narratives and the specific storylines they laid down for
interpretive work (Schafer, 1992).

If, finally, we ask ourselves, What is transference love, the preceding discussions, taken together, suggest that we can begin to respond to
that question only provisionally and only after getting answers to a long
series of other questions that have been asked from various related but
not identical points of view.

These queries include Who is asking the question? In connection with which specific clinical example? Which school of psychoanalytic thought has regulated and guided this analysis up to this point?
And just which hierarchy of variables or narrative preferences is the
questioner prepared to accept as the most useful for psychoanalytic
purposes? Questions of this sort were made possible by Freud's "Observations on Transference-Love," by his other papers on technique,
and by his entire body of work. They are among his legacies (Schafer,
1992, chap. 9). Fittingly, other psychoanalysts have not been content
to rest on Freud's laurels. For his part, he never did either.

5

Conversations with Elisabeth von R.

I

Breuer and Freud's (1893–1895) *Studies on Hysteria* provides us with an excellent place to begin celebrating the hundredth birthday of psychoanalysis. Nothing could be more fitting than to praise the revolutionary step Freud took in that work. If, however, it is asked in just what this revolutionary step consisted, one is confronted at once with all the complex questions of contemporary critical theory. For the Western world has been at work trying to answer that question from the time the work was published, and as we know, it has proposed answers that have changed as critical perspectives have changed.

During these hundred years, a great variety of critical perspectives have been in and out of favor both in psychoanalysis and in the humanities and sciences that surround it and nourish it. One must also take into account the fact that psychoanalysts have had one hundred years of experience working clinically with Freud's ideas and working theoretically not only with his sweeping propositions but with his highly particularized ones as well. Consequently, one can now ask questions and propose answers based on contemporary practice, our ideas about evidence and theoretical coherence, and our relations with reality, authority, and knowledge—questions and answers that were inconceivable one hundred years ago.

That is to say, one can approach the inquiry into Freud's revolutionary step in a postmodern fashion (Schafer, 1992). Working in this way, one finds in the *Studies on Hysteria* preconceptions and modes of thought about gender relations, clinical relations, and the goals of treatment that must be interrogated with the full force of present approaches to understanding. This I propose to do in my return to Freud's first immersion in the hot waters of clinical psychoanalysis: his report on his treatment of Elisabeth von R.

Using that report as my specimen, I shall first review critically Freud's understanding of hysteria in the period 1893 to 1895, and his correlated technical approach to its treatment. I shall pay particular attention to those aspects of Freud's early ideas and methods that I believe continued to color his later work. Second, I shall present my idea of how he might have, or could have, understood and approached this analysand some forty years later when he was concluding his world-shaking career of profound insight into the human condition. Too often, in my opinion, accounts of the early Freud are taken whole, that is, as the definitive accounts of Freud's ideas, if not as definitive accounts of all of psychoanalysis. That limited approach gives one the impression that neither he nor the discipline he created has a history—more exactly, a number of histories, depending on who is writing the history.

I share the common view that most of the best of Freud is to be found in the mature works written during the 1920s and 1930s. By then he had made new contributions of such scope and depth that, understandably, he was himself unprepared to appreciate them fully. I believe that they were far more consonant with general changes in the intellectual climate of the early decades of the twentieth century than he realized. In the concluding section of this essay, I shall touch on a few aspects of this lag in Freud's self-understanding. In the main, however, I shall develop a critique of some aspects of Freud's final position on Elisabeth (as I have constructed it), and I shall revise that hypothetical position, using for the purpose insights that I regard as among the most useful and deep that can be offered by the Freudian psychoanalysis of today.

II

In these *Studies on Hysteria*, Sigmund Freud wrote that when symptoms intrude into the treatment situation, they are "joining in the conversation"

(p. 148). What conversation can he have meant back then in the mid-1890s? On my reading, the assumptions and the resulting tone of the interchanges resemble detached medical interventions and passive responses far more than conversation or dialogue. That words are being used need not make it a true dialogue, that is, one evidently based on common understanding and with room for mutual influence. The record suggests that, for Freud, Elisabeth was a carrier of symptoms. Although he was already in a position to say that these symptoms should be regarded as voices speaking in other registers or languages, he was not acting on that understanding. Instead, he seemed to be limiting his role as psychotherapist to that of a zealous physician engaged in letting out the pus of festering traumatic experiences, as though that were the remedy for psychic pain and dysfunction. His technical concept of abreacting affects seems to have been organized around a medical metaphor.

Freud had already expressed his recognition that infections develop only in bodies and minds that make good hosts for the foreign invaders. Consequently, he did not inflate his claims; he emphasized that his therapy was aimed only at symptom cure and not, holistically, at transforming his analysands into organisms which would be well fortified against future infection. In support of this limited approach, he tended to take for granted that, in general, his analysands were mentally sound victims of traumatic circumstances. That they were not always readily or steadily collaborative in their treatments was noteworthy but another matter. Later on (Freud, 1912a), he would no longer think it was another matter, and in recent decades much has been written on the complex, often seriously ill, makeup of his presumably mostly normal analysands burdened by their neurotic symptoms.

It would be wrong to fault Freud for maintaining this narrow perspective and setting only this limited goal. We have only to take into account the historical–professional setting in which he was working at that time, the extraordinary methods he was devising, and the discoveries he was making and reporting, in order to appreciate how great a change he was beginning to introduce into the understanding and the therapy of the neuroses. If, however, we look at this work from our current perspective, we will be better able to understand not merely what Freud was and was not seeing and doing back then, but also where we stand now in the development of our discipline.

The historians of the late nineteenth century would generally agree that it was an era of flourishing materialism manifest in the smokestacks of industrial capitalism and its colonialist offshoots. Determined management, efficiency, productivity, and technical control and progress were leading ideals. I propose that Freud was being consistent with this ideology when he approached the neurotic symptom as one would approach a colony of primitive natives sitting on a wealth of untapped natural resources and artifacts. In Freud's case, those resources were intertwined with the buried memories he was mining; when successful, he would reach the sources of civilized life. By these means, he could, so to say, both bring home the riches and bring to these "natives" all the taken-for-granted benefits of a rational, controlling civilization. Later (1923a), he would say that where id is, there would ego be.

Consequently, one could hardly expect these verbal interchanges in his consulting room to amount to a "conversation." Today, they seem more like unfeeling interrogations or, in their milder versions, efficient paternalistic forms of taking control. Within its own pretty closed system, the prevailing ideology of the times would confirm both the productivity and the benevolence of this approach. Therefore, it would be safe for us today to assume that the intrusion of symptomatic actions into the treatment setting was not so much their joining in an ongoing conversation, as Freud thought, than it was an attempt by the analysand to initiate a conversation, a true dialogue. Like Anna O (Breuer and Freud, 1893–1895), Elisabeth needed a "talking cure" and was doing her best to change the format accordingly. In a conflicted, delinguisticized way, the symptomatic actions of both women were conveying that there had to be two human participants in the process, each having power and each having available a variety of ways to further the dialogue. Contemporary reflection on the emotional positions and needs of both parties to clinical analytic interactions requires that transference and countertransference, broadly conceived, be put at the very center of things.

Where did Freud stand in relation to transference and countertransference back in 1895? Of countertransference he was saying nothing; of transference he did have some immensely significant things to say. First of all, it is no small thing that he introduced the term. Then, in his later chapter on the psychotherapy of hysteria, he characterized transference as a "false connection"; by that phrase he meant that analysands transfer onto the therapist disturbed ideas about others who then prove to be central figures in the painful memories currently being elicited by the treatment.

In this regard, his technical approach to the transference lagged behind his preliminary understanding, in that his attitude toward it remained administrative or benignly paternalistic and in some cases simply forcing. His report shows that, in general, he was aiming at managing and removing any and all expectable intrusions of human feelings that would disturb his mining of the past. He believed that these alien elements should not be allowed to "obstruct" the treatment process. For example, he remarked on how the analysand's relation to the physician can be "disturbed" by erotic trains of thought—"especially in women"—and he recommended some substitute and limited gratifications, specifically "friendliness," to limit that disturbance. He realized that the disturbed woman's "cooperativeness" might turn into resistance should she experience—inappropriately, he implied—feelings of neglect, lack of appreciation, even humiliation, or a great fear of dependency and an aversion to feeling vulnerable to influence, or should she be exposed to criticism by others of the doctor or the method of treatment.

Consequently, he argued that the analyst should "remove" these false connections because they give rise to resistances. He proposed that the means to keep moving forward or, better yet, downward toward the buried traumatic memories is to make the transference "obstacle" conscious and show that the intrusion of the past in the present feeling has merely given rise to " a compulsion and an illusion." Only by that implicitly disapproving method would one hope that the obstructing transference would "melt away with the conclusion of the analysis."

Freud did not provide any adequate account of the therapeutic action of this rationalistic and judgmental approach. What he did provide, I suggest, was a clear picture of his determination to dominate the treatment. He felt justified in taking this approach because he saw himself engaged in a project of (in his memorable formulation) "transforming . . . hysterical misery into common unhappiness" (p. 305). Even though not thinking holistically, he did go so far as to state his belief that his method of symptom removal could yield prophylactic benefits, thereby broadening somewhat his claims for his new therapy. In his words, "with mental life that has been restored to health [the analysand] will be better armed against that unhappiness." But this he could not know. It is known now that *at that time*, and despite his disclaimers and cautious stance, Freud was not above making brash claims for his method. Moreover, as we now realize, it was in keeping with his patriarchal outlook that he manifested no awareness at all that he was unilaterally defining and deciding about neurotic misery and common unhappiness; specific goals were not the product of genuine dialogue with the analysand and mutual definition of results. It was, of course, the colonialist doctor of civilization who knew best.

Freud's patriarchal stance may also be inferred from his neglect of the mother's role in Elisabeth's neurosis. Too quickly, he centered his analysis on the daughter's relationship to her father and other "strong" male figures. He seemed to be relying on the stereotypical view of women as the weaker sex; presumably, their lives made sense to them only in relation to men. Today, mature clinical analysts would not grasp so readily at the material Elisabeth pushed forward. And critical appraisers of this report would also be alert to the extent to which this one-sided development took place under Freud's active guidance.

We have learned to be skeptical of material that is, so to say, served up on a silver platter. What was on Elisabeth's (and Freud's) platter was a sick father, his leg in her lap, the mother on the sidelines, the triangular rivalry for a man with her sister, the desirable widower, and the unfulfilled romantic dreams about the potential suitor who would rescue her—and, as the final result of this traumatic onslaught, symptoms of a broken heart. It is all rather like a Victorian romance. In Freud's posttherapy conclusion of his narrative—his seeing the heroine whirling past him in a dance and he then hearing that she married—he offers the reader the conventional comfort of a happy bourgeois ending. It is as if he assumes that we will derive satisfaction from knowing that, finally, Elisabeth came to her senses and accepted the conventional feminine role happily—exactly the role she had always rebelled against. It is not going too far to surmise that Freud was eager to restrict his analysis to what was on that silver platter, for it fit in too well with two interrelated factors: his patriarchal social orientation and his therapeutic zeal. Also, to the extent that he had gone after just that material, he would have welcomed compliance.

Today's analysts would not buy it. In the contemporary analytic way of telling lives, mothers cannot be kept on the sidelines. They are central players from the first. If the analysand is simply trying to keep away from material pertaining to mother, she or he will make that obvious pretty soon, and the avoidance can then be taken up analytically.

If, on the other hand, the mother seems to have made herself peripheral in the child's life, as by invalidism or absence, she can only have come to be seen as a figure profoundly threatening and burdensome to the child; for in unconscious fantasy, the child will experience the manifestly sidelined mother partly as an abandoning figure filled with disgust or hatred and partly as a damaged figure driven away by the child's own demands and hostility. The child's sense of worth and security in the world will be undermined. Mixed-up images as victim, helpless one, and omnipotent one will develop. The girl will have no basis for any straightforward erotic development, leading to reasonably uncomplicated positive oedipal desire for the father and father surrogates, and no wholehearted wishes for the conventional feminine role defined as subordinate wife, mother, and homemaker. Yet, in the end, this development and these wishes were just what Freud imputed to Elisabeth. One can surmise that, even later in his career, he would have done the same, seeing that he continued to pay inadequate attention to mothers in his theoretical and clinical accounts. Mostly, mothers remained unarticulated oedipal–sexual fantasy objects of desire and rivalry.

III

By the end of his career, Freud had already written "Mourning and Melancholia" (1917a), *Beyond the Pleasure Principle* (1920a), *Group Psychology and the Analysis of the Ego* (1921), *The Ego and the Id* (1923a), *Inhibitions, Symptoms and Anxiety* (1926), and a number of papers on gender development and differentiation. He had already recognized the role of identification in ordinary development and psychopathology. He had installed destructive aggression alongside libido at the center of his metapsychological narratives. He had organized his account of development around anxiety and guilt and the various infantile danger situations, defense and repetition. He had worked out a good deal about the interpretation of transference and acting out and their uses for the analyst's purposes of reconstruction of early development.

With regard to the results of analytic therapy, he had made his claims more modest, less symptom-oriented, and more articulated. With regard to the role played by the mother, however, I am not impressed by his effort in 1931, "Female Sexuality," to give more prominence to the infant–mother relationship, for by the time of his 1937 paper on termination (1937a) and his final "Outline of Psychoanalysis" (1940) he was showing that he had reverted to the castration complex and penis envy as "bedrocks"—a conclusion that again put the actual mother on the sidelines. Apart from this major factor, his rich, complex, eye-opening advances in theory and technique could readily have led him to reformulate the case of Elisabeth. I should like next to try my hand at formulating this case in the terms available to him in the late 1930s.

I begin with what Freud called "the harsher side" of Elisabeth's character (p. 140). In the end, I suggest, he would have viewed that side as expressing primarily a dominant identification with her father, and he would have tried to account for it primarily in terms of her castration complex and penis envy as well as a heightened negative oedipal orientation. He would have regarded this "masculine" constellation as overdetermined by a defensive switch away from the positive oedipal orientation. He would have seen the necessity for including this defensive factor after surmising that the positive had been dangerously intensified by Elisabeth's having been her father's favorite and by the mother's invalidism having left a vacuum in the father's life for Elisabeth to fill. Most likely, Freud would have also emphasized the likelihood that Elisabeth was struggling against a "sickly" identification with her sickly mother. However, I am inclined to think that he would have linked that struggle with the fantasy of the sick mother of the phallic period, that is, a castrated and therefore defective woman, very much as Annie Reich, for example, did in her studies of pathological self-esteem regulation (1953, 1960).

Continuing with this reanalysis, it is most likely that Freud would have also viewed Elisabeth's invalidism as, in part, her way of punishing herself for her rage against both of her parents and her sisters, for her infantile oedipal desires, and for her wishfulfilling sexual fantasies in her present setting. Taking into account her locomotor symptom, he might well have gone on to suggest that, like the homosexual woman he had discussed in 1920 (1920b), she was unconsciously imagining herself to be, or acting out, the part of being a fallen woman, perhaps even a pregnant woman.

With regard to gender preference and love-object orientation, Freud, at the time of the *Studies*, wrote this of Elisabeth, that when she was under pressure of her feelings of desperation and helplessness in her emotionally overburdened circumstance, she began finally to yearn for a strong man to love and help her. Freud presented this switch of deep-seated attitude in a way that can be regarded now as notably matter-of-fact, for he referred to this change simply as an erotically charged desire for love that grew out of her painful situation. By the end of his prodigious career, however, he would have had to cast some doubt on the depth of this change, for he had come to appreciate the great power of what he called the character resistances, the adhesiveness of the libido to instinctual positions once adopted, the power of repetition, and other such factors. Most likely he would have emphasized the inexorable and enduring power of penis envy. Additionally, with his relatively new systematic focus on destructive aggression, he would have assumed that this shift of orientation was accomplished with a good deal of rage or bitterness toward men, and he would have linked that rage to Elisabeth's envious response to both the anatomical distinction between the sexes and her unconscious masculine identification. The turning to men would have seemed a neurotic act of desperation.

With regard, then, to gender preference and love-object orientation, Elisabeth's *astasia abasia* would or could have been viewed by him as a compromise formation that at one and the same time expressed her unconscious fantasy of castratedness, an identification with the invalided mother, a protest through weakness against being forced into the role of a homebound caretaking child, and her simultaneous struggle against and assertion of the homosexual side of her personality (see in this last regard the Dora case [1905a] and "Hysterical Phantasies and Their Relation to Bisexuality" [1908]).

In his early years, Freud's therapeutic optimism led him to take a light attitude toward the recurrence of Elisabeth's symptoms subsequent to termination. In contrast, the later Freud would have shown a good deal of skepticism with regard to any suggestion of recovery from her neurosis. Although her apparently symptom-free "whirling past" him in a dance, and reportedly having been married, would have been of interest to him, he could have surmised that these outward changes and developments had been based far more on a strengthening of defenses rather than on insight and structural change (see in this regard "Analysis Terminable and Interminable" [1937a]).

This skeptical conclusion would have been consistent with his dictum that neuroses can be considered cured only if their underlying unconscious dynamics have appeared in the transference and been analyzed there—analyzed, that is, in the continuous, even if only tacit, conversation that constitutes the analytic relationship. The conclusion would have been consistent, too, with his having laid out both his structural theory and the sequence of infantile danger situations from which basic transferences and major defenses issue. The later Freud no longer believed that merely the recovery of memories, especially those of recent origin, can suffice to resolve neurotic conflict. And that was all that had taken place in Elisabeth's treatment! To top it off, he would have shown his much greater respect for the power of sexual masochism in symptom formation and elsewhere, by not leaping to conclusions about "cure."

IV

It remains now to develop my critique of what I have imagined to be Freud's much improved way of retelling the case in 1939. What could be still missing from this story, and what could be off-center or even wrong with it? I shall start with an overview before getting into the details. First of all, the foundation stones of this clinical story are poorly laid. The defining origins of Freud's narrative not being spelled out, it lacks a *developmental* foundation. His story of Elisabeth begins after the middle, that is, long after Elisabeth's early years of life, so that the "conversation" was necessarily quite limited in scope. Second, the *cultural setting* is ignored. Freud takes the mores of the time for granted. Unreflectively, he situates that young woman neither in her patriarchal society nor in her warped family setting—again, quite limited conversation. And third, the *philosophical preconceptions* regulating Freud's work are unsound, for his account rests on a naive positivism that allows him only to carry on limited conversations with himself about the questionable way he was trying to fit his interpretive work into his simple inductivist model of science (Schafer, 1983, 1992).

1. *Developmental.* This "study" contains no exploration, through the transference and the reconstructions that it makes possible, of the oedipal years and especially the preoedipal years—what I would prefer to call the dyadic years. I refer to the mother–daughter relationship from the time of birth onward. I share the view that the origin of later disturbances,

including those of gender identity formation and choice of love-object, must now be located in that early dyadic period. My reformulation is limited by there being no report of when the mother became sickly. If it was early, as Freud may have been suggesting when he said that Elisabeth was thrown together with her father from early on, then it is plausible that Elisabeth's initial experiences of mothering were far from satisfactory. Probably, she did not have a "good enough mother" (Winnicott, 1958). One could say so even while granting the presence of a satisfactory nanny.

On this defective dyadic basis, Elisabeth's capacity to differentiate herself from her mother would have been seriously interfered with. Her tolerance of dependency, separation, and loss would have hardly begun to develop. She would have been vulnerable to unbearable feelings of helplessness, worthlessness, and "omnipotent" guilt in relation to a mother she could only perceive both as damaged by her and rejecting of her. Accordingly, she would have been burdened with a crushing need to make reparation to this mother; indeed she seems to have tried to do just that in her adult years, especially after the death of her father. If, culturally, that was the role that everyone, including herself, would have expected of her, that cultural fit would have reinforced both her servitude and her defense against realizing how conflicted she felt about it.

It may be surmised that Elisabeth had no mother to serve as a model for an identification imbued with life, vitality, and vigorous sexuality. Support for this surmise may be derived from the impression given by Freud's narrative of the mother: a woman with few substantial social and cultural skills, interests, and pursuits; additionally, a woman quite alone in the world when Elisabeth was not there to look after her. Although it is certainly possible in this regard that Freud was both showing a customary lack of interest in noting or reporting the details of the mother's life, and, as a narrator, wanting to sharpen the drama of this story by impoverishing his account of that mother's life, it would not be straining too much to infer that, psychologically, Elisabeth's invalided mother was a relatively impoverished figure.

Enter the father—for Freud a positive oedipal figure of grand proportions, considering the father's preference for Elisabeth, her care of him, and Elisabeth's other disturbed life circumstances. But wouldn't one now have to suppose that Elisabeth would have found this man an ambiguous figure? In her psychic reality, he could well have been experienced as a combined maternal–paternal figure, a parental couple one might say, the one who provided care and concern: in some respects a strong model to identify with, in other respects an exciting person toward whom to develop sexual feelings. At the same time, however, he would have been experienced unconsciously as a powerful figure who was the object of envy and thus as a stimulus of wishes to attack, spoil, and reject (her "harsher side"). Additionally, he would have lent himself to fantasies that it was he who had damaged the mother in the primal scene, in which respect he would have come to be seen as an especially dangerous figure with whom to get close, even though she also found his closeness gratifying her needs for the care and love of a mother. And that dangerousness would have been augmented by projection into him of her anger and spoiling envy.

It is, therefore, reasonable to suppose that Elisabeth's readiness to be a caretaker of father involved the same guilty, reparative needs that seem to have controlled her relationship with her mother once her father had died. With both parents, the "altruistic surrender" (A. Freud, 1936) would have reinforced repression of her rage at these exploitative and burdensome parents who had forced on her a kind of reversal of generations and deprived her of significant elements of her youth. Those erotic feelings that would have been stimulated, especially by all the physical contact involved in taking care of the two of them, would also have been defensively useful in helping to ward off not only her destructive feelings and urges but her guilt as well. Libido camouflaging aggression is a common defense; in our culture it is quite common not only in male–female relations but in same-sex relations as well.

2. *Cultural.* The preceding remarks have already anticipated much of my critique of Freud's taken-for-granted attitude toward the mores of his time and place. I refer to his assigning narrative centrality to the father; portraying women as the weaker sex; implying that heterosexual desire, love, and marriage and motherhood are the natural culmination of women's psychosexual development; enacting the unilateral paternalistic authority of the physician; and his generally sponsoring the values of the middle European bourgeoisie that prescribed what is "masculine" and "feminine" and what is "rough" versus "gentle" or "agreeable." Then and there, Freud could safely assume that Elisabeth shared these values, however at odds with them some of her unconscious desires might be, so that she would rejoice in arriving finally at a conformist social role. He would have had no reason to question whether any other therapeutic goals would make sense for a young woman of her sort and with her developmental background, and so no reason to detect subtle signs that she might also be questioning his prescribing those goals.

Today's analysts are, I believe, slowly coming to realize that all such opening-up types of question should be considered possibly valuable, even essential in psychoanalytic treatment. Feminist critics and practitioners and gay and lesbian critics and practitioners have been forcing the issue by stringent critiques of hidden bourgeois, homophobic, and otherwise closed-minded valorizations of only certain conventional therapeutic goals. Also, certain segments of our social organization have changed enough to allow any analyst who might treat an Elisabeth today to analyze her apparent lack of female friends and the supportive network they can provide; similarly, it would be essential to analyze the apparently too tight family structure in which she was confined rather like a prisoner doing time as an aide in the prison infirmary twenty-four hours a day.

3. *Philosophical.* Freud's position in 1895 was uncompromisingly positivistic. Unreflectively, he saw himself founding a science modeled on the biological and physical sciences of his time: partly field research and partly lab research. For him, Darwin and Helmholtz were paradigmatic figures (Schafer, 1983). In his accounts of it, the clinical situation he devised was partly field and partly lab; he wrote about it using both types of discourse. Occasionally, he threw in archaeology as a variant of field research. To pursue either type of research, psychoanalysis required a strictly neutral, objective, genderless, uncompromising, purely inductivist inquirer and a compliant, submissive, or passive object of research. Subjective reactions—both his and his analysand's—were to be eliminated or at least kept to an absolute minimum, even though it was the analysand's subjective life that was the object of study. Further, it was necessary to develop explanatory narratives based on the "fact" of drives, especially the sexual drive that guaranteed the survival of the species. So many have already written on this subject that this portrayal of Freud's methodological and conceptual precommitments and their dominance in his self-understanding should be familiar to any audience familiar with psychoanalysis.

It can be argued now that it was not so much a case of self-understanding as self-*mis*understanding. Contrary to Freud's ideal and belief, his clinical method was thoroughly hermeneutic and, for his time, gender-specific, even in its interrogatory form, for he was guided in his explorations by the continuously interpenetrating factors of what he was looking for and what he was hearing. He could raise only certain questions about his cocreated data and he could propose only certain connections among them. This I have tried to show in sketching hypothetically his later formulation of the case of Elisabeth von R., and then adding my reformulation and some comments on the continuing influence of the cultural–historical setting in which Freud had framed his master narratives and the storylines they laid down.

Self-consciously, Freud had declared early that he drew back from writing only stories. I would say that he did so once he recognized that, inevitably, case histories and treatment histories are narratives. That is to say, they are *tellings* of human events, not measurements or simple records of process and materials in the physical universe. Furthermore, he could not come close to recognizing that his narratives were about Elisabeth's narratives, themselves already a product of her peculiar interaction with him. In addition, the final summary of them that he reconstructed first in his notes and then in his writing about her in the cultural and theory-laden context of his enterprise was no more than his final narrative of all the other narratives.

Mostly unknown to Freud, he was far from trafficking in naturalistic Darwinian observation and experimentally controlled lab tests. There was no "out there" to draw conclusions about directly. There was only an "in here," in the analytic space, where two storytellers were groping toward a true dialogue about the inner and outer worlds of both (Schafer, 1992). Only later in his career did Freud occasionally write about his divergence from straightforward positivism (e.g., Freud, 1937b).

In conclusion, what I have set before you was, first, my version of the version worked out by him and Elisabeth; second, the version of that version that Freud could have developed later on; and third, my version of the best review of both one might expect of contemporary Freudian psychoanalysis.

Part II

Further Clinical Explorations

Although it has already been evident in the preceding chapters that my clinical understanding and approach have been much influenced by the contemporary Kleinians of London, this change becomes even more obvious in the clinically focused chapters of Part II. I now intend to illustrate and show the advantages I believe I have gained from this broadening and deepening of my understanding. Part II fits well with my larger purpose in this book to present my version of the shift toward some form of object relational thinking that, in chapter 1, I claimed was well under way throughout the discipline of psychoanalysis.

In this vein I take up humiliation and mortification, introjection, enactment, and aloneness in the countertransference. Then, in chapter 10, I present a set of pieces on clinical problems. These pieces make it plain that the changes I have undertaken have not involved my renouncing the technical wisdom of ego psychological Freudian analysis. As I have argued elsewhere (1994a, 1994b), I do not see contemporary Kleinians and standard ego psychological Freudians as fundamentally alien to one another; nor do I see them as facing a huge problem of finding a good deal of common ground. Rather, I see them as having maintained in common a base in Freud and having gone on to develop two different but not antagonistic trends in Freud's thought. Each development has in its own way evolved an ego psychological emphasis in its concepts and techniques. Differences there are between the two, to be sure, but common Freudian principles continue to rule both of these dominant trends in psychoanalysis. In my view there has been a steady mingling of influence in the work of both groups and certainly an increased recognition by the standard Freudian group of the valuable contributions of the contemporary Kleinians.

6

Humiliation and Mortification in Unconscious Fantasy

A full understanding of the highly emotional and painful experiences of humiliation and mortification requires thorough analysis of the unconscious fantasies they express. These clinically inferred fantasies are themselves further analyzable. One tries to work out their complex dynamics, including the transformational processes from which they derive their specific features and influence. My investigation of these extremes of the experience of shame will consider their descriptive aspects, which include much that is of degrading, violent, and deadly significance, and then move on to the desires, feelings, and defensive modifications that help us understand and explain how these internal events become powerful regulators of human relations. Relevant analytic literature will be considered along the way.

DESCRIPTIVE

In unconscious fantasy, humiliation and mortification frequently involve not only disgrace but ostracism, that is, exclusion from one's community and total loss of its respect. Belonging to a community and feeling its respect, however qualified and variable they may be, contribute greatly to one's belief that one deserves to be alive. Consequently, the fantasy of being ostracized implies being sentenced to a kind of emotional or spiritual death. Once ostracized, one feels changed into a nonperson or a worthless and unwanted substance. We convey this implication of loss of spirit or of spiritual death in our expressive figurative language. For example, when we feel extremely ashamed, we are likely to say, "I could have sunk into the ground" or "I could have died from shame." In psychoanalysis, figurative language is, as we all know, another royal road to the unconscious.

My reference to sinking into the ground links up specifically with the experience of humiliation. Etymologically, the word *humiliation* derives from *humus* or earth and, in language usage, it shifts to "on the ground," "of the earth," or more indirectly, "lowly" or "lowdown." In the context of this extreme of shame, our use of the word *humiliation* can imply death and decay in the earth rather than the alternative, the birth and growth that spring from the earth.

The implied reference to death is even clearer in the case of mortification. Etymologically, the word *mortification* points toward death, dying, even killing; its stem *mort* appears in the words *mortal, immortal*, and *mortuary*. In common usage, mortification is usually represented as primarily an affair of the internal world (one just feels mortified), while humiliation frequently refers to believing that painful shame is being inflicted on one from without. In the subjective world, however, the mortification may turn out to have been inflicted by an introject rather than the self, in which case the experience might be better described as the passive one of humiliation.

The difference between humiliation and mortification seems therefore to rest on humiliation's more pronounced reliance on some internal or external object, one that may very well be the container of a projective identification.

Excrement and other human waste products have long been assigned a prominent place in analytic discussion of these experiences. Freud (1905b) and Abraham (1921) showed the extent to which the varieties of shame experiences are organized around anal fantasies. Experientially, the infantile linkage of shame to anal matters is thought to develop especially around the time of habit training generally and toilet training specifically. Ostensibly, that training carries only the message that one is being trained to be an appropriate, well-socialized, clean, and healthy person, thus an acceptable, respectable member of the community, first of all the immediate community, that is, the family. However, excrement in unconscious fantasy is a weapon, an explosion, and a murderously powerful regulator of pleasure and self-esteem, though it may also serve as a gift.

The equation of shame with excrement is made obvious when we try to humiliate others by calling them assholes or referring to what they say as bullshit or use some other scatological expression. With these words, we bring in ideas of waste, filth, stink, refuse—everything that has had the life taken out of it and is supposed to be avoided, left behind, or gotten rid of in disgust; more than worthless, it is repulsive and fit only to be destroyed. And to be "shit on" or "pissed on" can be felt to be a violent attack that calls for either despair or violent response, verbal or physical. Frequently, "garbage" is an intermediate or euphemistic form of anal derogation.

Then, there is the painful experience of losing face. Almost paradoxically, shame experience also gets organized around the face. The complexity of the psychology of face and its presentation to the world is such that its discussion calls for multidisciplinary approaches. Only a few aspects can be discussed here. More than displacement upward and feelings of exposure are involved. On primitive levels of thought, it is believed that, if one's face is not seen, one is not being seen at all. Therefore, losing face can be a devastating experience in unconscious fantasy in that it implies that one has been abandoned or banished, has been lost or has vanished, or in some other way has been utterly devalued and finished off. Consequently, saving face can imply saving life itself or at least salvaging what life is left in you and what community remains available to you.

Associated with losing face is the idea of *de*facing. Defacing usually refers to marking up something to spoil it and make it ugly. Therefore, on the level of deep fantasy, defacing something can imply depriving it of its identity through making it so changed and so ugly as to be unrecognizable, unacceptable, even dangerous to look at. It is felt to have been rendered strange, alien, worthless, even dead. In the extreme, there is *e*ffacing—total destruction by elimination.

Consequently, the common inclination to hide your face when feeling mortified or humiliated can express primitive fantasies of dying, death, and disappearance. Sinking into the ground and hiding your face may be viewed as different versions of the same act. The common expressive movement of hiding your face in shame can also signify, in the concreteness of unconscious fantasy, covering or burying the degraded excrement with which you now feel identified. Additionally, hiding your face is a way of defacing yourself, giving up your identity in order to ease the pain. By covering your face, by so to speak enshrouding yourself so that you are simultaneously seen and hidden, you may be unconsciously enacting your own death and burial—the final effacement. In another of its aspects, this face-covering may be a gesture of trying to ward off the defacing, the killing blow, or the punishment for being offensive.

Therefore, it may be inferred that, in unconscious fantasy, the hands that cover the face create a scene of violence, repudiation, death, and disappearance. The implied catastrophe is reversible, however, for that gesture can simultaneously signify destruction and its negation. Because the hidden face can always reappear fully and be seen to be intact, the gesture can signify the denial of catastrophe, specifically death and defense against it, perhaps death and resurrection. The unending psychic contest in unconscious fantasy of life against death may well be being enacted when, either literally or figuratively, the face of the mortified person appears from behind the hands. Then, it is like spring after winter, which is to say that life is being affirmed once again, much to everyone's relief. It is as though one has been penitent long enough. One has sunk down and died but "not really." One has traveled briefly to the underworld and is now permitted reentry into the world of the living.

Not only has an escape from responsibility and retribution been staged by going beyond the reach of the living for the moment, but persecutors have been pacified through the gesture of extreme self-punishment. In unconscious fantasy, one may be behaving much as ascetics do when they mortify their flesh symbolically, for in doing so they lend themselves to the fantasy that they are putting themselves to death or through the pangs of death, perhaps dying in Christ only to be finally resurrected as he was—all of which makes it a glorious death, too.

These are the versions of the extremes of shame that, during analysis, may be attributed to the latent thoughts of those analysands whose lives have been pervaded by an actual or impending sense of humiliation or mortification. These versions become interpretable through dreams, slips of the tongue, avoidable accidents, overreactions to situations that for others would call up only mild embarrassment, and distinctive uses of figurative language and expressive gestures. Typically, these analysands live with the experience of always being looked at and seen through by others disapprovingly, if not now then soon, and if not in the external world then in the internal. They remember shameful experiences of long ago so vividly that it is as if they are happening here and now. These sufferers are profoundly self-conscious and hyperalert to the environment's responses to them. They behave as though they feel cut off from developing a sense of looking and evaluating for themselves, that is, looking and judging independently, and also cut off from looking *to* themselves for affirmation and constructive criticism, again, independently.

DYNAMIC

What has happened developmentally is that the shaming eyes and sharp words of others, both real and imagined, have been internalized to the point where, unconsciously though sometimes even consciously, children come to feel constantly persecuted by those internal figures we call introjects. Some children go on to identify with these shaming, persecutory introjects so that they come to experience the criticism as self-criticism. Even then, however, it seems to be the case that, as a rule, the original shaming figures, who were a mix of actual persons and fantasies, are always waiting in the wings, as it were, ready to reappear as themselves, that is, as alienated, alienating, critical others. This is so because it seems difficult for those who live in great shame to identify fully with what they have internalized. For identification does imply, among other things, a move toward autonomy or independence, so that some victims may regard that next step as too rejecting of control by others; also, that step may involve too much sense of loss of the object, and it may even be imagined as murderous in relation to whichever object is owed the "loyalty" of merging, submission, and dependence. Here, the distinction between shame and guilt is quite plain.

In the treatment situation, these humiliated and mortified analysands quickly, repetitively, and unyieldingly use the transference to externalize their internal condemnations. Using projective identification,

they rapidly and rigidly cast the analyst in the role of a humiliating figure. In their experience, their own excessively critical minds are now
their analysts'; they begin to act as though they have no mind of their
own. Thereby, they maintain a familiar and safe, even if painful, relationship to the outer world while also gaining relief or achieving escape
from the internal world of shaming persecution and bottomless dread
of humiliation. From their internal worlds, they expect only unrelieved
and inescapable derogation.

In this way, what may have seemed on first acquaintance to be
these analysands' impartial self-appraisals quickly become transparent to the analyst for what they are. All too soon, the analysts see that
they are playing out fantasies of persecution by what they take to be
their overinvolved, sadomasochistic analysts. They fantasize their
analysts as maintaining close and hostile surveillance at all times. In
this transference situation, the analysts' reassuring words and tones of
voice can be of no avail, for fundamentally the analysands take reassurance as a confirmation of their worst fears; they see it as condescending, insincere evidence of their having had a damaging influence
on their analysts' judgment and standards, or evidence that their analysts, too, are worthless. It is well known how much hard work is required before analysts can effect change in this regard, if they succeed
in this at all.

Dynamically, humiliation and mortification can be situated within
the paranoid–schizoid position. In this position, as defined originally
by Melanie Klein (1946), emotional experience and concrete thinking
take precedence over the focused concern for others, sense of responsibility, and guilt feelings that characterize the more integrated, whole-
object-related, superego-based, thoughtful, depressive position (Klein,
1940). Being fantasized as a potential killer, the analyst is approached
or avoided with paranoid dread. This dread is implied, for example, when
analysands feel so undeserving or rotten or "shitty," as they often say,
that they regard it as inevitable that the analyst will just want to react
hatefully and treat them like dirt or excrement and abandon them with
disgust—in other words, effectively kill them off. The words *mortification* and *humiliation* capture the sense that one has fallen into the hands
of an external or internal executioner-by-derogation and that one is
undergoing spiritual as well as corporeal death and decay. That drastic
sense of it is not captured by the words *embarrassment* and *feeling*

foolish, and it is certainly obscured when, as is so often the case, shame is simply taken as an irreducible feeling.

Prime features of the paranoid–schizoid position include—along with heavy reliance on projective identification—envy, splitting, and grandiosity. Taking these four into account together firms up our grasp of the dynamics of humiliation and mortification.

The envious wish to spoil is often accomplished by humiliating looks, gestures, or words. Envy can destroy the object's own sense of personal worth, making it feel like excrement or refuse (Klein, 1957). Those who feel spoiled by envy say such things as, "I was made to feel like dirt." Along the same lines, envious friends or family members may try to spoil an analysand's enthusiasm for treatment, and when they are successful, the analysand often shows up somehow conveying the feeling that the treatment or the analyst seems rotten or suspect.

Analysands envy the analyst, though often they are afraid to show that this is so. They feel that the analyst is in possession of what they lack themselves: pure goodness, sanity, and happiness. Defensively, they may split off these positive assessments and then project their envious selves into the analyst and imagine him or her to be an envious spoiler of them. At this point, they may well experience the analyst's interpretations as envious efforts to make them feel worse or to think even less of themselves. No longer picturing themselves as spoilers but rather as victims of the analyst's spoiling intent, they go on to try to stimulate the analyst into overt countertransference responses of disgust and rejection, whereupon they will use even the slightest sign of departure from acceptance to validate and intensify their sense that they are innocent victims of envy in a rotten relationship.

Grandiose fantasies of the self seem to be implied by extreme vulnerability to shame. Vulnerability and omnipotence: it is a case of opposites meeting. The grandiose fantasies that are generated are fearfully protected. No sense of being flawed, deficient, or powerless must enter the internal scene. On this account, these grandiose analysands become intolerant of the virtues of others. Enviously and spitefully, they try to spoil the goodness of others so that they themselves will not have to face anything that would stimulate feelings of smallness, ugliness, inferiority, and vulnerability. For them, feeling needful or dependent on the other person implies powerlessness and is therefore taboo; technically, then, the best defense is to spoil anything that would constitute a temptation toward dependence, for then the critical judgment of others need not matter. This strategy requires that there be no reason to feel loss, responsibility, or guilt, all of which belong to the more integrated depressive position. In the paranoid–schizoid position, one attempts to feel godlike, able to give birth to oneself, and be totally self-sufficient.

This grandiose fantasy can take other forms, some of them initially quite deceptive. For example, the unconsciously maintained sense of omnipotence and blamelessness can be implied when, consciously, the analysand readily assumes total responsibility for his or her own humiliating experience. In this, there is no paradox, for one's sense of *total* blameworthiness precludes complaining against others for having contributed to the problem or even having created it. The opinions of others mustn't matter. Total blameworthiness blocks out resenting others for what may seem to be their relentless devaluations. In none of this self-blame is there evidence of that well-developed sense of responsibility that takes into account the feelings of others and so recognizes that others do matter. The grandiosity in this way of looking at things is betrayed by the predominance of self-referential thinking. Persecutory, yes, but that painful world is still focused on the self. The narcissism behind this grandiose strategy is all-powerful.

In melancholia, the blameworthiness is directed at incorporated objects, as Freud pointed out (1917a). Although that may be a factor, too, in the cases under discussion here, diagnosable melancholia is not part of the presenting picture.

In this grandiose setting, mortification may be imagined unconsciously as a glorious death at the center of the universe, a saintly fate, similar to what I mentioned earlier in connection with asceticism and what Erik Erikson (1959) took up when discussing triumph through the attainment of negative identity.

A few brief clinical examples may help crystallize this account of envy, grandiosity, and allied tendencies. One female analysand was profusely apologetic for having a critical thought about the analyst's clothes. It was as though so much harm had been inflicted that serious retaliation had to be expected. The contempt was based on her own unconscious identification with a scornful mother, a dominant internal object. Most of all, she was identified with a particular pained expression she believed she saw on her mother's face whenever she looked at her. Unconsciously, the analysand was seeing the analyst through what she experienced as her mother's contemptuous eyes. To justify her contempt and thereby support her precarious conscious sense of strength, worth, and superiority, she had projected her fragile, vulnerable, humiliated but envious and vengeful child self into the analyst. In this case, it was more fear of retaliation than guilt that led to her being so apologetic; it was also a sign of omnipotent fantasy. Saying that you are sorry doesn't necessarily mean that you are feeling guilty.

In another case, a male analysand's expression of contempt for his unsupported idea of his analyst's politics was also tied to an identification with a mother he experienced as contemptuous. Analysis of that contempt led to recognition that he had made a strong and pervasive feminine identification with that internal object. He had been trying to exclude that "female" self from his consciousness, hiding it anxiously behind a superior "masculine" self representation and a good deal of arrogant, implicitly omnipotent behavior.

In a third case, the analysand was hiding from himself and others noteworthy assets in the realm of intelligence, charm, sense of style, and perceptiveness; he did so in order to protect the self-esteem of fragile and potentially envious parental figures who were also afraid of intimacy. It was through analysis of transference and countertransference that these assets, along with some adventurousness, imaginativeness, and livelier experience of sexuality, could be freed from this unconscious strategy and allowed to develop further.

Ms. M. This young woman was extremely vulnerable to feelings of humiliation and mortification. These feelings had much of their origin in the consistently shaming environment in which she had grown up. Her self-esteem had been shattered by judgmental, persecutory responses to her spontaneity and self-assertiveness. To compensate and also to identify with her aggressors she had developed unconscious fantasies of omnipotence. She expressed these fantasies in exasperated, contemptuous, judgmentally persecutory attitudes toward others, being always ready to blame them for their shortcomings and blunders. Also, she could not tolerate being dependent on another person recognized as being different from her and with other interests and values. All of which dominated her transference; she alternated between unworthiness and superiority, and she felt that analysis always put her in a humiliated position. It made her "so ordinary." One day she appeared with a cast on her arm, having broken a small bone in a fall on the ice. She reported that she was aware of having felt a bit of a shock when she was shown the X ray of the bones of her wrist and hand. She reflected that it was "so ordinary" to have a skeleton like everybody else and to be vulnerable like them. She was mortified. "It was degrading!" All her fantasies of being special were threatened by this confrontation with her humanness.

Returning now to the overall dynamics of humiliation and mortification, mention should be made of interpersonal influences. Humiliation is often inflicted on others in the form of the challenging question, "Who do you think you are?" The question is often put into words, though it may be conveyed through gestures such as raised eyebrows or mocking looks. When this confrontation is repetitive and intense and when it comes particularly from parental figures throughout childhood, it can humiliate children to the point where, as time goes on, they feel driven to internalize the confrontational attitude and try to identify with their persecutory objects, as mentioned earlier. Compliantly, they become constantly self-deprecatory. They may then shift the emphasis away from humiliation toward mortification—the extreme shame that seems to come from the self. A thoroughly humiliated or mortified man will unfailingly "know his place," that place being lowly, always at the foot of the table, so to say, or even on the outside, in exile. Often he will find, through projective identification, slights and scorn where none is apparent to others, and often he will try to provoke this abuse from others to validate his pathological strategy.

It is well known that there are defensive advantages to be gained by identifying with the aggressor—in this case, the deprecator, both real and imagined. On this basis, children (and later, adults) come to feel relatively safe from unexpected criticism from others. Feeling already traumatized as they do, they feel particularly pained by unexpected criticism. Such a person might say, "I always beat my critics to the draw," or "beat them to the punch," and by using these combative metaphors of shoot-out and brawl, they suggest the unconscious fantasy of traumatic violence that is involved in being all too readily shamed.

Another defensive advantage of seeming to remain small, humble, and humbled, is the reinforcement of defenses against manifestations of the latent grandiose tendencies mentioned earlier. Heinz Kohut (1977) has put much emphasis on the need for defense against latent grandiosity. We are able to infer the fear of grandiosity from the various metaphors for conceitedness, such as swellheaded, too big for your britches, and too good for this world. Most of those who feel chronically humiliated or mortified prefer to feel small as a way of insuring safety or at least the possibility of being safe from ostracism or other retaliation. It is better to remain inconspicuous and unpretentious in a world viewed as entirely unwelcoming. That world may include the self itself, as Groucho Marx indicated when he said he would never stoop to join a club that would have him as a member.

Yet another advantage of directing the question, "Who do you think you are?" at oneself is that it works against stirring up the envy of others. The potential for being the target of that envy is indicated by the popular terms: showy and show-off. You cannot be envied for what you hide successfully.

The internalization of the humiliating attitude generally results in one's becoming ever more envious of others for their freer and fuller achievements, their relatedness to others, their self-assurance, and their multiple pleasure possibilities. Then the humiliated or mortified person joins the ranks of the persecutors, unconsciously as well as consciously looking for opportunities to be disparaging and contemptuous. In this way that person hopes to acquire feelings of power and superiority; however, the momentary satisfaction to be gained this way is a nasty one, and it backfires, for the mental representation of the community you are living in, if not the entire world, will be crowded with failures, isolates, betrayers, and persecutors. In the end, going down this road leads to meaninglessness and despair because everyone and everything is leveled to the ground.

In transitional cases, some guilt feelings may accompany the destructiveness of this policy. In that case, the analyst may gain some therapeutic leverage in this extremely difficult therapeutic context.

It is also well known, however, that there are many disadvantages that follow from cringing before the question, "Who do you think you are?" no matter whether it arises interpersonally or in the internal world. Obviously, to diminish yourself as a form of self-protection is also to impair yourself or damage yourself. Various forms of self-destructiveness may be involved: inhibited use of your capacities; warped reality testing in relation to your actual achievements; a split in your sense of self necessitated by always having to be on guard against the spontaneity that might reveal your own enviable talents or assertive self-interest or pride. When relying too heavily on this defensive strategy, you will impose limitations on your social relations and your career through excessive caution and self-consciousness. By becoming mindless through projective identification (others must do your thinking for you) and by reducing your actual achievements, you will also limit the possibility of being recognized by others as a worthwhile or interesting person. Finally, you will be excluding normal pride from your subjective experience. Excluding rightful pride may reach the extreme of eliminating the beneficial effect of recognized good performance on your own sense of identity and worth. When you leave all self-definition and self-appraisal to others, you remain in a totally vulnerable position.

Upon beginning treatment, the analyst assumes that somewhere and somehow the analysand's internal world contains aspirations toward something better: a way out of the dismal narcissistic world of isolated omnipotence, self-crippling, and vulnerability and a way to free or restore the capacity to love and care. On the strength of this wish, the analysand can form an alliance, however compromised and tenuous, with the analyst.

DISCUSSION

The preceding study has remained close to the disruptions and nuances of here-and-now clinical relationships. Instead of emphasizing shame in general, it has centered on the extremes of humiliation and mortification, in which regard it has clarified differences between the two in their unconscious fantasies and the defensive operations they express. Here, they have been treated as complex experiences rather than simple affects, the understanding of which lies in clarifying their complex developmental histories and working out their metapsychological explanations. Prominent among the basic constituents of these affects seem to be splitting, primitive aggression and narcissism, projective identification, envy, and grandiosity—all of them features of Melanie Klein's paranoid–schizoid position; also, defenses against these tendencies and the ways in which they themselves may be used defensively. In certain respects, this account departs from what has become traditional in the ego psychological Freudian psychoanalytic literature. A useful 1984 paper by Spero on an object-relational approach to shame was conceived along lines compatible with the present argument, although it also seems to try to link itself to the metapsychological tradition and so to end up as something of a transitional effort.

The ego-psychological Freudian approach is exemplified by a set of papers in *The Psychoanalytic Study of the Child* (Ablon, 1990; Gillman, 1990; Yorke, and collaborators, 1990; Abrams, 1990). These authors present scholarly, clinically knowledgeable, informative essays on shame, and their lists of references provide a fine coverage of the preceding Freudian literature. Typically, they start out from shame not as a complex experience but as a simple, implicitly irreducible affect. Whatever cognitive or fantasy content shame may have is presented as being acquired during the time when this mental element is proceeding through the psychosexual phases of development and the constituting of the ego, ego ideal, and superego; concurrently the subject is developing self–other differentiation with accompanying rises and falls of self-esteem. In these writings, the fantasy content features loss of control, dirtiness, inferiority, and a sense of physical and mental exposure based on phallic–oedipal conflict over exhibitionism and voyeurism.

What stands out to this reader is the constant pressure felt in these essays to present a full developmental account and a full structural formulation; the experiential data seem to be relegated too quickly into the service of these theoretical imperatives. A steady march toward a comprehensive theory of affect is constantly in evidence. The rest, as Yorke et al. put it, is "descriptive rather than analytic" (p. 377). In contrast, this reader would be inclined to say that, when it is pursued in detail, the descriptive along with the dynamic *is the* analytic in the strict sense, while the rest is developmental psychology, speculatively overdetailed reconstructions, and ambitious model-building. Even that model-building can no longer claim to be the only kind that is "analytic," for there is now, for example, self psychological model-building of quite another kind (Kohut, 1977). That approach has its own extensive literature on shame; it differs in fundamental ways both from the ego psychological Freudian and the views presented here.

Another feature of the traditional ego psychological literature that must be emphasized is its dedication to subordinating the preoedipal and pregenital to the phallic-oedipal, especially of the positive libidinal sort. This practice differs significantly from the increasing tendency in the psychoanalytic literature to give greater weight to primitive levels of mental experience and infantile fantasy formulations—material that is not closely tied to what seems, to the external observer, to be environmental input. The traditional emphasis continues to be present, however, in more recent publications than those already cited (e.g., Rizzuto, 1991; Rothstein, 1994).

I have tried to develop a way of analyzing the phenomena of humiliation and mortification that pursues them into the concrete thinking characteristic of primitive unconscious fantasy. For example, as we see in the figurative language that we all use, the deeply ashamed person would equate himself or herself with dirt itself and not be thinking only in terms of a conceptually and self representationally higher level of "dirtiness" or being treated by clearly defined others "like dirt." The latter expressions only point the way toward the concrete unconscious fantasies, so that it would appear to be superficial to let matters rest with them. Similarly, the experience of inferiority is likely to be imagined unconsciously in terms of concrete physical attributes related to seductive or brute power of the child's own invention, and not be tied exclusively to specific toilet-training experiences and presumably actual observations of the anatomical differences between the sexes and the generations. And, as already mentioned, violence, death, and annihilation are typically at the heart of the unconscious experience of humiliation and mortification.

In my view, the limitation in the Freudian ego psychological tradition that I have been emphasizing is not systematically required by ego psychology itself. That psychology leaves plenty of room for exploring the primitive, concrete unconscious fantasies that enter into subjective experience (e.g., Kris [1939] on inspiration). Rather, the fault lies with those analysts who tend toward premature classification of feelings, structurally oriented placings and explanations of them, and metapsychological speculations about affects and the developmental workings of the "mental apparatus" as a whole. It seems that programmatic concerns often take precedence over sustained analytic curiosity.

I have tried to reduce this limitation by centering this discussion on certain unconsciously elaborated fantasies that I believe it necessary to construct through interpretation in the course of clinical analytic work. At the same time, I must emphasize that I regard my essay as a supplement to the existing *clinical* literature, not as an alternative to it. That, for example, I mentioned castration fantasies and exhibitionism just in passing and did not dwell on them in this context indicates only that I am not presenting this essay as a comprehensive discussion of the topic of shame in all its degrees and colorations. Nor has it been my goal to survey or integrate the mass of writings on the ego ideal and self-esteem and their relations to superego functioning. Further, I have not concerned myself with those mild or occasional shame experiences we refer to as embarrassment or moments of feeling foolish. Finally, while my comments do bear significantly on the goals of clinical exploration, they are not intended as technical directives to proceed directly to the depths of unconscious experience.

SUMMARY

Different in their etymologies, humiliation and mortification come together as prominent members of a family of forms of experiencing debasement. Debasement may extend as far as a sense of annihilation associated with fantasies of deserving to die, being made to die, even causing oneself to die. These fantasies and the figurative language and gestures corresponding to them may also imply retention of the power to reverse the process, thereby to regain existence and acceptance through penance and rehabilitation. Mortification and humiliation are constituents of dynamic contexts in which opposites meet, so that analysts are able to infer as well the presence of omnipotent fantasies and envious, contemptuous, and persecutory attitudes in just those unfortunates ostensibly leading only debased lives. All of which is understandable in terms of the strategic and tactical defenses characteristic of the primitively narcissistic paranoid–schizoid position as described by Melanie Klein (1946). To the extent that the analysand has moved toward the depressive position, a position in which he or she can assume responsibility and feel reparative wishes along with guilt, and not merely a desire to placate others in order to ward off their retaliations, to that extent will it be easier to work through these problems in analysis. In extreme cases, however, much time may have to be spent helping the analysand move far enough into the depressive position to begin to accomplish this working through. This part of the work requires much analysis of primitive ego functioning as expressed in the transference and felt in the countertransference. In these ways, psychoanalysis may make significant contributions to the development of all those analysands, of whom there are so many, who have lived their lives in states of extreme shame and who, upon entering analysis, take on the immense job of change toward greater autonomy, pride, and regulation of self-esteem through truly mutual relations with others in both the internal and external worlds.

7

Blocked Introjection/
Blocked Incorporation

I

The first time I heard "blocked introjection" used in a clinical discussion was at a meeting at which Hanna Segal was the featured discussant. It was a meeting of the psychotherapy staff of the Yale University Health Services, sometime around 1970. Dr. Segal used "blocked introjection" masterfully to pull together some basic but disparate issues in a case presentation. In the years since then I have frequently witnessed her (or read her) doing equivalently impressive things of that sort, so much so that she has established herself for me as a model of acute clinical listening and shrewd interpretation. But it is just with the idea of blocked introjection that I shall be concerned here.

The sources of this idea can be traced all the way back, first, to Freud (1905b, 1917a) and perhaps especially Karl Abraham (1916, 1924) in their essays on the oral phase and depression and, subsequently, to the firm psychoanalytic foundation provided by Melanie Klein. I believe, however, that all of us have experienced moments when a known, interesting, but until then perhaps only subsidiary idea was transformed into an important instrument of understanding by someone's felicitous use of

111

it. One thing we mean when we say of an idea that "it clicked into place" is that we have successfully introjected an aspect of a mind at work in such a way as to change a piece of learned content into an essential tool for coping with consequential issues. Still, at that moment the process is not yet complete, for further transformation will take place as one becomes more familiar with that new tool, extends its uses by adapting it to unexpected problems, and defines its limits. This process of mastery may be unending. So it has been for me with "blocked introjection."

In this essay, in order to detail my present understanding of blocked introjection, I shall explain my preferring to call this unconscious fantasy "blocked incorporation," then cover some of the complex theoretical and clinical issues that I have encountered in interpreting it, and go on to give some brief clinical illustrations of my uses of those interpretations.

II

Introjection belongs to a family of terms that includes identification and incorporation, the three of them falling under the general heading of *internalization* (Schafer, 1968). Of these, only incorporation refers directly to the unconscious fantasy of taking into the bodily self something perceived as existing outside that self. Elsewhere (1974) I have argued that the entire language of internalization is founded on the fantasy of incorporation. That incorporation fantasy concretizes self, mind, learning, restraint of action, and other such ideas, changing each into a substance existing in, or a physical process taking place in, spaces with more or less distinct and confining boundaries. The language of internalization organizes mental events in the terms of a spatial *metaphor* or *story line*. Mental events are not things that travel in space as things may in the everyday physical world. The spatial metaphor of internalization actualizes an unconscious fantasy.

Usually, the concrete incorporation fantasy is cast in oral terms: sucking, biting, chewing, swallowing, gastrointestinal events, and the like. Although the fantasy can be cast in anal, visual, tactile, and other bodily terms, it is not easily divested entirely of its oral origins; we see that this is so in those familiar interpretations that point out the use of the anus, vagina, eyes, or ears as mouths.

Certainly, the literature developed by Mrs. Klein and her follow-ers contains an abundance of references to incorporation. In general, the physical, bodily, substantial prototypes of modes of object relatedness have figured prominently in that literature. It has seemed to me, there-fore, that the most apt term for the process in question is *blocked incor-poration*, not *blocked introjection*. The concept implies the mouth (or its equivalent) shut tight against intruding objects. "Blocked" itself adds to the concreteness of the idea. For this reason I depart a bit from the more common Kleinian usage: blocked introjection.

I have also argued (1968) that a place should be made in our think-ing for "primary process presences," more simply "presences." These presences are the influential fantasy figures who are not necessarily located within the bodily self and whose psychic existence does not necessarily raise questions about how they got to be "inside." They may be imagined anywhere: alongside one, lurking in the shadows, and so forth; they may not be placed in any definite space, simply having the attributes of thereness, as in "I felt your presence even though I know you were not in the room." The presence may be a whole person or only a voice or a pair of eyes or ears or a skeleton rattling in the closet. *Pres-ences*, in my sense of the term, are part of common experience, and they do not qualify as malignant hallucinatory events; rather, they may best be regarded as daydream fragments so vivid as to feel real without com-promising seriously the person's current reality testing. They need not be "borderline" phenomena. Perhaps "momentary dreamlike states" comes close to it.

Incorporation may culminate in the experience, conscious or oth-erwise, of an introject or, if carried further, in an identification whereby the subject takes on its characteristics as his or her own. Here, I shall not be concerned with end points; rather, my concern is with incorpora-tion as a mediating and enabling process.

III

In certain contexts the fantasy of blocked incorporation may be prima-rily defensive of the self; for example, in the exclusion from the bodily self of bad objects or substances and their less concrete manifestations in bad ideas or feelings. The fantasy may, however, be in the service of protecting the object; for example, not damaging it by destructively cannibalizing it or immersing it in the badness or destructiveness of one's internal world. The reverse of both these dynamics may also be indicated at times, that is, one may be blocking the incorporation of another's goodness in order to avoid destabilizing a defensive posture of one's own that features an anhedonic, bitter or dead mode of function ("not getting my hopes up" or "not letting my defenses down"). Similarly, one may be using blocked incorporation as an instrument of war in object relations by employing it as a punitive refusal of invasive or controlling caretaking and reparative efforts (spurning embraces or "food that's good for you"). On account of this reversibility, the meaning of blocked incorporation must be arrived at only in specific, individualized clinical contexts.

When blocked incorporation figures importantly in the analysand's emotional life, it will control his or her development of transference and attempted manipulations of countertransference. To avoid confusion in this realm, it will be well to remind ourselves of a major fact of life in psychic reality: the coexistence of more than one unconscious fantasy pertaining to the same relationships and issues and the inevitable contradictions that are tolerated unconsciously. We have been introduced to examples of this fact of life in many places in Freud's work and, with regard to internalization, in Abraham's as well. For present purposes, consider the case of the analysand who refuses food owing to the fantasized cannibalistic significance of eating, even though the depression itself testifies to the existence of an unconscious fantasy of having already devoured the ambivalently regarded object. A second example is the fantasy of containing the container of the self, as in the instance of maintaining a sense of contact with the "containing" analyst during separations by imagining that one has incorporated the analyst; in this instance, Euclidean space is inadequate to the job of mapping out the domain of unconscious fantasy. A third example is the adult male fantasy of being both a boy and a girl and also both the child and the parent of his parents.

It is probably never fully warranted to claim with certainty that one understands and can designate exactly the sequence or hierarchy of fantasies pertaining to incorporation. Technically, it seems, there is much to be gained by the analyst's tolerating the contradictoriness of many unconscious fantasies and conveying that tolerance to the analysand.

The alternative of making too much order among unconscious fantasies is most likely to support intellectualization and the analysand's
idealization of the analyst as omniscient or omnipotent. Tolerance of
contradiction need not entail launching chaotic barrages of interpretation, resorting too rapidly to the concept of overdetermination, or sub-
stituting what is merely thinkable as a possibility for what is strongly
implied in the ongoing analytic dialogue or otherwise shown in the
interaction.

Do we require the concept of *partial* incorporation, as Abraham
seemed to think? I believe so. Although our view of unconscious fantasy is that it is predisposed toward all-or-none, black-or-white, and *pars
pro toto* thinking, and although, in self-contradiction, unconscious fantasy may include partial and total incorporation at the same time, there
does seem to be value in reserving some interpretations for what is primarily partial; for example, incorporation of only a penis, a breast, a
damaged leg, or blind eyes. Again, making false choices and acting on
too great a need for order may lead the analyst astray or limit the effectiveness of his or her analytic work. An example of usefully mixing the
partial and the total would be the following: a female analysand unconsciously fantasizes during holidays that, because the analyst does not
think of her, she no longer exists, so that in her subjective experience
and actions she feels deadened for the duration; she may be said to have
incorporated the analyst as an empty container, which in one respect is
totalistic but in another respect only partial in that it allows the analyst
to be away and to have a mind filled with other things and people. There
is no single correct way to take up this partial/total fantasy; more than
one approach to it may be necessary.

Similarly, the placement of the fantasized figure need not be fixed
or limited to one spot. A figure may be inside and outside simultaneously,
as in the melancholic's simultaneously representing the object as already
incorporated and as being kept outside. Also, depending on (or manifesting) changes in attitude, the locale of the figure may shift rapidly
from inside to outside and back again. For example, a dreaded incorporation may seem to have taken place when the analyst's figure is unexpectedly experienced as being within, this then quickly followed by that
figure's expulsion or reprojection and its characterization as repugnant.
In the analysis of transference, the locale of the analyst cannot be taken
for granted; in the same way, owing to projective identification, the

locale of the self or some aspect of it, such as understanding or feeling, may not remain effectively and consistently "within."

IV

Case Example 1

Mr. A. This young man, son of a highly demanding, critical, competitive father, manifested extensive disruption of cognitive functions. He could not perceive accurately, remember with certainty, or communicate with any clarity what he had encountered in his studies, social relationships, or activities. Approximate locutions such as "something like that" and "in a way" filled his analytic communications. He misremembered numbers, and he mispronounced words and names. Almost invariably he recalled the analyst's comments in a distorted way. It seemed that "blocked incorporation" was a useful designation of the fantastic foundation of many of these phenomena. Because it was important to the analysand not to become like his father, blocking any incorporation of, and subsequent introjective identification with, father seemed to have a very high priority. In this case, one primary motive seemed to be to enact a castrated role in relation to his father and, in the analysis, to his analyst. This castrated role lived out the negative identity unconsciously being deposited in him by the father's projective identifications. Enacting this role was also to engage in a form of warfare with the father, experienced in this connection as a demander of achievement. Additionally, the analysand's cognitive impairment seemed to blind him to evident limitations in the father's actual professional and social achievements; thereby, he was protecting the "fragile father" whose fragility was supposed to be entirely lodged in him. This fragility included "feminine" or "castrated" aspects of the father's self now being enacted by the analysand in his characteristic mode of function. He played all of this out in his transference and tried to stimulate countertransferences of a "paternal" type.

I have presented only enough of this analysand's total emotional situation to show that incorporation of the father's aggressiveness and weakness both had and had not taken place, and that this contradictory state of affairs in the analysand's self was in the service of his seeking some equilibrium in his internal world. It is implied that a certain amount of introjective identification had developed in the wake of those incorporations that did take place.

Case Example 2

Mr. B. This young man had fought his way out of a rigidly Marxist upbringing. He had felt "brainwashed" by that upbringing, indicating by his use of the term *brainwashed* the interiority of the fanatical parental pressures. Also, he had felt under constant surveillance and criticism, in which respect he was subject to the experience of presences in the form of eyes upon him and voices at him. For a time during his adolescence, he had been a firm believer in his parents' creed; later he had become "disillusioned" and had "broken away from them."

In the course of analyzing his struggle against feelings in the transference, it emerged that he was trying to believe that, in effect, he had purged himself (his internal world) of a variety of controlling and persecutory part- and whole-figures. Consequently, he believed that if he let the analyst become important to him, and certainly if he let himself feel the analyst's presence within him, it would culminate in a repetition of brainwashing and willing bondage. This outcome he was determined to prevent. This incorporation had to be blocked. It did, therefore, occasion brief panic whenever he noted, as time went on and rapport grew, a sense of the analyst's presence with him or in him. He would then stabilize himself by launching into scathing critiques of the idealism of psychoanalysis, the bourgeois values of psychoanalysts, and the personal faults of his analyst. Beyond expulsion, a wall of disgust had to be erected, in order, he hoped, to block any further ingestion. Also, a wall of negative countertransference, if possible.

Case Example 3

Ms. C's mother had been severely depressed and hospitalized on more than one occasion, some of them early in the analysand's life. In the analysis, this young woman gave signs of having attempted desperately to repress her incorporation of her mother. Blocking incorporation in general seemed to have become a general strategy of life. Her mother had seemed to view the world around her and all the figures in it, including the analysand, with distaste. This distaste was covered with a shallow show of benevolence.

The young woman carried over this distaste, looking at the world through her mother's (incorporated) eyes in what might be regarded as a partial identification. But she also felt that she had to be wary of engaging in incorporation in relation not only to her mother but to all other "maternal" figures, including the analyst, for all were regarded as forces of noxious (depressive) influence. Thus, her attack on incorporation was two-pronged and powerful. Her strategy in the analysis was this: to hold the analyst at bay by affectlessness. This affectlessness would also serve, she hoped, to protect the analyst from rude surprises, such as unsettling shows of feeling or independence; in part, that same concerned mode of function had been developed to protect the fragile mother. Thus, the analyst as depressive mother was both being held at bay and being protected, and additionally was being regarded as repugnant just as the analysand felt she had been by her mother. Like her mother, she was superficially compliant, but her compliance was thin even though firmly in place.

More so than in the cases of Mr. A and Mr. B, this analysand fought against incorporation in the transference with great success. Almost entirely, she made use of the analyst only from a great psychic distance; she improved her lot to some extent and then stood pat until the analysis was ended.

I believe that for this analysand the greatest fear of all was the uncovering of the already incorporated, depressively mad mother. While the character trait of distaste could be analyzed with some effect, approaches to the other major issues usually led to increased freezing of feeling, some suspiciousness, and regression to other symptomatic positions that, over time, had been relieved. They had been relieved by the combination of analytic work closer to the surface and the achievement of some differentiation of the analyst from the malignant mother, and some more realistic incorporation of him, a combination that allowed her to derive a limited amount of support from the analytic relationship.

V

To summarize: I organized my presentation around the clinically valuable concept of blocked incorporation. Interpreting unconscious fantasies of incorporation, achieved or blocked, is a subtle, often seemingly contradictory enterprise. The conception of unconscious fantasy as fluid, non-Euclidean, illogical, fragmented, and concretistic, which should be an essential part of every analyst's equipment, is never more needed than in working out the vicissitudes of anti-incorporative strategies. These strategies play major roles in structuring and limiting transference and the analysand's designs on the countertransference. Several brief case examples were adduced to illustrate these complexities.

Good learning from others cannot do without substantial contributions of one's own, but these contributions cannot come to much without those core ideas and attitudes one incorporates from good teachers and good models, Hanna Segal being an outstanding example of both virtues.

8

Some Reflections on the Concept of Enactment

Currently, the concept of enactment is very much in the psychoanalytic air, so much so that it qualifies for the description "buzz word," meaning that by using it you establish yourself as an up-to-date, if not avant garde analyst—or so you hope. This being so, some conceptual working through is called for; otherwise "enactment" may lose its value in the psychoanalytic vocabulary. In this essay I shall begin with a much needed discussion of "enactment's" conceptual boundaries, proceed to its clinical manifestations, then its overuse, its vicissitudes in different schools of psychoanalytic thought, and a set of summarizing and concluding comments. I see this essay as a step toward clarification and consistency of discourse, not as an attempt to have the final word on the topic. In psychoanalysis, as in all other disciplines, there never has been, and never will be, a final word on any topic.

ON CONCEPTUAL BOUNDARIES

It is most useful when enactment is not taken to be just another term for what Freud called acting out and what is sometimes called acting in when it refers to events within the analytic session. Freud (1914a) used acting out to refer to those instances in which memories were, so to say, performed in current life rather than remembered. He saw this performing as a sign of resistance on the one hand and of the need to repeat on the other.

He was emphasizing the therapeutic importance of recovering early pathogenic memories. That recovery was to be effected by reducing the infantile amnesia through the analysis of resistance (Freud, 1912a). Freud never fully relinquished this emphasis on the curative power of remembering. His topographic model of mental functioning, neurosogenesis, and the analytic process had a permanent, though not exclusive, hold on his thinking (see, for example, his *Outline*, 1940).

Later on, in the careless usage of some analysts and others, acting out has been used to imply being bad, specifically by getting oneself, the analyst, or the analysis in administrative, emotional, or legal difficulties. On the whole, however, this corruption of analytic meaning does not seem to have affected the current usage of "enactment," though history warns us to be ready for that eventuality sooner or later.

The vocabulary of "enactment" is also not identical with others that have developed around well-established psychoanalytic concepts. One of these concepts is *character*, when that word is used to refer to habitual modes of action that will show up in the analytic relationship as they do elsewhere. Character, however, is a rather general term; additionally, unlike enactment, it is fixed on traits rather than processes, positions, or scenarios that are constantly in flux. Thus, it does not address itself as finely as enactment to the nuances of the immediate give-and-take in the analytic situation.

Another well-established term to consider here is *repetition*. That term, however, tends to be so centered on the idea of an independently operating compulsion that it, too, can blur the analytic focus on the complexity of the here-and-now engagement of the two parties to the analysis.

Compromise formation, to consider that next, is oriented far more to impulse–defense conflict and its outcome within the mind than it is to the object relational playing out of unconscious fantasies.

Then there is nonverbal communication: Used especially by the Kleinian analysts to characterize many enactments, it does sometimes seem to have been extended too far, in that it takes in occurrences that have never been established in the analytic dialogue as having the intent of communication. In these instances, it is just that the phenomena are interpretable enough to be brought into the analysis by the perceptive analyst; however, it does not make matters clearer when we equate the interpretability of nonverbal phenomena with communicative enactments.

"Enactment" is perhaps closest to the idea of participation. "Participation" does imply that, even when they seem most unresponsive or uncommunicative, analysands may still be viewed as participating in the analytic process. For example, instead of the analyst thinking that these analysands are psychically dead or too resistant for analytic work to get done, or simply paralyzed by anxiety, any of which is a static and probably essentialist trait characterization, he or she may view them as participating in the analysis in a manner that is deadening, restrictive, or frightened to the extreme. In other words, they may be viewed as engaged in actions relevant to the treatment even when they are most inactive. This version of analysands is analytically affirmative rather than negative, and frequently it is more effective in initiating and sustaining collaborative analytic work (Schafer, 1976, 1983).

ON IDENTIFYING ENACTMENTS

The analyst identifies enactments through close analysis of the moment-to-moment interplay of language, physical movement, emotional expression, associative content, and already established dynamic context. Correlatively, the interpretation of enactment is oriented primarily toward the present rather than the past. This way of working defers explicit interpretations about the past and does not necessarily cast present-oriented interpretations in language that refers to typical infantile prototypes, such as the oedipal triangle. To begin with, the analyst might refer only to an emotional atmosphere of coldness or defensiveness or solicitousness. It is the phenomenology far more than the explanation or cause that is to be worked out as fully as possible before going any further. One does not want to presume too much or to get too far ahead of the analysand and certainly not to start playing the role of the omniscient healer. Thus, the idea of enactment is a vehicle for always keeping alive the questions, What is going on here right now? What am

I being told indirectly or being shown concerning the analysand's way of experiencing this moment in the analytic relationship or of trying to structure it? How might I be stimulating or supporting that performance?

It is recognized always that the analyst makes his or her own contribution to any countertransference enactment, and, in extreme instances, that contribution may far outweigh the analysand's and therefore not lead to understanding and useful interpretation. In the main, however, the analyst is regarded rather more as a sensitive, responsive listener in whom a variety of reactions may be stimulated and who can observe these reactions and put them to good interpretive use by clarifying the analysand's role in bringing them about. In this latter regard, the analyst's countertransference enactments have been attributed either to the analysand's projective identifications (a Kleinian emphasis) or to what Sandler (1976) has called role-responsiveness and regarded as the analyst's participation in "actualizing" unconscious fantasies (1987). In either case, the point would be that the analyst may be viewed as complying with an unspoken need or manipulation. Both the need or manipulation and the response to it take place more or less unconsciously.

With this general understanding, the analyst is technically prepared to identify enactments. And the heightened attention to the present moment works against untimely, exclusive, possibly avoidant and intellectualized preoccupation with the past or with current matters far removed from immediate transference–countertransference interactions.

We cannot, however, fix "enactment" in one place forever. It is not possible to establish permanently the meaning of any psychoanalytic term or of any other term for that matter. Meanings evolve in psychoanalysis as they do in law: They take on meaning as cases are processed and decisions rendered; to begin with they are virtually empty vessels waiting to be filled and refilled by a more or less changing history of usage and challenge. Consequently, both what I have already summarized about the meaning of the term *enactment*, and what I shall go on to say about it, cannot claim to settle anything permanently.

Nor can a term be fixed in just one place even at the given moment. As soon as one reflects on what is being enacted, one comes face-to-face with the recognition that what seems to be a simple matter of perception is controlled, even if not fully determined, by preferred interpretive story lines (Schafer, 1992). These story lines, derived from master narratives, tell us how to conceive of unconscious mental functioning and unconscious intersubjectivity. For example, we may prefer to think in the traditional metapsychological manner of defenses struggling to ward off impulses and ending up in compromise formations; we may prefer to think of shifts between paranoid–schizoid and depressive positions (Segal, 1964), of fluctuations in the states of cohesiveness of the self (Kohut, 1977), or of changes in the "representational world" of self, objects, and their relationships that the ego, as one of its functions, builds up and then uses in constructing all new emotional–cognitive experience (Sandler and Rosenblatt, 1962). When we do confront this recognition, we realize that we must give up the assumption that what we do when we analyze is *un*cover or *dis*cover or *re*cover what is already there in fully developed form. Instead, we are prepared to assume that there is little or nothing that exists "out there" in a well-formed manner. It does not exist until it is brought into being and given a shape by an act of naming and characterization within some kind of psychoanalytic context and ongoing dialogue. For example, the analytic observer, in dialogue with the analysand, constructs a version of the analysand's representational world and its constructive principles.

Thus, as analytic data, enactments must be regarded as constructions. One analyst might say to an analysand who, at that moment, is acting in a clinging manner, "You are showing me your anxiety about not controlling me totally"; another might say about that same moment, "You are frightened that I may try to seduce you if you appeared more womanly to me"; a third might say, "You are building a wall of anxiety around yourself to preclude, through your appearance of fragility, yet another shattering experience at my hands"; and a fourth, "You must be seeing yourself as altogether helpless in relation to me right now." All four are interpretations of one enactment—a clinging manner—and each may elicit a different response that further defines or clarifies or perhaps obscures all that is being enacted in that analytic moment.

Viewed in its most general sense, enactment has always been a significant item in psychoanalytic interpretation. We can see this in Freud's early writings, for instance, when he talks about the motoric betrayal of secrets by analysands in the *Studies on Hysteria* (Breuer and Freud, 1893–1895). Yet, there has been an evolution in understanding and technique in this respect. Now, there are many more options on how to interpret enactments and how much emphasis to put on them. In other words, as we attempt to develop or drive home an interpretation and to go on to work it through, we know and accept that we have available to us different ways of characterizing the momentary total situation and relationship. Always, we are engaged in construction.

Perception itself is a constructive activity, so that what people say they see, however well their seeing conforms to convention, is no more than one possible version, and there is no answer really to the question of what it is a version of, since any other statement is itself a version. Even what I called "clinging" in my earlier example is a version; it could have been put otherwise as we see when we consider the kinds of redescriptions that the analyst's comments imply. There is no perception, therefore, that can escape this constructivist viewpoint. The case is the same and even more compelling when we think of interpretation. On this basis we are better prepared now to show how, again and again and in many modalities, the analysand is showing as well as telling (or showing instead of telling) the same conflict, the same feeling of alienation, the same compromise, or whatever. We do strive, of course, to be in tune, but we do not idealize exactness or exclusiveness once we understand that we are working with only one of a number of possible versions of what is taking place.

ON THE OVERUSE OF "ENACTMENT"

It is possible to overemphasize both transference and countertransference enactments. Enactment is sometimes used in relation to the analysand as though it applies to any analytic material that can be interpreted as having transference significance. That this amounts to overuse can be recognized once we realize that it renders the term superfluous if not meaningless; enactment then has become a synonym for being in analysis. When things reach that pass, one knows that the analytic discourse is being controlled by fashion rather than thought-through understanding. Certainly, a dream, a memory, a comment about the analyst can be part of an enactment, but it can be more useful in many instances to view it as just that much more analytic material available for understanding and interpretation.

With regard to countertransference, similar problems arise, although with an added problematic twist. For sometimes analysts seem to feel licensed to be freely and demonstratively responsive to an analysand's manipulations; they participate in this way on the assumption that this is what analysis is all about and that it can be made into a valuable source of information and remediation through later understanding and interpretation. What may happen instead, however, is that the analyst's loose rein on his or her acting out (in the old sense) confirms the analysand's unconscious fantasies to such an extent that subsequent interpretation will seem to the analysand to amount to little more than a confession of guilt, an attempt at further seduction, a cover-up, or something that extends the enactment rather than explains it. Whatever the case may be, then, interpretation becomes progressively less influential. Too much reality confirmation cannot be undone by interpretation, and by "too much" I refer not only to numerous instances but even to one serious or traumatic enactment on the order of a sexual approach or a scathing denunciation.

ON BEING COMMITTED
TO ONE SCHOOL OF THOUGHT

The emphasis on countertransference enactment has developed particularly in connection with attempts to begin and continue analytic work with exceptionally difficult cases. These cases may be those that are stagnating or frequently in explosive or life-threatening states. Once we have been trained and have gathered some experience, however, we are never entirely without interpretive resources or the capacity for suspended judgment. Our analytic resources are embodied in expectations of what we are likely to encounter, in the sense of readiness to articulate or modify these expectations step-by-step as the analytic work proceeds, all with a reasonable sense of assurance that it will be possible to do further sorting out of the important issues at a later time. In these ways analysts never approach a clinical situation from scratch. At the same time, the history of our field shows that these aspects of preparedness do not preclude surprise, revision, or the development of new ideas and techniques.

An essential resource in this regard is one's readiness to orient oneself on the basis of commitment to a single school of analytic thought. The school of thought provides the theoretical guidelines or the interpretive story lines of analytic work. The boundaries between schools of analysis are not altogether sharp, but neither are they unknown or easily breached in either direction. Some analysts have played down the importance of these guidelines or story lines and these boundaries, so that they draw on a number of schools of thought in interpreting enactments. Their doing so gives some cause for uneasiness, for they may be manifesting a form of intellectual claustrophobia, rebelliousness, or confused understanding, and dressing it up as an assertion of flexibility, spontaneity, and even an implied assertion of romantic individualism. It then begins to seem that doing analysis is perhaps being equated with one's own life-style.

This questionable free-spiritedness raises an epistemological and methodological set of problems, too, for it is inherently positivistic in a naive way. In effect, it asserts the outmoded idea of being "natural," which idea depends on the notion that there are essences out there that are simply waiting to be uncovered, discovered, or recovered and that are better revealed when there are no strong preexisting commitments to get in the way. Acceptance of the ideas of the constructivist nature of perception and interpretation, and of the multiple options available for developing one or another version of the analytic moment, does not allow any implication that one truly gets at the essence of the one-and-only reality there is to deal with (Schafer, 1992).

CONCLUDING COMMENTS

"Enactment's" long history within psychoanalysis has been registered under a variety of partly overlapping names and has been placed within a variety of overlapping contexts. Analysts have always been interpreting enactments, though less so on the side of countertransference in the past than they do now. At least, they have been in a position to interpret both types of enactments (e.g., Fenichel, 1941).

Changes have taken place, however. Of these changes I would emphasize the following. (1) Closer attention is paid now to how, unconsciously, the analyst may be drawn into an enactment through changes in the countertransference that have been more or less induced by the analysand. (2) Greater emphasis is usually placed on the present moment than on reconstruction. (3) There is greater acceptance of the idea that the analyst's participation in enactments is an inescapable part of any analytic endeavor, although it is not, on that account, to be recommended or treated casually. (4) It is more clearly recognized that, inevitably, the specification of what is being enacted or jointly enacted is strongly influenced by the interpretive story lines of the school of analysis to which one is primarily allied. (5) Analysts who freely shift among the interpretive lines of different schools of analysis arouse three sets of suspicions, the first being that their demonstrations of learnedness and authenticity may amount to little more than intellectualized expressions of claustrophobia, rebelliousness, or confusion; the second being that they are subscribing in an epistemologically naive way to a simple form of positivistic thinking that is allegedly theory-free; and the third is that they have an inadequate grasp of the entailments or more or less well-defined and system-bound theoretical and technical terms and tactics. On whatever basis, one must consider whether some countertransference enactment is involved in this allegedly free-spirited flexibility. Admittedly, it is not always easy to differentiate analytically what is excessive from what is different, unexpected, or creative work in a new mode, so that here again we should not rush to analytic judgment.

9

Aloneness in the Countertransference

The practice of psychoanalysis has gained a great deal from narrative innovations. These usually appear in the form of themes or headlines to use in giving accounts of clinical work. I prefer to call these innovations story lines because, in an interesting and instructive way, they lay down a line to follow in telling others about a single case or representative instances of a type of case or a type of clinical problem. To mention only a few of them, there is Freud's (1916) "those wrecked by success" and "the exceptions," Anna Freud's (1936) "altruistic surrender," and Winnicott's (1958) "true" and "false self." By following these story lines, the authors were able to organize and keep in focus a large array of clinical phenomena and a set of dynamic variables that seemed to underlie them. Usually, these dramatic and illuminating clinical narratives were not designed to replace more or less standard, systematic formulations, Winnicott (1958) perhaps being the exception here.

To apply the narrational model more exactly than I just did, it should be said that what we call the phenomena of the clinical situation are themselves modes of description that implement a narrative strategy. Thus, it is not that the phenomena are there in the material, simply waiting for a suitable narrative; rather, the designation of these phenomena indicates that narrative practices are already in play. For example, if in writing a case history you simply say that a man is "unmarried" or "still single," you already place him in the context of a matrimonial narrative, not to speak of your performing an ideological act that upholds the value of the social convention of marriage. You might instead say only that he is "single," which, though related to unmarried, introduces the shadows of aloneness, or you might not mention marital status at all until it becomes particularly relevant, say in giving the man's sexual or social history in detail, which itself will be a narrative account.

I just wrote, "until it becomes particularly relevant." What does? What is the "it"? "It" is nothing except as it is endowed with meaning by a choice of wording that establishes a narrative context: unmarried, single, bachelor, unattached, divorced, widowed, lives by himself or with a male friend or female lover or his mother.

My introductory emphasis on narrative and story line is needed to illuminate a core aspect of my general theme for this essay, which is countertransference, and also my specific theme, which is aloneness in the countertransference. *For I could have referred to both differently.* Because I shall be using countertransference in its broadest sense, I have committed myself to a story line concerning the analytic relationship that is not the same as the somewhat narrower one required by reference to Sandler's (1987) "role responsiveness"; as I understand it, Sandler's concept does not emphasize adequately the continuity between emotional responsiveness and unconscious fantasies that we find in Heimann (1950), Racker (1968), and Joseph (1985).

Most likely, as I develop my argument, at least some of my readers will think of still other names for what I am establishing in my account of significant phenomena in some or many analytic relationships. And the reader may even explain my choice of words as revealing something about my problems, and refer to my essay as an effort to legitimize these problems. I would not rush to object to the use of other terms or to deny personal expressiveness in my choice of narrative; in fact, it is precisely my point that any narrative account is open to that kind of applied analytic interpretation. Is Sandler's "role responsiveness," for example, so perfectly objectivist, impersonal, and neutral that one could not view it as a choice? And, in certain contexts, could one even venture a hypothesis about this choice, especially after taking into account the tensions within the British Psychoanalytical Society between the conservative leanings of the standard Freudian group and the Kleinian group which uses, as I now do, a broad idea of countertransference?

Every narrative enterprise takes its chances in the way I have been discussing. It has always been this way. In another place (Schafer, 1992), I tried to show that Freud's emphasis on resistance as a core concept said something about a countertransference problem he had in his clinical work. I would argue that those who keep searching for definitive and exclusive terms for any aspect of the analytic process are continuing to think in the objectivist or realist tradition. Fidelity to that epistemological tradition requires one to maintain a blind spot concerning the existence and the further possibility of multiple versions of what it is that we talk about or write about, that is, what we bring into being through narrating it. In my discussion section I shall take up further the question of alternative designations of the experiences subsumed here under aloneness.

ALONENESS

There are times when analysts feel alone in their analytic sessions. At first they may notice only that they are feeling listless, impatient, distracted, or irritable. Upon reflection, however, they will often recognize in the background that feeling which, here, I call aloneness, though others, in line with their sensitivities and interests, might call it something else, even something with no evident links to feeling alone.

Reactive aloneness, which I shall soon detail, might occur during certain phases of most analyses; for example, when the analysand is intensely defensive. However, the aloneness on which I shall be focusing is the one evoked particularly by certain analysands, those who are acutely anxious, guilty, defensive, or "omnipotent" to the point where they stir up aloneness so frequently that it begins to seem continuous and unmodifiable. Sooner or later in these cases, the analyst may be tempted to conclude grimly that the analysand cannot be reached, that his or her words keep falling on deaf ears or on ears that can only hear interventions as irrational, inappropriate, incomprehensible, or damaging, and that the analytic enterprise was ill-advised to begin with and is in the end doomed.

The feeling of aloneness need not arise when there are long silences, many latenesses, or unexplained absences; nor need it be present during controversy, bursts of verbal abuse, or difficulty in getting the drift or even the sense of the analysand's associations. Any one of these events may signify close engagement. But when aloneness does set in, it is likely to indicate the existence of some technical problem serious enough to require close attention, reflection, and perhaps intervention.

When I say the analyst feels alone, I do not mean acutely lonely; "acutely lonely" suggests that the analyst is grossly dependent on the analysand to gratify personal needs for company. It is when that loneliness is acute that the analyst is locked into a position that precludes effective analysis of the analysand's contributions to the difficulty. But because, in the usually shadowy realm of countertransference, it is not possible to draw sharp distinctions with confidence or to rule out a mix of influences, one must allow that, to varying degrees, loneliness can and often does enter into the feeling of aloneness. In addition, however, I do believe that many analysts share a longing for a special kind of company that they achieve only through their work, and that ordinarily this longing can both facilitate that work and expose the analyst to being manipulated destructively.

A large part of what follows from this point on is a detailed survey of the phenomena shaped and organized by the story line that the analysand is trying to induce the analyst to feel alone. Knowing how endlessly innovative analysands seem to be and how varied analysts may be in their emotional responses to these analysands, I neither aim at nor claim an exhaustive survey of transference or countertransference. In addition to the interpretation already built into the story line of aloneness, simply by giving it that name, I shall include some interpretations of the unconscious fantasies that this kind of analysand may be enacting. Later on I shall offer some tentative technical suggestions for working through some problems in this area.

In the first type of induced "aloneness" to be considered, the analysands limit much or most of their contribution to the analytic dialogue to citation or quotation. For instance, they refer to previous details of this dialogue by saying, "You said I was feeling depressed"; "We talked about the idea that I didn't like what you said"; "When I said that, I felt mad. . . ." They speak as though they were the keepers of the analytic archives and reading from files rather than participants in a highly personal dialogue. They convey no sense of having assimilated what they have said themselves or have heard or imagined. They give the impression that nothing has been allowed to work on them or in them. Their fidelity as analysands is limited to acts of remembering; however, the remembering is often inexact, owing to their making much use of projection and issuing many provocative invitations to be abused. Protective distortion and "seduction of the aggressor" (Loewenstein, 1975) ought to be expected from any analysand who is so well defended.

These analysands contrast sharply with the many who engage with others in more or less conventional ways, that is, those who usually mention simply what they felt, meant, discovered, rejected, or took into themselves as valid, however one-sided or exaggerated or misleading these mentionings might be. For example, they will say, "That time I got so angry," or "When I knew you were wrong"; they are less likely to try to limit themselves to saying only, "When you said I was angry," and "When I said you were wrong." The archival analysand may talk this other, more personal way more and more if and when the analysis is able to effect change.

Surely, we never expect every one of our interventions to be incorporated and assimilated or even to be remembered exactly. We are prepared to find that much has been modified or transformed, if not repudiated or repressed. And surely, citation or quotation always has a place in psychoanalytic dialogue. Here, I am referring to an extreme quantitative shift that creates the strong impression that the analysand is in so different a place psychologically as to seem inaccessible and to leave the analyst feeling quite alone.

Heavy reliance on citation is a sign that the analysand is trying strenuously to submerge her or his emotional life. These analysands come across as affectless, and their affectlessness announces that any sense of engaged togetherness is not to be hoped for. Consequently, there seems to be no hope of obtaining any of those essential confirmations of the analyst's own identity that depend on the two-way traffic of introjection and projection. Betty Joseph has been much occupied with these analysands in her writings; in one place (1993), she describes them as making it impossible to "resonate" with their subjective experience.

It has been recognized that empathy depends on that two-way emotional traffic. Without that traffic, effective mutual identification is blocked and usable empathy precluded. The conscientious analyst may be tempted to persist in trying to convey an empathic orientation, as, for example, by trying to empathize aloud with the desperateness that underlies and motivates the extreme detachment. However, if one hopes for quick or clear results in doing so, one will end up disappointed. Persisting further in this effort will certainly feel forced, dutiful, artificial, and basically defeating to analyst and analysand alike.

It is the analyst's effortful, overconscientious hopefulness that plays into the analysand's transference. For at that point the analysand's intended transference–countertransference enactment will have begun to take effect. The ground will have been adequately prepared for the full-blown countertransference of discouragement tending toward despair, or of resentment tending toward rage. Either of these reactions may then be compensated for by some impetuous friendliness that is more likely to be a last resort of manic defense than a spontaneous expression of good will. At such times the analyst would be better advised to defer activity and to reexamine the felt need to remain active in the old way, or expressively empathic in a persistent way, or too eager for results. Usually, the analyst can be more helpful by confronting the indications that, at least inwardly and for the time being, the analysand must insist unconsciously that the situation is hopeless and to stimulate despair in the analyst. And that insistence on mutual hopelessness may not even be just for the moment; it may be permanent. Winnicott somewhere advised the analyst to be prepared to acknowledge his or her genuine hopelessness and helplessness. As I recall, he suggested that the preparedness may even have a catalytic effect on a stalled therapeutic process. I have had some experiences that are consistent with Winnicott's advice. It is, however, a judgment call that is not easy to make and certainly difficult to communicate usefully to one's analysand.

To return directly to citation, it should be useful to mention some of its relatives. One noteworthy cousin is that curious form of continuing self-observation in which the analysand comes across as a bystander or reporter witnessing a steady stream of inner experience. For example, the analysand might make stereotyped use of the immediate past tense, regularly giving associations of this sort: "I was just thinking of my father," "I was just feeling kind of grumpy," and "A second ago I was afraid you weren't listening," or even a day later, "I was wishing you would say something about that." What is missing in these cases are straightforward, declarative, present tense statements that are the most definite signs that an analysand is engaged in dialogue with a sense of immediacy and not acting as if reporting to, or sharing observations with, an analytic record-keeper who might just as well be a tape recorder or, if not that, then simply a dulled listener.

Another cousin has been described by Ernst Kris (1956), the so-called Proustian analysand who dwells and dwells on memories in a self-loving way, quite possibly a masochistic way, to the exclusion of effective dialogue. Noteworthy in this case is the impression one gains of the self-indulgence through remembering that is very like enactment of masturbation on the couch. When that is the case, the analyst, as imagined by the analysand, is limited to the role of isolated and perhaps turned-on voyeur. Remembering has become a preferred form of sexual activity; it has been sexualized.

A transitional version of this isolating performance is being enacted when the analysand fills the sessions with self-analytic observations that have been made between appointments. This kind of analysis in the past tense may well be another form of masturbatory soloing, and perhaps a masturbatory confession as well. Nor should its competitive, envious, or omnipotent elements be disregarded.

Sometimes these remote analysands refer to emotion by way of inference or speculation. These are the analysands who say such things as, "I think I must be anxious"; "I would have to be depressed to be having these thoughts"; and "I must have been in a rage to have done that." Traditionally, this mode of function has been classified as showing the effects of extreme obsessional reliance on the defense mechanisms of isolation and intellectualization. These analysands counterfeit being engaged in dialogue. Often they strive so hard to give the appearance of bending over backward to be cooperative and responsive that, in the end, they only heighten the analyst's feeling of isolation. That feeling might be further heightened when they try to whip themselves into an intense emotional state by flooding themselves with intellectualized variations on an emotional theme; for instance, getting tearful or irate or enthusiastic over some speculated feeling state in the present or past. In these instances, the analyst experiences no resonance (Joseph, 1993); if anything, his or her feelings run in an opposite direction, so much so that it can be realized after some self-critical self-analysis that he or she is being maneuvered into worrying inappropriately about being cold or hard. These analysands might even complain that the analyst is a "cold fish," hoping thereby to shift attention away from themselves as strangers to themselves, wanderers in a desert of pulverized affect who seem not even to cast a shadow.

Another narrative account of this conduct is this: These analysands are enacting a form of sleuthing for emotional experiences rather than spontaneously letting feeling be included in whatever it is they are saying. However, because they never really get a good look or make a secure inference, their sleuthing is never conclusive and the suspect always gets away, if indeed there ever was a real suspect or even a real search. Their researches are, of course, to be conducted in apparent isolation.

A similar manipulation may be encountered in the realm of ideas. This phenomenon is commonly called "running an idea into the ground." The analysand takes a word, phrase, or sentence that encapsulates an interpretation with emotional impact, and then repetitively invokes it in one context after another; this is often done in such a crudely reductive and mechanical manner as to induce in the analyst regrets for having ventured to convey the idea to begin with. Ostensibly, the analysand is complying, perhaps even "gratefully," by taking up the interpretation and going all out with it; however, the movement seems to be in circles, the words become meaningless, and once again the analyst is left feeling alone. For the analysand's purposes, any words will do: anxiety, envy, compliance, low self-esteem, triangle, and so on and so forth. These incantatory enactments demolish what is often a good enough conjecture or even a firm interpretation and perhaps as well an initial strong emotional response on the part of the analysand.

I turn next to another form of unrelatedness that tends to induce the countertransference of aloneness: the blatantly omnipotent narcissistic surface presented by some analysands. Because this surface has been amply described by many authors in recent years, once by me (e.g., Kernberg, 1975; Kohut, 1977; Schafer, 1992a), I shall limit myself here to some brief comments. These analysands set themselves up as authorities, passing judgment on their analysts, weighing their interventions judiciously, and when impressed, making sure to say so approvingly, perhaps only after noting with implied surprise that that good idea is something they hadn't thought of themselves. Also, they may hold forth at such length about the analyst, themselves, and the world at large that the analyst may well feel reduced to the role of someone who can only hope to get in a few words edgewise. In this posture the analysands are aloof connoisseurs, omniscient persons who are not really needful, masters who are not willing to let the slave/analyst try his or her hand at doing something useful. One may say that at best these analysands limit themselves to tasting what the analyst offers rather than ingesting it and expecting to metabolize it. Often, instead, they act as though all they are hearing is noise and all they are tasting is poisonous, and if they do not become scornful or suspicious, they become confused and difficult to understand or have difficulty remembering. Most likely, any one of these reactions forcefully enacts their experiencing the analyst as some-one who exerts a bad influence by daring to interpret or even to speak, or in other words, interrupt. It is implied that the analyst would do best just to keep out of it, at least for now, that things have gone far enough and may get out of hand.

Not all analysands who are set against feeling needfulness will act in this exaggeratedly lordly manner. It is well known that the defense against feeling needful is extremely widespread. Its extreme forms in-variably involve powerful unconscious fantasies of omnipotence. Be-cause for these analysands it is imperative that they never ask for help, they develop the position that they can meet all their needs by them-selves. Meeting this pathological requirement for total independence calls for much rationalization, projection of needfulness and responsi-bility, and wariness of what they experience as being seduced by the analyst into a "dependent" position. They often use the idea of depen-dency as a synonym for abject surrender, humiliating weakness, totally vulnerable helplessness or slavishness. They cannot envision experiences of needfulness as part of the give-and-take of any emotionally intense, ongoing human relationship; however, the practiced eye of the analyst can see signs of warded-off intense feelings of emptiness and ravenous hunger. Even the fact of coming for treatment, with its implied expres-sion of the need for some help, is experienced resentfully by them. And though they continue to come for appointments, they try strenuously to keep out of an unrestrictedly dialogic treatment process and to create in the analyst the feeling of being on the outside, alone, with no one really to talk to and restricted only to being talked at.

The last family of clinical narratives I shall consider before taking up a few technical points, involves those who "catch only a glimpse." Catching only a glimpse is one way to limit contact with whatever the individual considers to be the external world. Some analysands show that they belong to this family by never looking at the analyst directly or for more than a split second; a quick look out of the corner of the eye is the most they will venture on their way in and out of the office, and perhaps only after a long while. As the treatment proceeds, the analyst learns that, in various guises, this glimpsing is characteristic of their relationships with persons and events in general. Consequently, these analysands are often unsure of what they have seen or encountered, and they spend much effort in trying to decide. Alternatively, they may slowly let it be known in the analysis that they have not taken the good look that initially they claimed or implied and that they are in fact feeling more or less confused most of the time.

I am especially aware of two major factors that contribute to this mode of functioning: previous traumatization and a sense of forbiddenness. In the first instance, coping with traumatization seems to have eventuated in a heightened stimulus barrier against the possibility of encounters with more external stimuli that could do further damage. These glimpsers may have witnessed terrible events, such as psychotic breakdowns or gruesome deaths, or they may have been exposed repeatedly to versions of primal scenes. The second instance, forbiddenness, implies a taboo against seeing clearly. This taboo may express a desperate need to subserve family myths that eliminate recognition and memory of serious transgressions, breakdowns, and deviance of every kind. Traumatization and forbiddenness may also operate together, even synergistically. No doubt, other factors are involved as well.

These two major contributing factors seem to stimulate or reinforce unconscious strategies of always keeping channels for projection open and those for introjection closed. There is overlap here with the group I described as relying on citation. In preference to projection and introjection, however, I prefer to say expulsion and incorporation or, even more concretely, open and closed. My preference is based on these words carrying more bodily connotations and so being more likely to capture the force of what is being unconsciously fantasized. Catching only a glimpse limits what is available to be incorporated, and at the same time it prepares the ground for expelling badness into what the analysand designates as being "out there." By expulsive projections, what is "out there" is made to seem dangerous or disgusting and therefore not safe or fit for human consumption. Instead of badness, however, it may be one's own goodness or sense of power that is expelled and then used to idealize the object to the point where it is out of reach of one's destructive influence. In other words, unconsciously the analysand's commerce with his or her surround moves only one way: bad out and nothing in, or perhaps some good and some strength out, too, and still nothing in.

In chapter 7, I took up some aspects of this problem in terms of blocked incorporation. Blocked incorporation can be protective of the object as well as of the self, in that the rejected object is being spared the fate of immersion in one's inner badness and destructiveness. I believe that both Melanie Klein (1946) and Fairbairn (1954) were describing something close to this phenomenon, she in connection with what she named the paranoid–schizoid position, and he in connection with what he called schizoid and described as involving centrally the extremely disruptive conviction that one's love is dangerous (see also Schafer, 1995). When one-way commerce is dominant, it may delay the appearance of signs of effective analysis for some time. It is a transference that seems altogether unapproachable by interpretation. In some contexts, it suggests a massive negative therapeutic reaction, which in a way it can be. Most likely, this sort of analysand feels the analyst's interventions as humiliating criticisms, boasts, rotten ideas, evil productions, or commands from on high that had best be obeyed. The analysand blocks any sense of being party to a personal relationship, or so it would seem from the standpoint of the analyst who persists in using the usual array of interventions.

It may well be that in the world of unconscious fantasy these analysands have had extremely painful and infuriating experiences of being the captives of harsh introjects or "presences" (Schafer, 1968). These experiences seem to date from an early age, and owing to repression, they will seem to have retained much of their initial vividness once they are registered consciously. On this basis, these analysands will feel that they have lived their lives in enemy territory or as though they were standing before burning bushes into which they do not dare to look. Therefore, anything that resembles fraternizing with the analyst, such as eye contact, informality, or familiarity, remains out of the question. Hence, their avoidance or furtive looks around. In one respect, their eyes seem to serve as mouths shut tight except for occasional nibbles at what might well be poisonous material around them.

Frightened they are; yet, when described along another line, they may be characterized differently, specifically as occupying positions of omnipotence. They are omnipotent in a limited universe: in one way, rulers of all they survey; in another way, rulers of all they overlook or banish. What they can't see can't hurt them—so they hope! And, in its more benevolent aspect, what they don't see can't hurt their objects either.

This fantasized omnipotence has other dimensions, such as screening out all evidence that might confront one with a warded-off sense of helplessness and guilt. That these analysands can still readily feel humiliated or overwhelmed does not contradict their ideas of omnipotence, for on further analysis the negative feelings about themselves do not appear to be fundamental. Rather, they are experienced with only partial conviction; it remains most important for these analysands to believe that they cannot be touched by anyone else. Even the painfulness arises only on their terms, by which I mean that the humiliation is that of the extremely vain person and not that of someone trying to preserve ordinary human dignity. In these cases, the great powers ostensibly wielded by others are merely delegated powers that can be exercised only in the analysand's own projective scenario. This aspect of omnipotence plays a crucial role in the analyst's countertransference feelings of fatigue, impatience, anger, even despair in being alone. Because of these feelings, the analyst experiences his or her resources of empathy, neutrality, shrewdness, and tact as being drained without apparent effect, if not put to negative use. It would not be wrong, however, for the analyst to infer that the analysand's implicitly and constantly reiterating, "You can't touch me!" gives a clue that unrelatedness is all there is to it. Far from it. The countertransference of aloneness is only part of the story.

Other members of this family of glimpsers manifest not so much the avoidance of looking as chronic vagueness of perception or perhaps indefiniteness of registration. In these instances, they look but do not see, consciously at any rate. Sometimes they seem unable to focus; sometimes they are distracted from what lies directly before them. In these cases, it seems that disruption has been shifted somewhat toward the internal world. These analysands may not readily retrieve names, addresses, quantities, pronunciations, and times and dates. What they do retrieve is full of gaps, approximations, and expressions of uncertainty or uncommittedness, such as "sort of," "somehow," and "something like that." Sometimes they carry this vagueness so far as to make it seem that they are clear-cut cases of cognitive deficit or severely arrested ego development. Eventually, however, the path of interpretation through conflictual enactments of traumatization and a sense of forbiddenness or destructiveness leads to their being able to deliver definite versions after first having floundered. It is this change that shows that it is retrieval rather than initial registration that is disrupted. Despite their trying to appear agreeably engaged socially and often succeeding at that, they rather obviously invite the condescension, if not abuse, of many around them.

Consequently, of these analysands, too, it may be said that they are engaged in blocking incorporation and facilitating acts of expulsion. In other terms, it becomes apparent that what seemed like deficits are interpretable as enactments of unconscious fantasies in the context of transference–countertransference. It is, I believe, well known that enacted castration fantasies may be involved (a recent approach to this aspect may be found in Kalinich [1993]); more often than not, however, the analytic work will fall short if it does not take into account more primitive factors, such as omnipotence, envy, and depression. The analyst's search for these essential conflictual enactments must be sustained if it is to result in the definition of neurotic disturbance of ego functions rather than primary deficits. Indeed, it is not rare to find, after extensive analysis, that these analysands are unusually sharp perceivers and that they fear the consequences of realizing or expressing what they have actually picked up. In these instances, the problem is not deficit, it is dangerous or rebellious nonmasochistic use of assets.

ADDITIONAL
TECHNICAL CONSIDERATIONS

I have been emphasizing that it is difficult to deal interpretively with transference that is designed to keep the analyst feeling alone. One must, of course, always be patient, but beyond a certain point, analysands who exert this effect are likely to experience any exercise of patience as a withdrawal into silence, that is, as a retaliatory, submissive, despairing, or abandoning response. Although I know of no intervention that is guaranteed to work with every such analysand or even with any regularity with any one analysand, I will venture to make a few suggestions in addition to those I have already made along the way.

With analysands who are pathologically sensitive to real and imagined criticism, it can help to suggest that some kind of unclear communication is taking place. For example, at times I have found it helpful to say that an atmosphere has developed in the room that may be responsive to an as yet unrecognized attempt by the analysand to make some point to the analyst; it is an atmosphere of personal isolation, and as yet it is difficult to grasp or understand what point he or she is trying to make and about whom. By putting it this way, I ascribed (in my terms) no heavy responsibility to either party to the analysis and in that way tried to avoid reinforcing the analysand's readiness to feel abused. In other instances, I have said that so far I have not been able to think of anything to say that will not come across as disruptive or disapproving, and have then gone on to raise the question why that might be.

It is best to defer reconstructive references to paradigmatic relationships in the past that were equally isolating; it helps to wait until the point has been reached where the analysand is able to acknowledge that there is important meaning to be derived from the apparent impasse in the analytic relationship. It has often been suggested that the analyst might remark that the analysand is letting her or him know now, by showing it or recreating it in reverse, how it felt during early development when one was put in such an alone position by absent, negligent, uncomprehending, persecutory, or exhibitionistic parents or other caretakers. When it is put that way, the interpretation keeps the focus mainly on the present, where it should fall.

One analysand who left me feeling quite alone because she spoke so softly as to be virtually inaudible, responded productively *for a while* to my commenting, "You're talking as if you don't expect to be listened to," an intervention which, while it took in the past, remained directed at the present situation. Another analysand, one who relied heavily on citation and implicit forlornness, responded productively *for a while* to my saying that he seemed to be laboring against an overwhelming prohibition and that it was a prohibition against having a felt relationship with me. When I then mentioned his having told me during early sessions that he had felt this way in relation to his mother when the two of them were constantly under the surveillance of his seemingly fantastically possessive father, the effect of this further intervention did not last for long. In another case, I remarked to an analysand who held forth so rapidly that I felt quite excluded, "I always have the feeling that I'm interrupting you or barging in on you when I have anything to say, much as though I'm an outsider. Does it feel that way to you?"

These groping examples are shaped by my sense of the importance of avoiding formulations that come across unequivocally as demanding or blaming, not in the vain hope that I can forestall all projection of demand or blame in this way but in order to maintain a platform from which to speak about distortion, incorporation, and expulsion. Sometimes, a consistent way of speaking in that manner to these extremely guarded analysands can have a progressive effect. With them, it may be necessary to maintain this meditative tone up to the very end. In effect, one is always somehow asking reflectively, "How is it between us?"—a question which does its best to minimize the appearance of invasiveness, controllingness, intolerance, sadistic manipulation, humiliating intent, and the like, and yet is not overcontrolled by the analysand who would like to limit the analyst's response to hopefulness based on denial of despair.

Just as it is important not to be lured into overambitiousness, it is important not to succumb to despair and inactivity. The creation of despair should be taken up once it is unmistakably in play. For example, the citation that runs the analyst's words into the ground must be addressed in some way that brings out the anxiety, the guardedness, and the sadism in it, the analyst all the while being prepared to find that those efforts, too, may be run into the ground for extended periods.

DISCUSSION

In taking as my theme the analysand's inducing in the analyst a feeling of aloneness, I have not intended to place that transference maneuver at the base of the hierarchy of motivational and affective factors governing the personality. Rather, I have been trying to construct a narrative of the therapeutic relationship that highlights aloneness. The value of that narrative lies in its both defining and organizing a variety of clinical phenomena and dynamics along lines that stay close to the framing of interventions. Along the way I have emphasized the potential interpretations of omnipotence, sadomasochism, masturbation, narcissistic preening, and so on.

In developing therapeutically oriented narratives of this sort, we do better when we invoke dynamic factors when and where they seem clinically "in tune" than we do when we try too hard to conform to the requirements of one or another developmental or dynamic schema of personality organization and psychopathology. We do better because we convey more accurately the give-and-take of clinical dialogue. Although, necessarily, that dialogue does imply the analyst's being guided by a preferred schema of development and psychopathology, it still retains the advantage of individualization, concreteness, and timeliness. That kind of dialogue evidently reflects the analyst's empathic estimate of what the analyst as well as the analysand is prepared to deal with.

Narrative flexibility is not fluidity. Its point is to suggest by word and tone that right now and perhaps for some time it is one theme in particular and not some other that seems to be the most profitable one to try to develop. In this way, what might be regarded by outside observers to be essentially the same issue may be talked about quite differently at different times or with different analysands. There need be no strict limit put on major themes. Only what I have called the master narratives of a system of analytic thought need to be limited (Schafer, 1992). But analytic therapy of individual cases presents the potential for a multitude of useful narratives. Existing technical emphases on tact, timing, and dosage imply this thematic flexibility.

Thus, the kinds of cases I have discussed might lend themselves to interpretive themes that center not on aloneness but, for example, on the idea that the analyst is supposed to feel responsible for all the reflective thinking in the room while the analysand feels—what? Forbidden to participate? Shamed into silence? Waiting for the ax to fall? Alternatively, the analyst's narrative line might be the psychic deadness founded on identification with a lost object or the emptiness consequent to having been invaded and depleted by powerful persecutory figures in the past. With any of the types of analysands I mentioned earlier, these alternative story lines may have to be included in the analytic dialogue along with aloneness.

One theme I have not emphasized is the place of aggression as a key factor underlying the experience of aloneness in the countertransference. One might readily think of aloneness as the result of the analyst's not taking up the aggression or the sadism in the analysand's inducing this countertransference. My reluctance to emphasize aggression prominently *in this context* is based on the following considerations. (1) Empathy with the unconscious terror of change that besets analysands can justifiably lead the analyst to view the aggressive elements correctly as mostly secondary and defensive and therefore not as assaultive as they might seem otherwise. (2) When the aggression in the room escalates rapidly, the first question the analyst might ask is whether he or she is too eager to be in control of the relationship or too needful of the analysand's cordial company; that is, too ready to feel rebuffed and alone on his or her personal account and thus too easily frustrated. In this respect, the anger may indicate first of all that a narcissistic countertransference is in play and that it is crowding out empathy with the analysand's dread of changing.

In these cases, it usually hinders the analysis to take up the aggressive aspects quickly and directly. It may be more facilitating to place the aggression in the context of great anxiety and guilt over deep-lying problems with relationships or of the need for omnipotence, and to do so later on. Thus, I do not propose neglecting aggression altogether. As a way of being punitively isolating and frustrating, it must be taken up. Rather, the first requirement is that the ground be adequately prepared by the analyst's emphasis on dread, defensive needs, and omnipotent fantasies and controlling enactments.

Finally, I must stress that it does not follow from my emphasis on narration that the analysand's psychic reality is simply whatever the analyst makes of it interpretively. I do not believe that it is the case that "anything goes," as is sometimes charged or celebrated. What does follow is that all we ever have are different versions of what we have chosen to call psychic reality. There is no one ultimate, correct version. It is likely that many more than one version will be helpful in any one analysis. The main point is the potential usefulness of flexibly applying narrative lines. A 1994 issue of *Psychoanalytic Inquiry* shows, for example, how a group of Kleinian analysts in London employ to good effect a variety of thematic headings for a number of cases, each of which has many descriptive features in common with the others. This thematic variety has always been valued by clinical analysts for sparking their imagination and technical resourcefulness as they go on trying to be as helpful as possible to each of their analysands.

10

An Analyst's Notebook

AUTHOR'S NOTE

During their successful ten-year tenure as coeditors of The Round Robin, *Drs. Mary Libbey and Gil Katz invited me to submit a series of short reflections on recurrent or special problems that arise in the course of clinical analytic work.* The Round Robin *had been established as an informal newsletter of the Section of Psychoanalytic-Psychologist Practitioners (Section 1) of the Division of Psychoanalysis (Division 39) of the American Psychological Association. Libbey and Katz succeeded in transforming* The Round Robin *into an informal journal in which members could share experiences and reflections and debate clinical and professional issues, review books, post notices, and make announcements. It was, therefore, deeply gratifying to receive this invitation to become a regular "journal" contributor and I accepted readily. Over the next two years (1992–1993), I submitted six short pieces under the heading they suggested, "An Analyst's Notebook," now the title of this chapter.*

In this chapter, I have assembled those six pieces and added two more. One had already been published in The Round Robin *as an applied analytic discussion of the movie* Thelma and Louise; *in it, I focused on the theme of violence in the internal world as well as the external, and especially on the regular exposure of women in our society to attitudinal, verbal, and physical violence. The second piece, "Authoritarianism in the Countertransference," was unfinished at the time I gave up writing for* The Round Robin. *It would have been my next piece.*

Although this reprinting of these eight short pieces hardly qualifies this chapter as any kind of survey, I do view the chapter as a whole both as a potentially useful guide through some of the trouble spots that analysts regularly encounter in their daily practice and as an introduction to, or reinforcement of, some of the newer developments in the theory of the psychoanalytic process and its results.

All the previously printed pieces have been edited in an effort to sharpen their focus and otherwise enhance their presentation. They are reprinted here in the sequence in which they were written.

THELMA AND LOUISE AND VIOLENCE

Manifestly, the movie *Thelma and Louise* (1991) confronts us with both the violence that is endemic in our society and the sense of ultimate helplessness and doom that enters into our experience of this situation. Although the movie centers on violence between men and women, it does not totally neglect intragender and interracial violence (e.g., Thelma's attitudinally brutal husband arbitrarily upbraiding a workman he knows well enough to call by name; the cackling and envious motel coffee-shop waitress who puts a porno spin on the lingering, tender, sad, and erotic kiss between Louise and her departing lover; the African-American, seemingly alienated bicyclist "shitting" on the state trooper when he blows marijuana smoke into the car trunk in which the officer is imprisoned).

In a world seething with feelings of victimization and bitter resentment, if not hatred, one cannot avoid experiencing oneself at times as having to choose between being imprisoned and being a fugitive—or, most likely, being both simultaneously. In this movie, this ambivalence is depicted, enacted, and told. Louise's chief symbol of hell seems to be Texas, where she'd been violated in some unnamed but terrible way (rape, we think, or gang rape). It is so much a hell, in fact, that she'd rather risk her life by driving the long way to get around Texas on the way to safety in Mexico. She is a fugitive even from the memory of Texas, being permanently unable to talk about her victimization there. She imprisons it in herself while simultaneously imprisoning herself in it. For Thelma, her hellish prison is at home with her bullying, unrelated husband, and her previous pathetic "escape" from the prison had been her sneaking bits of candy bars, watching soap operas, and adopting an oblivious manner of living.

Much of the press, with the help of box-office oriented ads, has played up the movie as a road movie, a buddy movie, a switcheroo on *Butch Cassidy and the Sundance Kid*. That instead it is *No Exit*—or no living exit—all over again has been pretty much glossed over. It also seems that many viewers would rather debate whether or not the movie is male-bashing, an idea that is only a cut above ideas like "Quayle-bashing," that is, a way of saying to the movie, "Shut up already!"

Viewing it as a new version of Sartre's *No Exit*, however, makes it more understandable why so many in the audience I sat with cheered the final drive toward death over the canyon cliff. They seemed be cheering it as a triumph of the spirit, thereby helping us all temporarily escape the grimness of it all and not go home in shock. Just as there are cheers for Thelma when she tells her husband over the phone to go fuck himself, in the final death drive, when implicitly Thelma and Louise tell the whole world, "Go fuck yourself—you can't fuck with us any more (in all senses)!"—the audience is thrilled despite its deeper sense of the despair that is depicted and, I would say, shared to one or another extent by the audience.

One might think there is punishment for sin at this moment of death. Unconsciously, that is probably a part of the unconscious experience of many viewers. That conclusion of the movie may also have been a "box-office" concession to middle American piety. I believe that a more vital part of that experience is its conveying a two-sided version of the Last Judgment: both that the protagonists rise up to heaven, blessed (up and out into space) and that they fall into the pit (out of which the demon helicopter has risen to pin down their location for the forces [the killing force] of law).

All along, the movie develops the complex psychology of the idea of the fugitive. Thelma and Louise are in motion: defiantly separate, progressively more alive in spirit, increasingly capable of being enchanted with the grandeur and beauty of the nature through which they are passing. In this, and with the noteworthy help of manic denial, they are hoping to be on their way to freedom and discovery. For them, not to be on the go, as they now are, would be to return to a living death. Analysts recognize this aspect of living death in many of their analysands: those who have succumbed to symbiosis and persecution, real and imagined, during their development; those who have served as the trash cans of parental projective identifications of all that the parents hate in themselves; those who serve as guilt-ridden prostheses and life-support systems, real or imagined, of fragile but tyrannical parents or parent surrogates; those who, inwardly, exist as objects with little or no entitlement for desires, aims, and standards of their own; those who present such formidable challenges to our analytic efforts.

In these last few lines I have, I believe, also been describing women's common experience in our world of being reduced to the role of object, in that way more or less consigned to the living dead, to being trash cans for men's projective identifications, too, as well as victims of men's physical and moral abuse, and props to their insecurity. Other women do the same to them, too: mothers, peers, and rivals who have identified with the enemy and unconsciously despise their own femaleness. And as do the psychically unseparated analysands I mentioned, many women have adopted the role of object and have colluded in their subjugation, having hoped thereby to keep their own psychic economies in balance. Except in their role of caretakers and so always on behalf of others (and in line with Anna Freud's concept of "altruistic surrender"), they unconsciously give up (repress) claims to desires, aims, and standards of their own. They believe that to rise out of this living death would be to confront the great risks of the fugitive, the exile, and the alien: new forms of persecution and aloneness and also the destructive envy of those who have remained behind. A woman asserting her distinct identity is all too often treated by conventional society as a dangerous, perhaps bewitching "witch" or "whore." The risks are high. In the words of the "good guy" cop in the movie, "Brains will only get you so far, and luck always runs out." In short, the impulses to turn rebel or fugitive are all too often countermanded by fear of its consequences.

The movie seems to be jolted into its fast and furious action by the attempted rape of Thelma in the parking lot and Louise's murder of the would-be rapist. But rape and murder pervade the movie, provided only that one takes into account those symbolic forms of them in tune with which we resonate unconsciously and powerfully. Think of the coarse truckdriver making obscene (masturbatory) gestures in their faces; or of the would-be rapist's "Suck my cock" to Louise, which prompts her pulling the trigger; or the two-bit con man unscrupulously seducing and pleasuring a pathetically vulnerable, consciously uncomprehending Thelma en route to stealing her money. By reducing a woman to utter helplessness and objecthood, rape (in this instance capped by verbal rape of Louise) is shown to be a form of attempted murder of the spirit; consequently, the audience, while shocked, is also heartened when Louise "kills him back." The talion law that prevails in unconscious reactivity is observed. He was heartless, so she shot him in the heart. Momentarily, she establishes a sense of symmetry in the world.

The violent world is literally and symbolically (unconsciously) murderous. The phallocratic structure of much of our world rapes and kills women, literally and symbolically. But when we resonate with the movie's counterviolence, it is not only with our attention turned outward; in our inner worlds, too, there is much that is violent and murderous. On this account, the movie helps us achieve some release with a sense of justice (the pity and terror of tragedy), and for this reason I believe the movie's wide appeal does not derive from some totalistic condemnation of men as victimizers of women; although the movie simplifies a lot, it is not *that* simplistic—it also shows men who are foolish, limited, and playful. Instead, the appeal of *Thelma and Louise* resides in its materializing our struggles with fantasied violence in our inner worlds as these become enmeshed with our all too frequent encounters with violence in the world around us. The inner world of violence of *both sexes* includes sexual violence, too, experienced actively and passively, painfully and pleasurably, and with repugnance and curiosity. For women in our world, this enmeshment occasions special and intense forms of pain, rage, and depression.

BEING SELF-CONTAINED
AND FUNCTIONING AS A CONTAINER

As a supervisor I've often been stimulated to tell a smart, well-intentioned, insightful therapist or analyst-in-training to interpret less and listen more,

to interpret later rather than sooner, and to look within to try to determine what made it seem necessary to intervene at all at this or that time.
Sometimes the supervisee's loquaciousness seems to be based on some
transference to me, such as trying to impress or perhaps compete with
me; sometimes, in the anxiety-arousing situation of being a therapist,
the supervisee is being self-reassuring that he or she can understand and
does understand. The instigation may be a reparative need to reassure
the analysand that the therapist or analyst is listening and understanding and caring. It could be something else or all of these. Whatever the
case, I get the impression that the interventions seem not only too rapid
and not well attuned, but not well received. To get a handle on this frequent problem, I've thought back to the times when our ideas about technique began to crystallize.

The technical ideal that developed out of Freud's papers on technique and all the later advances in ego psychology or structural theory
required of us analysts and therapists strict neutrality in our dealing with
analysands. Neutrality would be manifested in maintaining a position
that Anna Freud (1936) described as equidistant from all parties to the
conflicts under consideration. Particularly after the discussions by
Hartmann, Kris, and Loewenstein (1964), "all parties" has been understood to refer not just to id, ego, and superego, but to the tendencies
involved in intrasystemic conflict as well, such as unintegrated superego strictures or ego interests.

What I infer from these teachings, often by reading between the
lines, is that our conduct is supposed to come across as "contained"; that
is to say, we should contain ourselves in looks, voice, and timing of
interventions. Be impersonal and restrained, and you won't muck up
the analysis of transference by injecting your responsiveness into the
process! The idea of the analyst as "participant," implied in the ego
psychological advocacy of the analyst's ego being both observer and
experiencer, is not a recommendation to depart from containedness.
"Experiencing" should refer only to experiencing *inwardly*, as in fantasy, associational processes, and shifts of feeling. By intervening interpretively, we are merely fulfilling our therapeutic responsibility to
report observations as objectively as we can. Central among these observations are the ones that report the analysand's transference fantasies
and point to their extraanalytic origins, these origins usually being familial and early. Self-containedness makes it all possible, and, in turn,

that containedness is made possible by our relevant ego functions being maintained on a high level of relative autonomy from drives, superego pressures, and rigid unconscious ego defenses—disruptive factors that get expressed in countertransferences, counterresistances, and counteridentifications. This is the message to us from Freudian ego psychology. If not transformed into a straitjacket, it has more than proved its worth.

In recent years, however, there has been increasing interest in the idea of the analyst not as contained, but as container. Containing in this sense derives from Kleinian object relations theory and practice. The analyst functioning as a container? Is it an idea that is antithetical to the ego psychological ideal? I don't think so. Instead of being focused on psychic structure, it is focused on unconscious fantasy—more exactly, the Kleinian version of unconscious fantasy. As I understand Bion's development of Melanie Klein's ideas, much of the transference involves projection into the analyst from the analysand's internal world—projective identification so-called—which the analyst is in a position to contain (for the time being, to let it be).

By interpreting the projection, we are attempting to restore the extruded part of the analysand's internal world to its place of origin, that is, to induce a reintrojection of the troublesome content. Doing so once the indications are clear would seem to constitute sound handling of the therapeutic relationship, especially the transference. This principle applies only on the assumption that our analytic orientation to technique is strictly fixed on maximizing rationality and consciousness *at all times*. The thing is, though, that we ought first to understand the motives behind the projective identification. Why hurry to interpret? Perhaps the projective identification is an emergency measure to protect whatever precarious psychic equilibrium seemed possible at that moment to an extremely threatened analysand. Perhaps it is needed to reduce intolerable psychic pain by ejecting an undesirable part of the self or a threatening internal object. Perhaps it is a "good" part of the self that needs protection and that the analysand fears would be destroyed by other parts of the self and other figures in the internal world. (Remember, please, that we are talking here of unconscious fantasy, which, typically, is concrete and highly personified.) Therefore, when a transference interpretation of a projection is made too soon, it can be hurtful or damaging on any of these grounds. It might also be understood by the analysand not only as sadistically rejecting and condemnatory, but as conveying a sense of insecurity or fragility on the part of the analyst. In both ways, it may then induce further anxiety or guilt.

The point is that, for the moment, analysands may be making an adaptive move by using us to contain the role of villain (persecutor, depriver), or good soul (safekeeper), or sharer and acceptor of painful or exciting experiences. On their part, however, analytic therapists may feel stimulated toward an unhelpful countertransference, such as having to prove "goodness," "humility," or "understanding." They would hope, therefore, to reassure themselves—narcissistically, really—that they are not at all hostile or destructive, grandiosely accepting idealization, or so helplessly passive that there is nothing they "can do about it." Under the influence of these countertransferences, analytic therapists are likely to add to the analysand's problems rather than reduce them or resolve them. Therapeutic rapport can only suffer. We present ourselves then as poor containers at best.

Thus, less reality can be more when the analysand's tensions are running high and are of a certain sort. Our delaying overt response can allow time for mutual emotional experience to become more concentrated, attain greater richness and complexity, and extend deeper into the inner world.

With patience, timing, and tact, we can begin sooner or later to interpret in a manner that does not increase panic but rather conveys that what the analysand experiences as intolerable or endangered can be contained and thereby transformed into something more manageable.

Consequently, it seems correct to say that to be an effective container, one must remain self-contained in the Freudian ego psychological sense of the world as described earlier. The two ideas fit together. In my view, however, it does not follow that in that role, as Freud would have it, one is proceeding aseptically into scientifically objective and therefore persuasive transference analysis. Psychologically, it is more illuminating to say that we are participating sensitively in a transformational dialogue, much of it unspoken, that is both supportive and interpretive in the most subtle, nonnarcissistic, and truly analytic way.

In the 1960s, during a visit to New Haven, Heinz Kohut said to me that, as he went on listening to his analysands moment to moment and session to session, he often bit his tongue for his having spoken too soon. It was not so much talking itself that he was questioning; rather, he was emphasizing the advantages of patience, timing, and tolerating or empathizing with ("containing") the needs of analysands *on their behalf.* In my early supervision with Hans Loewald, I got the same advice. It's good advice.

BETTY JOSEPH LIVE

I was bowled over by the reception given Betty Joseph's three clinical case discussions on November 7 and 8, 1992, at the Institute for Psychoanalytic Training and Research (IPTAR) in New York City. Not that there was universal acceptance of her ideas about dynamics, interpretation, and technique, for she was challenged by some participants in the workshop. And not that it became absolutely clear that hers was the only possible way to understand and deal with the material presented to her from the analyses by three quite different analysts of three quite different analysands. What stood out for me in her reception was an increasing buzz of excitement as the weekend progressed, the likes of which I have rarely encountered at any of the psychoanalytic meetings I have attended in recent years. It was as though all the well-trained and experienced participants, including a fair number of senior analysts of undisputed competence, were beginning to enter wide-eyed into a new mode of analytic experience. It was, I sensed, a mode of increased freedom, of increased interpretive possibilities, of heightened and liberating self-awareness of oneself as practicing analyst—an analyst trying, through interpretation, to maintain both a consistently analytic frame for the treatment and a place for the analysand's attacks on that very frame.

Before thinking further about this "fresh air" phenomenon, I should also state that Betty Joseph, one of the two leading modern Kleinian analysts in London (the other being Hanna Segal), showed us an energy, enthusiasm, tact, wit, brilliance of understanding, and versatility of clinical approach that we are not often enough privileged to witness and enjoy at a public meeting. She is a teacher in every sense of the word, so that some of the workshop's excitement could well have been the joy of reviving the experience of being a student listening to a superb teacher. Several of us at least felt her helpfully accompanying us when we returned to work on Monday.

Also, Betty Joseph did a lot to disabuse those participants who came with the oppressive stereotype of "the Kleinians." This stereotype is based very loosely on the writings of Melanie Klein and her earlier followers that are by now quite old and have been transformed in many significant ways. So effective was she at this disabusing that one member of the audience asked her where the Kleinianism was in her approach. Though not discontinuous with its origins, it was there, she showed, in its evolved, significantly modified form.

What she was making clear was a significant development of here-and-now analytic method that is focused consistently on the transference and countertransference. This method is expressed in one-step-at-a-time, jargon-free interpretations that come across almost always as clarifications rather than formal explanations. She emphasized that the chief thing is to try to show the analysand *from the analysand's own material* just what he or she is doing in the analytic relationship right now, and to let the historical connections emerge only in the fully developed, live context of immediate experience. Thus, she advocated none of those frequent, long-winded, symbol-laden, part-object defined reconstructions of earliest infancy based on fragments of manifest content—the kind of interventions that make up the "Kleinian" stereotype. With this aspect of her demonstration, Miss Joseph helped the participants see how their usual work on here-and-now transference stands in relation to hers and that of her colleagues. She also helped us understand why she objects to the designation "Kleinian," for there are quite good reasons to claim that the work is consistently Freudian though developed along one turn in the road, inaugurated by Melanie Klein, rather than another that we tend to call, schismatically, "Freudian" or "ego psychological." There is much to ponder in this, I think.

There is more, too much, in fact, that I could go into: concrete examples of Betty Joseph's illustrations of the modern "Kleinian" approach, the events of the meeting itself, the context of cultural history generally and psychoanalytic history specifically in which this meeting took place. But I shall limit myself to one major theme: destructiveness. Miss Joseph focused much attention on the pervasive presence of destructiveness in the analytic sessions, especially in the transference, and she developed a meaningful interpretive approach to it. It is here that one of the distinctive "Kleinian" contributions became clearest and seemed to me to elicit some of the excitement as the three workshop sessions progressed. Unlike contemporary "Freudians," contemporary "Kleinians" still hew to the idea of the death instinct. In my view, however, they no longer have any well-developed instinct theory, and, as she showed, in practice they are referring essentially to self and other directed destructiveness, not just in the treatment room but as a built-in part of life, and so as a continuing problem for all human beings. *At the same time, they do not neglect signs of various degrees of love and concern that signify advances in development.* For them, the destructiveness is the major obstacle in the way of goodness and lovingness.

I see no great gap between this clinical approach to destructiveness, Freud's original death instinct theorizing, and Hartmann's "aggressive energy" modifications of Freud. Freud spoke of fusion and defusion, Hartmann of degrees of neutralization, and the "Kleinians" of the various forms and degrees of destructiveness that are all mixed up with erotized transferences as well as sadomasochistic manipulations. The formal modes of theorizing about destructiveness differ far more among these three figures than the content of their clinical interpretations, except in this respect: The "Kleinians," if anything, remaining hyperalert to the insidious forms of destructiveness directed at the very possibility of analysis and of the analyst's retaining the identity of the "good analyst." With keen perceptiveness, Miss Joseph showed how often it was the case that pressing issues of this sort were not being adequately engaged in the otherwise competent analyses being presented to her. She also showed that, as a result of that shortcoming, there was unwitting collusion with the analysand's creating continuing impasses, misunderstandings, and repetitive enactments instead of opening up possibilities to develop insight and change.

And with tact and concern for the analysand's anxieties (and, in my opinion, the presenters' as well), she showed us how one might intervene helpfully with a variety of difficult-to-treat analysands in destructiveness-laden transference–countertransference situations. She did the same on Monday in one case conference held at the New York University Postdoctoral Program. As a dedicated teacher, she developed her critiques meticulously, never formulaically, always with reference to the process notes being presented. It could not have been altogether comfortable for any of the presenters despite her best efforts to keep each of them at ease.

Why did the development of this theme of destructiveness play so important a role in the excitement she generated? I think, at least in part, she helped us clarify the problems we all encounter *again and again* in trying to keep our work effective. She was, so to speak, giving us a better handle on our work. It was a relief as well as exciting to be listening to someone so helpful. During the discussion period, it was remarked from the floor that, too often, our training in the United States, including perhaps our own personal analyses, prepares us inadequately to deal with aggression or destructiveness in the countertransference as well as the transference, and murmurs of assent to this were heard in the room. Whatever the reason, however, the larger implication of the relief was, as Betty Joseph might say, that we saw more clearly how, in order to move closer to the "good analyst" of our ideals, we must be able to accept without paralyzing anxiety and guilt the presence of destructiveness as a constant force in ourselves and in our analysands.

Among other things, Miss Joseph helped us appreciate more fully the fact that unconscious destructiveness in the transference–countertransference engagement is a central part of the truth of psychoanalysis.

TRIANGULATION AND SPLITTING WITHIN THE TRANSFERENCE

Many years ago, in the course of analyzing a seriously disturbed young man, I encountered what I took to be a clear-cut, though subtle, instance of oedipal triangulation within what manifestly seemed to be the transference twosome. The triangle comprised him and a split version of me: on the one hand the cold, undemonstrative, critical mother, and on the other the warm, sympathetic, indulgent father. I played the mother's part, he felt, by what he experienced as my mechanical, strict adherence to the rules of "correct analytic technique." Behind that technique, however, he believed that he sensed a paternal caring response to him, subdued in me as it had been in his father by the mother's control over his upbringing. He, then, was the yearning, needful, frustrated, and deprived child. Clearly, I thought, a negative oedipal configuration.

At that time, though still "a younger analyst"—that indefinitely extended designation!—I was no longer a rank beginner. This analytic development had been achieved by me and the analysand jointly. It was a significant step forward, and I expected significant new change to ensue as we worked through this insight. But nothing of the sort took place. We remained with what was, for him, not fantasy or "subjective" experience, but concrete reality. As he saw it, the problem was that, like his father, I was truly "pussywhipped" by maternally cold analytic rules.

In recent years, as I have gained more confidence in pushing back beyond oedipal triangulations into primitive preoedipal dynamics and phenomena, especially when working with more seriously disturbed analysands, I have in my own mind reanalyzed that analytic impasse. Now, I would focus not on the oedipal triangle primarily but on his primitive relations with his mother in his internal world, for that is where I believe the primary action takes place in seriously disturbed cases. It is the site of dangerously ambivalent love, splitting of single object representations into good and bad, and secondary distributions (projections and displacements) of these part objects into other fantasy figures who are only loosely related to the "real" figures in the analysand's life. Thus, it would have been useful to surmise that, in this analysand's mind, the kindly father was largely a surrogate for the displaced or projected good mother-figure—the idealized, omnipotent caretaker whose strict rules and controlling attitudes are inherently right, while the child's rage and needfulness are inherently wrong and cause for fears of retaliation and perhaps as well some primitive guilt and feelings of unworthiness.

I would now see the analysand as reenacting his attempted infantile solution of his troubled relations with his inner-world mother, quite possibly an exaggeratedly cruel version of the mother he had. Today, I would try to take up his problems with containing his ambivalence toward me as a transference stand-in for her, his idealization of my "correctness," his own fearful and despondent feelings in relation to me, and his clinging unconsciously as well as consciously to the role of passive victim who is entitled to be righteously angry at the same time as he is quite prepared to love me wholeheartedly in my guise as the maternally suppressed good father. I would not dismiss the triangulation as false material. Because it is authentic material in its reflecting one aspect of his attempted infantile solution. I would approach it as an element of the major problem and not as the core of it. Concurrently, I would be wary of his reliance on splitting and projection, for this reliance bespeaks a readiness to become paranoid. The analysand did present initially as inclined toward paranoid fantasies, though not, in my judgment, of psychotic quality. Later in the treatment, however, he entered into a severely paranoid phase of the transference from which, using the ego psychological approach to which I was then committed, I was not able to extricate him. He left treatment with many gains but with much bitterness toward me.

I now believe that things might have turned out at least somewhat better were I to have addressed four issues intensively: the projection of his own rage and destructiveness onto or into me, in order to protect his "innocent victim" idea of himself (i.e., a split in his own self representation); his subsequent rage at what he experienced as my "real" coldness and deprivingness; his destructive orientation to me and his fear of and guilt over its negative consequences; and his always trying to stimulate rage in my countertransference as well as guilt over my alleged harshness toward him. I cannot be sure this latter approach would have made a difference. But I do believe it would have given both of us a better chance to accomplish more of the necessary analytic work. This then could have led to a better conclusion of the analysis. One cannot be sure of this, because accurate interpretation and empathy never guarantee positive results in severely disturbed cases.

ADAPTATION AND PSYCHIC REALITY

In the course of my daily work it is not unusual to hear analysands give "progress reports." This kind of report is exemplified by a male analysand, early in his analysis, recounting that, upon feeling somewhat more sure of himself, he had openly addressed an emotional problem he had been having in relation to his parents. To his surprise and relief, the problem was pretty much resolved. He then expressed gratitude to me and was pleased over his increased self-confidence. His parents had not been as obstinate, mean, prejudiced, rigid, and competitive as he had expected them to be. On his part, he had been more self-confident than he had expected. Although not everything had gone smoothly, the confrontation had more or less eased the problem. The air of daily life had been cleared, and the clinical air seemed to have become fragrant with improved adaptation. Although in my estimation the analysand was a bit manic at this point, I did think he had been putting to good use the hard analytic work we had been doing. Nevertheless, to avoid joining him in his elated state, I did have to keep his new step and his report of it open to further analytic investigation.

In my opening chapter on termination and the self in *Retelling a Life* (1992), I discussed some aspects of this type of change *during the termination period*. For example, I mentioned times when the analysand reports bringing out the best in others rather than the worst and then emphasizing what a difference that change has made. At that late time, these changes may be relatively stable and analytically transparent. In this case, however, and not unexpectedly, the reported change was only temporary, and the sequel had some clearly negative features. Thus, his early enthusiastic presentation of significant change does warrant my skeptical label, "progress report." Such skepticism can be useful if not quickly and indiscriminately imposed on the analysand.

Often, these "progress reports" are introduced at particular moments in the thick of searching analytic work. Sometimes, it seems they are attempts to turn attention away from those difficult aspects of psychic or internal reality that are *at that time* under consideration: fearful fantasies, painful memories, ambivalence in the transference, and the like. The "progress reports" are brought in as if to say that reassuring developments in daily life have put an end to not-yet-worked-through conflicts of long duration and multiple manifestations. It then feels as though I am supposed to believe that both of us have gotten over a very high hurdle, which, as the subsequent course of the analytic work will show, may be far from the truth. The fears persist, the pain lingers on, relationships get even worse, and so on. It seems then that the analysand has overemphasized a benign turn in external reality at the expense of confronting internal reality, that is, that subterranean reality where things change slowly and painfully and where reassuring developments in daily life are never as powerful as one would hope.

In this regard, Freud referred to flights into health. He also quoted the writer Nestroy on the skeptical point that every advance is only half as great as it first seems, to which I would add two points: On the one hand are the advances that are underestimated; on the other hand are those that prove to be not even half as great as they first appear. We must remain prepared for ensuing negative therapeutic reactions of defeat and despair.

The basic point to keep in mind is this: In doing analysis, we are most helpfully positioned when we assume that it is never the case *in important matters* that we are dealing *primarily* with problems of adaptation to external reality. For in these contexts, the parents, spouse, lover,

or whoever else is always heavily freighted with the analysand's unconscious fantasies, and these involve still unanalyzed major transferences,
ambivalence, needs for repetition, provocativeness, and so on. To keep
this principle firmly in place, one has only to ask either. If an oppressive parent dies, is the analysand then emotionally free of that parent?
or, If the analysand has moved East from the West Coast, has he or she
escaped malign family influence? For then one realizes that these external changes usually fail to reduce or eliminate problems; indeed, they
may even exacerbate them by adding burdens of guilt or persecution in
unconscious fantasy. Which is not to say that these events—death, the
move—make no difference at all or have no adaptive potential; by themselves, however, they are analytically ungrounded and so they are never
adequate to resolve important conflicts. This much is obvious to all
experienced analysts. It is best to take a wait-and-see attitude toward
early, enthusiastically reported changes in external relations initiated by
the analysand, such as long-desired reversals of passivity to activity and
a turning away from regularly and overtly playing the role of victim or
loser.

Technically, then, upon hearing these reports, I might begin to feel
put in the position of either being a destructive skeptic who takes the
wind out of the analysand's full sails or a dupe who colludes with his or
her defenses by uncritically accepting or affirming the "good work"
being reported. But, on reflection, I realize (at the times that I do) that I
need not feel put in a bind. It does seem that the analysand is trying
to frame our relationship that way and so to induce a "trapped" countertransference in me. In practice, I can always and appropriately wait and
watch for signs of what she or he makes of my deferred response. Using
whichever signs the analysand then gives of how my analytic posture is
being interpreted, such as that I am indifferent, dismissive, or envious,
I can show that she or he is opening a dialogue within the transference
on the present status of the internal conflict under analytic scrutiny. In
other words, the "progress report" being brought up within that trans-
ferential context, its relevance to it should be the first thing to work out.
Was the report a transference gift of love, a competitive thrust, a bid for
reassuring praise that, it is hoped, will alleviate guilt or persecutory
anxiety? Was it a propitiary move to soothe my imagined rage and impatience with lack of "progress"? Or, as may be the case later on in an
analysis that has been going well, it could be that the preponderant

feeling is pride, self-respect, and an unexpressed wish to share that experience with me as analyst-collaborator.

One cannot always tell which it is or which mixture it is and in which proportions, but usually there is enough in the sequel to the "progress report" to provide a lead into a productive inquiry or comment. The result, if there is one that is definable, may then shed light on what persists of the internal problem that seemed to have been surmounted by that adjustment to circumstances or even by a well-grounded adaptation.

On this understanding, I have come to believe that, as a rule, it is best not to take for granted and certainly not to encourage and praise seemingly adaptive actions. It is more helpful to enable analysands to contain their doubts, ambivalences, and pain while myself maintaining an open, inquiring attitude toward the place of that "progress" in his or her inner life. Usually, to do otherwise, as by being reassuringly appreciative, would be to encourage repression, conformity, and ultimately counterproductive immediate peace of mind. It would have this deleterious effect through supporting archaic ego ideal and superego pressures as well as infantile dependency in the transference. It is the analyst's obligation to try to avoid depriving the analysand of opportunities to mature into relative autonomy, with all the burdens as well as gains that go with this development's becoming stable and subjectively owned. I believe that it helps to accomplish this if, upon hearing those abruptly introduced "progress reports," I limit or analyze my own reactively hypomanic response in the countertransference. I try to remember that these reports are always introduced in a context of transference, defense, and either actual countertransference or positive or negative countertransference that the analysand wishes to induce.

SCYLLA AND CHARYBDIS
IN DISCOURSE ON COUNTERTRANSFERENCE

More than fifty years ago, in his *Problems of Psychoanalytic Technique* (1941), Otto Fenichel described as the Scylla and Charybdis of psychoanalytic technique the analyst's stimulating either too much or too little emotionality on the part of the analysand. Thinking about the growing interest of analysts in countertransference, one soon realizes that an equivalent pair of dangers confront the analyst's relation to his or her own emotionality. I am referring to countertransference in its broad sense, the sense first developed in Kleinian analysis. In this sense, countertransference refers to all aspects of analysts' responsiveness to their analysands and not just disruptive intrusions of personal factors into their analytic way of working. So understood, countertransference includes what ego psychological Freudian analysts might want to call incipient affect signals that point to developing issues in the transference, such as the analyst's feeling a bit of impatience or flagging attention or a too zealous wish to be helpful or protective.

For my part, I agree with those who argue that the designation countertransference is warranted and helpful to whatever extent some personal emotional coloring enters into the interaction, unconsciously or preconsciously. Once analysts open their eyes and minds fully to this coloring, they are likely to discover that it is not only a regular feature of the relationship but an informative one as well.

And this is where the metaphor Scylla and Charybdis becomes applicable. Once attention is being paid, the analyst can feel the pull in two directions at once and end up either paralyzed or moving impulsively to one extreme or the other. One extreme seems to be the emotionality conveyed, for example, by the language of Heinrich Racker (1968), a pioneer in this area. In his writing, countertransference coloring becomes quite dramatic. His language goes directly to the primitive, as when he freely uses terms like *manic* and *depressed*. As I read him, however, Racker himself is clear that he is not referring to breakdowns of functioning; rather, he is pointing to trends or shades of feeling that influence the analyst's actions both quantitatively and qualitatively. He is using the extreme terms as reference points and is allowing much room for differences of degree. And when we are honest with ourselves, we can grasp the presence and the variations of Racker's type of emotional responsiveness.

Nevertheless, the use of extreme terms has its hazards. It does tend to make one think of the analyst as being necessarily involved in something like a stormy ambivalent romance or pathologically volatile childrearing, and it even seems to legitimize it. Consequently, the analyst seems to be expected to be steadily prone to noteworthy and counteranalytic countertransference enactments. The results I would regard as an idealization of emotionality in the countertransference and a rationalization for the analyst's acting out. On the basis of that idealization, those analysts who prefer to think literally in Racker's terms of responsiveness may well regard with suspicion or disdain those who work otherwise; that is to say, they may regard them as lying to themselves, not entirely candid, or just wooden. Call this the Scylla.

On the other hand, Charybdis: Here the ideal of neutrality holds complete sway. The analyst finds no help at all in the broad concept of countertransference. She or he does not see any basis at all for dramatic primitive designations of ongoing responsiveness to analysands. Instead, that analyst's discourse may feature relatively autonomous ego functions, the analyzing instrument, or, as I mentioned, affect signals in the service of the ego's reality testing function in the analytic situation. "Charybdis" applies when this analyst makes excessive claims, internally as well as to colleagues, about having reached or closely approximated an ideal neutrality just about all the time, and who would therefore think it a sign of significant disturbance should words with any early developmental coloring be used to describe usual or desirable analytic functioning. I mean such words as *empty, abandoned, deprived, envious, hateful,* or *alone.* This Charybdis I regard as based on an idealization of sanity combined with a rationalization of inhibitedness on the analyst's part. It denies the analyst all access to those primitive layers of the personality that are bound to be touched by similar layers of the analysand as they are expressed in the transference. That analyst is ignoring Freud's advice to bend one's unconscious to the analysand's.

A case has been made for the heuristic potential of both Scylla and Charybdis. Each orientation has been said to lead to greater understanding of the analytic process and its results. There is, however, no way of measuring quantitative difference in this regard. Consequently, the positions analysts take in these treacherous waters will reflect characterological preferences, and these in turn will express values in the realm of human relatedness. When viewed in this way, each analyst may be expected, at times, to exert unverbalized pressures on the analysand of the sort described by Fenichel (1941): too much emotionality or too little. Then, the analyst's own implied values can show up in what seems to him or her to be simply the type or intensity of the analysand's self-induced transferences.

Here, the matter is no different from the way it often is in connection with dreams, acting out, and remembering. The analysand may be getting a latent message from the analyst and responding either seductively or defiantly or both. The analyst who attends only to the transference implications of these developments, while not wrong, is incomplete and inexact in his or her understanding of the analytic process. When Freud discussed the psychoanalytic process, he showed that he was well aware that, in this regard, there is useful analytic material implied in examining countertransferences and their influence, such as responsiveness to the analysand's assuming a false posture based on frightened or manipulative compliance.

Though unavoidable, the resulting ambiguity or undecidability need not pervade the work and be fatal to it. For there are navigable channels between this Scylla and Charybdis. With experience, the analyst can often find and follow one such characterologically comfortable channel and also quickly return to it when it has been lost under pressure. With experience, the analyst can come to believe more and more in the idea that, with much or most of the analysand's material, there is no immediate basis for deciding what to see it *as*. In my view, countertransference enthusiasts tend to decide too quickly what to see things as, in which regard they seem to practice a form of wild analysis. They seem to demand of themselves omniscience as a way of protecting themselves against anxious or depressing feelings of uncertainty. Some simplified examples of the countertransference ambiguities that these overzealous analysts may deny: Irritability may forecast either mounting anger against an analysand or intensification of defense against feelings of love; mixing up appointments may signify either a reluctance to see the analysand or a defense against too much eagerness; finding oneself with nothing to say for a long time may be a sign either of blocking understanding or of an intuitive response to the analysand's need for simply being heard and contained through a stressful period. The ambiguity may well turn out in the end to have been a mixture or layering of factors specific to that one analysand and that one analyst. And in the end not every one of these questions will have been answered.

Consequently, the experienced analyst will develop an ever greater capacity for a suspension of attitude, a hovering, a delay of responsiveness and understanding, and a tolerance for long periods of ambiguity and undecidability in the countertransference as well as the transference. All of which demonstrates a capacity for self-containment as well as containment of the analysand's projective identifications.

Once that navigational skill is well established, the analyst is in a position to use any noteworthy shading of feeling or change in functional capacity to infer from it with reasonable confidence some aspect of the analysand's transference, perhaps some response the analysand is pulling for in the relationship. In that way, which often includes what Kris (1952) called "regression in the service of the ego," access may be gained to the analysand's as-yet unverbalized primitive fantasies. Prior to that time, the analyst does best to remain careful about jumping to conclusions. It is quite enough that the analysand can be counted on to jump to conclusions, consciously or unconsciously, all through the analysis.

One should not, however, idealize "experience," that is, uncritically equate it with navigational skill in these treacherous waters. I believe it was in his book *Nausea* that Sartre (1938) made his trenchant remark concerning the validity of "experience": Too often, he said, it consists of someone's having repeated the same mistake enough times to begin to regard it as wisdom. In a similar vein, a well-known movie maker once said that, as time went on, his creative mind felt more and more like one of those midtown garages that has a sign outside saying, "Sorry. Full."

HAVING SOMETHING TO SAY

In this discussion I return to the issues raised in the course of discussing containment and self-containment in the section of this chapter entitled "Being Self-Contained and Functioning as a Container," specifically the problem of the analyst's talking too much.

Observations of both myself and my supervisees at work suggests to me that we practitioners often begin laboring under a countertransference pressure the essence of which is the feeling that we should always have something to say. I mean that we should have something to say about whatever the analysand brings up even if that is only the analysand's asking a question or dropping into silence. My baseline for regarding this sense of pressure as a countertransference is the principle that, almost entirely, it is desirable that we speak only when we feel that there is something to say that will further the analytic process. Inevitably, we make exceptions, as in the case of emergencies or rearrangements of schedule, or when working with certain extreme cases. Also, this baseline does not call for absolute certainty in intervening; sometimes it takes into account the value of floating some conjectures to help get our bearings. For it to be suggestive of countertransference, having something to say must include a steady feeling of internal pressure. This countertransference can also be expressed in the form of feeling obliged always to deliver interpretations when we speak, or to keep on making sounds or asking questions, in order to reassure the analysand that we are listening attentively, seeking to understand, or feeling with the analysand.

I have been able to sort out several major dynamic factors that are conducive to developing this countertransference. (I do not include for discussion here all the personal, life-historical factors that make us vulnerable to these countertransferences.) One factor is guilt. The analyst feels obliged to show that he or she is worth it, that is, worth the analysand's time and money and effort. The analysand has come for help; the analyst must keep on delivering it. When not burdened by this countertransference, the analyst or psychotherapist does properly feel obligated to try to do his or her best. But the analyst ought to be able to include under "best" refraining from saying anything and to do so without anxiety or guilt. If this guilt steadily intrudes in our work, it may well be that the analysand has succeeded in getting us to enact a guilty role in relation to his or her transference at that time.

The second countertransference factor is the need to feel that we are retaining control. We may speak up too often and too soon not only to seem to be steadily in on the process but to feel in charge of it. The countertransferential idea seems to be that if we keep talking, the treatment won't slip away from us or we won't lose control of the analysand. Action of this sort is no substitute for taking up the analysand's own controllingness that may be creating the sense that there is a problem of control. Analysands may well be playing on us to feel that things are getting away from you.

A third factor is omnipotence. Analysts often act as though they feel that, within themselves, they should know what it is necessary to say or to talk about at every moment. Then, they will have something to say about every life detail that the analysand brings up. In this case as in the others, the analyst may often end up on a wild goose chase as the analysand meanders from one topic to another, often ignoring what we have just said after briefly acknowledging it. Meanwhile, we may be making sure for our own purposes that the analysand doesn't develop an independent train of thought that may raise unexpected problems of understanding and so rattle our insecure self-confidence.

A fourth factor is difficulty with containment. The analyst's role necessarily involves containing a good deal of amorphous, painful, confusing, overstimulated, and overstimulating material, including our own countertransferences. When this is problematic, the analyst's talking a great deal can be a way of unpacking this material so as not to feel overloaded. If it's a case of the analysand's behaving in a way that consistently has this overloading consequence, the analyst will not be dealing with the situation just by having a lot to say. The analysand may be inducing that countertransference through projective identification. It is, however, always possible that the analysand may, for the time being, require that much containment; in response the analyst may just be feeling overtaxed by silence. When we are tired, ill, troubled in our own lives and preoccupied, we may feel too full of things as it is and so not be able to contain what is needed by the analysand. Then we may go on yakking away for our own sake—a narcissistic response in one way and, in another, a gesture of helplessness. When we are dominated by the need to keep open the sluices of speech, the result may be called "sluice talk."

Other factors of a countertransferential sort might be added to this list; however, at this point I want to say that when a countertransference is creating the feeling of having to have something to say, the analysand is either *avoiding* or *being prevented* from developing a line of thought, however circuitously, that will lead to expression and clarification of major conflict. Perhaps it will lead more to defensive needs and efforts, perhaps to material that is difficult to speak about. Frequently the conflict will be centered in the transference. When we are saying too much, we cannot be sure at any given time where the analysand is emotionally or psychically. The treatment has lost its rudder and its compass.

There is yet another major hazard to consider in this regard. Under most circumstances, the analyst's talking too soon and too much has the counterproductive effect of fixing the analysand on a certain level of mental organization and discourse. This stabilizing effect can prevent that fluctuation of levels of functioning that plays so major a role in the progress of any psychoanalytically conceived therapy. Flux is an invaluable source of understanding and interpretation. When this is problematic, the talking analyst's obstructiveness points to a fifth countertransference to be noted here, specifically the fear of encountering expressions of regressive or negativistic shifts owing to their disorienting effects. Or the problem may be fear of flux itself. Without flux, analyses become lifeless.

Certainly, allowances should be made for stylistic differences among analysts. Some are better able to think and feel along with the analysand if they do not remain silent for long periods of time. Others may do best by allowing themselves to vary from periods of relative inactivity to periods of increased activity, depending on what is going on in each analytic session. And still others may do best responding only occasionally and letting the analysand grope for longer stretches of time during which the many-faceted aspects of the analysand's current situation may become plainer and more readily interpretable. My discussion is not intended to prescribe one level of activity, and my earlier reference to limiting speaking to times when it will move the treatment forward must be understood to allow the analyst latitude to move it forward in his or her own way.

In general, though, for purposes of supervision and self-supervision, it does not hurt from time to time to raise these questions about an intervention already made: "Why was it said *just then*?" "Why *that* just then?" "For *whose sake* was it made?"

AUTHORITARIANISM
IN THE COUNTERTRANSFERENCE

Analytic investigation regularly provides clues that just about everything significant in an analysand's life has grown out of conflict or at least carries traces of conflict. We find this to be true in what appear to be happy marriages, gratifying sexuality, successful careers, favorite recreations, and dominant interests. These findings steadily remind us that the "conflict-free sphere of the ego" and the "autonomy" of ego functions are always relative matters, so that, periodically, as the tides of conflict rise and fall, there will occur at the sites of adaptive functioning tinges or floods of doubt, worry, anger, depression, envy, mistrust, embarrassment, guilt, competitiveness, grandiosity, and so on.

Analysands often attack themselves as abnormal when they feel affected in any of these ways. This we can infer when we see them trying to justify themselves by insisting, defensively, that, now and then, it is "normal" to feel this way or that "everyone has this problem," and so on. Then it is as though they are answering some kind of ethical charge, that they have a responsibility to conform to some norm, and that we share their concern in this regard. Furthermore, these analysands may try to manipulate us into a position where we enact with them their internal struggle with their own superego dictates; this we do if we begin to become impatient with them and directive.

This commonplace observation brings us face-to-face with one aspect of authoritarianism in the countertransference. Analysts generally agree that they should not intercede directively in their analysand's lives. They are not to become directive about sexual preferences, infidelities of various sorts, painful patterns of family interaction, obviously irrational social beliefs, or career plans or activities that do not proceed along conventionally approved lines. It is part of the analytic attitude to wait for signs of conflict, especially as it invades the transference and is sensed in the countertransference, before thinking of intervening; even then, the analyst is to prefer interpretation and to minimize directiveness by intervening tactfully.

Much of the time, we do not know what it would be warranted to take up at any given moment as we listen to the variety of life problems being presented to us. Nor do we know how take it up, to what extent, and to what purpose. The amount of ambiguity in the usual run of analytic material is enormous. Not that we analysts are helpless or paralyzed in the face of ambiguity. We do have resources for drawing out the analysand in order to reduce ambiguity. Even so, in some instances we may decide that, for the time being, it is more appropriate to defer intervention.

One of our resources is the capacity to bide our time. If we intervene prematurely we are likely to imply a wish to make important life decisions for the analysand. In turn, acting on this wish implies that we are relying on generalizations rather than the psychoanalytic specifics of the case at hand. Invariably, analysands respond poorly to what are in effect platitudinous interventions. They sense that we are choosing an ungrounded subjective sense of certainty in order to escape from our own anxiety about not understanding owing to the ambiguities of the situation. They experience us as narcissistically trying to counteract our own problems with helplessness, aloneness, inferiority, and depression. And at best they experience our directiveness as a form of benevolent despotism. Briefly, they see us as caught up in an authoritarian countertransference. They may, of course, repress, deny, or idealize this perception in order to ward off their mistrust, rage, or contempt, and any or all of these to protect us in our insecurity. When the countertransference is powerful, we in turn will not recognize the analysand's guarded or guarding response.

It seems to me that there is a kind of mental health perfectionism that often contributes to this countertransferential authoritarianism. It is as if the analyst feels that he or she already knows or should aim to know exactly not only what makes the analysand tick but how he or she should live life. In this, the analyst is taking sides in a somewhat grandiose way in the analysand's conflicts, behaving rather more like impatient and coercive parents whose "best intentions" do not warrant their obstructive controllingness.

In recent years, with the tides of change running high in psychoanalysis, I believe that nondirectiveness is being taken ever more seriously. Many analysts are moving beyond merely paying lip service to it. On a deeper level, they are accepting the idea that the business of analysis is that of finding out, understanding, and opening up issues; it is not that of setting goals for the analysand or specifying the best means–end relations to guide their activities.

In this way, analysts are rediscovering the side of Freud that is nonauthoritarian or even antiauthoritarian. This is the side that said that analysis should aim to help the analysand's ego to be in the best position to deal with its own conflicts; it is not the side that subscribed to the official Victorian ideals of the right way to work or the right way to love. For Freud did, I think, show in a number of places a strong need to bring his analysands into conformity with his ideas about health and proper conduct; these ideas were often quite conventional. He wrote as though he knew what was "moral," "worthwhile," "feminine," and genuinely "sublimated." Meanwhile, however, he was creating a psychoanalysis that undercut this authoritarian, conformist bias. The wonder is that he could do so much on this other, noninterventionist side of things.

Many of Freud's followers later translated and extended this conventional side of Freud into a very narrow conception of the right way to analyze. What is "right" too often has been rationalized on the basis of a shallow or confused grasp of ego psychology in general and its concept of adaptation in particular. Also part of this scene are idealizing ideas about sublimation, authenticity, and true selfhood.

The authoritarian countertransference often seems to be linked with a patriarchal orientation, perhaps Freud's own. In the past, many female analysts seem to have identified with this orientation. At the present time, however, along with the growing number of women in the field, there is a growing proportion of women who are resisting patriarchal indoctrination. They are stimulating or at least reinforcing the antiauthoritarianism that has been developing among men.

At present, no one can anticipate all the problems that will arise in connection with this arduous and slow dispensing with authoritarian traditions. One of the confusing problems is the ever present difficulty of defining standards of training, practice, and reporting.

We can be sure that each new advance brings new problems. The development of our discipline from old problems to new is not at all different from the personal development of those who are undergoing analysis. To think otherwise is to think that progress means getting absolutely in the clear, and to think that is to reintroduce the authoritarian perfectionism we have been trying to get rid of.

Part III

Authority, Morality, Conformity

The essays in Part III continue the theoretical and clinical discussions initiated in Part I, but they have been grouped here to tease out a particular red thread that runs through them: The thread of moral values and their effects on conceptual and technical practices. I try to show that, in important respects, these effects have encouraged conformity owing to the frequently authoritarian rhetoric that can be discerned in teaching and writing in our field. That rhetoric itself seems to originate in large part from an authoritarian tradition that colored Freud's otherwise exemplary humanist, nonconformist investigations. I have taken up some manifestations of this tradition in earlier chapters, for example in chapters 3, 4, and 5 on the psychology of women.

Here, first, I approach the topic broadly, as I did in chapters 1 and 2. I focus in chapter 11 on the complex question of evidence as it develops in the clinical relationship; that is, in the setting of transference, countertransference, and competing claims of authority. Next I take up, and take on, Hartmann's powerful, sophisticated, midcentury approach to the mostly neglected topic of moral values. There follows an appreciation and critique of a contribution by Kurt Eissler on technique that for many years had exerted powerful conformist consequences on ego psychological technique (see also in this regard Orgel, 1995). Eissler can be said to have been an especially faithful follower of Hartmann's bold yet also conservative contributions to theory.

In my concluding chapter I return to moral values, now in the psychoanalytic psychology of the nonconformist practices of gay and lesbian men and women. I use as my format an account of my own development so far as it has gone. This covers my progress from the ideas (read: prejudices) I was taught and too readily accepted during my training and early years in psychoanalysis. I believe that much remains to be remedied as well as to be worked out in this aspect of psychoanalytic thought and practice.

11

Authority, Evidence, and Knowledge in the Psychoanalytic Relationship

This discussion traces the complex interplay of transference and counter-transference in the clinical construction of evidence and knowledge and the establishing of *analytic* authority in the psychoanalytic relationship. Both participants are variably reliable sources of evidence on their own subjective experiences and on those of the other. By reliable demonstrations of understanding, responsibility, capacity for containment, openness, and flexibility, the analyst not only earns analytic authority but contributes to the analysand's development toward authority in coauthoring the analysis. The discussion closes with comments on the epistemological controversy concerning evidence and truth within a perspective that is narrativistic and pluralistic.

WHO IS TO BE BELIEVED?

Complex transference–countertransference processes play major roles in determining the availability, communication, and consequences of clinical psychoanalytic evidence. To a large extent, these processes decide which evidence will be regarded as convincing and why that is so. Consequently, it can only be the slow, arduous analysis of transference and countertransference that will lead the coparticipants to durable, rational, and useful agreements on evidential matters. The alternatives are confusion, controversy, or the analysand's submissive compliance—though sometimes, in subtle ways, it is the analyst's submissive compliance with the analysand. In these instances of compliance we deal not so much with knowledge as with new compromise formations based on distributions of power that can fall outside the analytic frame.

Often, analysts unreflectively package their role in these redistributions of power in claims of invariably superior psychological understanding and clinical experience. On their part, analysands often claim that they are the final authorities on their own subjectivities: after all, they assert, who can know better than they what they think, feel, wish, and intend? As a rule, it is exceptionally difficult for both participants to sort out what is legitimate and what is illegitimate in these controversial claims, or, if legitimacy is not the issue, then it is difficult to sort out what will be most useful to reflect on at the moment. This difficulty exists in part because, in the heat of emotion, there can be no guarantee that even the best-grounded assertions will be accepted by the other participant, or, if accepted, be used to move ahead. For example, an analysand may use potentially liberating insight into a difficult-to-accept unconscious motive to reinforce habitual self-recrimination. In another instance, an analysand may use the analyst's help in achieving an integrative insight to reinforce an existing counterproductive idealization of the analyst. On the analyst's part, he or she may use stabilizing insight into a countertransference enactment only to retaliate against the enactment-provoking analysand.

Thus, the questions concerning knowledge that it might be best to address are these: On each occasion, who is to be believed and why? And what are the consequences of doing so? In analysis, much time and effort are spent on these questions, although they may be put in other terms entirely. At their best, analysts do not stint in this regard and do not regret that necessary expenditure of time and effort, for they understand that fundamentally they are then engaged in analytic work of the utmost importance.

AUTHORITATIVE RHETORIC

In order to develop the points I have just made, I shall have to bypass other significant areas of potential confusion and controversy: the roles of authority, evidence, and knowledge in analysts' discussions with each other orally and in their writings and readings, and, relatedly, what they use in their teachings. I believe, however, that so much of what can be said about the clinical relationship applies as well to these other areas of psychoanalytic discourse—transference and counter-transference being ubiquitous—that it should not prove difficult to extrapolate to those areas any conclusions reached here about the clinical dialogue.

It would, however, be wrong to leave only to extrapolation a few observations about confusing rhetoric that I should like to mention before moving ahead. How commonly we encounter in all forms of professional discourse such locutions as, "Freud himself said . . . ," "As I have repeatedly emphasized . . . ," "Everyone knows that . . . ," and "In fact . . . ," none of which constitutes adequate support for any new theses being put forward. Citation alone never guarantees new knowledge. In addition, there are all those frequently used reallys, onlys, obviouslys, certainlys, clearlys, always, and nevers that, most of the time and until proved otherwise, are best taken as warning signs that a speaker or writer feels on thin ice and may be reassuringly encouraging a suspension of critical listening or reading in favor of an idealizing transference, a masochistic surrender, or a yielding to affiliative needs. The reassurance may be mostly self-directed in order to retain courage while developing a new point of view. Freud was a master of these rhetorical ploys, and while many of them paid off in the long run, some have created lasting problems in the realm of psychoanalytic knowledge.

These brief comments on rhetoric belong here, in my opinion, because the analyst's sense of authority in clinical work often derives in significant measure from all these other nonclinical engagements in psychoanalytic discourse. Consequently, we cannot afford to look into authority, evidence, and knowledge in the psychoanalytic relationship without at least making some reference to our other discursive ventures and exposures.

UNCONSCIOUS FANTASY AND REALITY TESTING

When working effectively, analysts steadily maintain a two-sided view of their authority on the matter of evidence in the analytic process itself. On the one hand, they must assume that, ultimately, they bear the responsibility that comes with claiming expertise in constructing evidence bearing on unconscious conflicts and fantasy. In this context, they must assume that their analysands cannot speak as authoritatively as they; otherwise, they would be forfeiting the right to use the traditional name for what they are practicing, namely, psychoanalysis. Their claim of expertise is grounded in their relative neutrality regarding the constituents of their analysand's unconscious conflicts and fantasies, their own didactic and technical education in detecting clues and constructing evidence bearing on disturbing unconscious mental processes, and whatever other qualifications they may have in the realm of personal sensitivity, experience, psychological mindedness, analytic knowledge of themselves gained though personal analysis and supervision, and scholarship. In trying to understand the human beings in subjective distress with whom they consult, they have prepared minds.

In assuming this role and this responsibility, analysts provisionally take for granted that they can count on some support from their analysands. They count on their having retained some capacity to remain aware of, and responsive to, the analysis as a treatment relationship. If this will not be so all the time in a clear and decisive way, then it will be so enough of the time, or it will be recoverable should it get lost during periods of stress; at least, it is a deeply buried potential that will become accessible in due time. Analysts count on this awareness or potential on the basis of their initial assessments of their analysands' *ego strength*. Ego strength is a flexible term that pertains both to more or less convincing evidence in their analysands' life histories and to the observations analysts can make during initial interviews that seem to promise a reasonably steady capacity to be realistic, focused, in contact with others, and adaptive even when under stress. If that is not quite attainable, as in some so-called borderline conditions, then the availability of some sizable fragments of this capacity may be assumed to exist, enough to promise a starting point for a treatment relationship, however tenuous.

Also, when analysts begin their treatments, they assume that in their analysands are sufficient glimmers of hope and yearning for something better in their lives to contribute to their siding with the treatment, enough to be able to counteract those frequent and inevitable waves of destructiveness and despair. From this more benign aspect of their orientation there flows from the analysands some willingness, however meager, to grant that their analysts are knowledgeable and deserve authority with respect to analytic evidence. The analysts count on their interventions *also* being registered as constructive efforts to understand and help. All will not be seen through a glass darkly.

All of which is on the one hand—the facilitating one. On the other hand—the manifestly hampering one—are a host of considerations. For one thing, analysts have well-grounded expectations that, unconsciously, no analysand is altogether ready to grant them the authority I have just described. Unconsciously, analysands more or less fear, mistrust, despise, hate, rebel against, and aim to seduce in various ways these figures to whom, consciously, they have turned for help with their problems and whom they may even respect, depend on, and adore. In this regard, analysts anticipate that their analysands frequently, perhaps even regularly and for a long time, will take their understanding interventions and evidential claims as confirmations of their (the analysands') own worst fears. To judge by their emotional reactions on so many occasions, the analysands' own best reality testing and their respect for their analysts' reality testing are frequently overruled by those authorities in the inner world which we have traditionally designated as superego, ego ideal, hostile introjects, ego defenses, self-destructiveness, and dominant fixations on narcissistic and omnipotent infantile wishes.

For example, those analysts who act in a kindly manner may well be regarded in very large part as feeling guilty, frightened of aggression (their own, their analysands', or both), frightened of madness (their own, their analysands', or both), or acting under their analysands' omnipotent control. When analysts feel that threatened or controlled, it becomes understandable that they feel compelled to offer their analysands support through reassurance. Or it may be supposed that these analysts are being kindly because they are dependent on their analysands' affection, duped by their analysands' defensive misrepresentations, are stupid dolts, or something else of a disqualifying nature. Likewise, those analysts who adhere firmly to a disciplined, judicious analytic mode of work may well be regarded as showing indifference, rigidity, or sadism, while those who maintain a somewhat informal manner may be taken to be seductive and to encourage acting out. And if, in their expertise, these analysts recognize the signs of these latent reactions and interpret them, they are likely to find that, at least initially, their analysands will take any such follow-through as proving only how dogmatic, defensive, relentless, or overexcited their analysts are. Furthermore their analysts' explicit and careful marshaling of evidence may well be taken as betraying either a prosecutorial attitude or a good deal of insecurity.

In these ways analysts are often made to feel up against a closed system. Analysands may sugarcoat these adverse and aversive reactions with shows of compliance and gratitude. But even the analysands' sincere, rational agreement may be limited to conscious attitudes. It is not at all rare, however, that instead of sugarcoating, all these negative responses are shown openly, even triumphantly, and in a way that puts the analysands in the role of prosecutor.

Still on the manifestly difficult second hand, the problems may take other forms. The reactions to the style and the content of the analyst's interventions may not be adverse or aversive in the ways I have just described. For example, an analysand may idealize or romanticize the analytic relationship, in which case he or she may take a kindly manner as an artificially (technically) restrained show of love or desire or some other profound attachment of that sort that violates the bounds of analytic decorum. It is not unusual to encounter analysands who think of their analysts as naturally warm but artificially confined and even frustrated by their dutiful attempts to observe the rules of "correct" technique. I described one such case in chapter 10. And, again, analysands may take their analysts' further interpretations of this kind of transference fantasy as evidence that supports their own eroticized interpretation of what is going on; for example, merely as instances of defensively protesting too much. Thus, once cast in a positive oedipal–parental role, the analyst will be seen as confirming that fantasy by interpreting ("sexually aggressive") or remaining silent ("anxiously inhibited"). Also, analysts have learned to watch for signs that one major function of these idealizations, romanticizings, and eroticizations is to block the way to analysis of suspicion, fear, guilt, envy, and hatred in the transference.

However it may develop in these respects, the analysands' major unconscious fantasies serve to limit or block their accepting in any reliable way that they are in an analytic treatment relationship. For unconscious reasons, they must believe that they are in a predominantly social or familial context or, one step removed from that or combined with it, in a clandestine affair. They do not believe that interpretation is that and no more. Consequently, the analyst's claims to authority and possession of valid evidence and knowledge remain contestable for a long time.

All of these "on the other hand" factors are anticipated, and to the extent possible, dealt with patiently by analysts who retain sufficient poise in the stress and strain of the clinical relationship. How they deal with them will vary according to each analyst's individualized version of his or her school of thought, plus his or her best judgment about each analysand's readiness for intervention or nonintervention. I emphasize *individualized* versions of schools of thought because it is these versions that determine differential weighting and selective presentation of evidence and differential sensitivity to the varied forms of transference.

It is in analysts' individualities that temporary and lasting characterological countertransferences come into play (Reich, 1951). The analysts' own neurotic and narcissistic countertransferences may intrude. Then they may assume or relinquish authority over evidence inappropriately, or they may misjudge evidence, seeing it when most others of their persuasion would not, or missing it when others would consider it conspicuous. They may decide to emphasize evidence that is of less moment, for example, switching to reconstruction when hints of hostility begin to fill the air. Of the temporary, situation-bound countertransfences, one must say that their inevitability has been recognized as providing important information or reasonable conjectures about undercurrents in the analytic relationship. In the interplay of transference and countertransference those undercurrents may eventuate in mutual enactments of the analysand's unconscious fantasies. But no matter whether the countertransference intrusions are characterological and generalized or temporary and situation-bound, they create a huge realm of potential ambiguity and confusion on the matter of authority, evidence and knowledge in the analytic relationship. It is as important as it is difficult to develop an analysis in which, so far as possible, these various influences can be sorted out. The required self-analysis of countertransference may be helped by scanning earlier dialogue for signs of helpful "supervision" by the analysand, followed perhaps by further dialogue to bring the analysand's evidence to the surface.

My reference to this "supervision" is meant to emphasize the value of taking into account those aspects of effective reality testing that analysands have retained. These aspects may yield some very keen perceptions of their analysts' countertransferences. In this respect, analysands can be acknowledged authorities on evidence concerning certain aspects of the analytic relationship, thus on what is going on in the room. Those analysts who respect this potential ability will also pay close attention to what their analysands do with the fruits of their reality testing of countertransference. Useful analytic evidence may emerge concerning the problems of both participants and how these have shaped the analytic process as a whole. For example, an analysand who sees quite a lot may give signs of feeling frightened or too protective of the analyst ever to mention it. The analyst who picks up those signs is likely to find that they are keys to large areas of conflict involving not only the analysand's guilt and persecutory fantasies but also the analyst's tendency to back off from analyzing frankly sexual and hostile features of the transference. The analyst who cannot recognize this protectiveness may have a smooth but unproductive time of it. On a deeper level, however, that analyst will be seen as confirming unconscious fantasies that it is the analyst who is ruthless, fragile, frightened, or under the analysand's control.

To summarize the points I have made on this second, ostensibly hampering hand: Analysts must realize that they regularly confront an exceptionally tangled situation. In this tangle, only some of the time is the analyst regarded as a reliable and knowledgeable authority on analytic evidence. Sometimes the analysand claims independent authority on evidence pertaining to the analyst's claims, and the claims made some of those times may be realistic and to the point. At other times, the analyst engages in a follow-through effort and uses as further analytic evidence how the analysand has constructed evidence about the analyst as abuser or seducer and what the analysand has then done with that "evidence" or "knowledge." Sometimes the analysand then uses that analytic follow-through to doubly confirm her or his negative or positive views; and there are times when, finally, he or she gets the point and moves ahead, though it may have to be the analyst who first gets the point and then puts it to good use.

In my view, one would have to be an exceedingly dogmatic analyst to insist that this sense of a tangle needlessly complicates an already complex picture of what it is like to do analysis. For myself, I would say that the tangle is even more complex than I have so far described. So much goes on in the analytic dialogue that there is always a need for further and finer sorting out of the variables. Closure must be permanently deferred, even though there are many times when decisiveness of intervention is appropriate and effective.

EARNING RESPECT

For the most part, I have been describing the two parties to the analytic relationship as they are in the early stages of analysis. In terms of absolute time these "early" stages may last for quite a while. I want now to discuss briefly how and why things may change for the better or change in the direction of shared authority and collaboration on matters of evidence—in that direction, because the analytic pair never altogether arrives at that end point in an irreversible way. The "early" stages often return, even if in modified form; their recurrence during termination periods is a phenomenon well known to analysts.

The particular factor I want to emphasize here, however, is the analyst's steadily, if not absolutely continuously, *earning respect* for his or her authority. I mean earning that respect *analytically*. How this comes about is itself a complex question that has stimulated various answers in the literature—far too many and various to be reviewed here. I shall limit myself to mentioning some of the main factors that I think help effect this change. Ideally, each analyst approaches each analysand in as individualized a way as possible. To maintain this approach requires not only the prepared mind that I described before, but a capacity on the analyst's part to keep that preparation in the background. Only when it is in the background is ample room left for hunches, novelty, surprise, definition of unfamiliar angles on old problems, and entertaining not well-understood connections and impressions. This capacity is the analyst's counterpart to the analysand's increasing freedom to associate on the couch.

It is not easy to describe or explain the analyst's fluid balance in this regard. Ernst Kris (1952) and his followers have written about a temporary, readily reversible, creative regression in the service of the analyst's ego. Earlier, Freud (1912b) had written of the analyst's bending his unconscious to that of the analysand with an evenly hovering attention. And Bion (1967) wrote of approaching each analysand without memory or desire. Although I do not believe that any of these ways of putting it stands up well when subjected to close conceptual scrutiny and careful introspection of how one changes while at work oneself, being descriptively incomplete and too dependent on rhetorical forcefulness, I do credit each with giving some sense of the analyst's flexible–fluid relationship to his or her own preparedness.

Along with this individualization and manifestations of this flexible–fluid position, the analyst earns some respect and authority within the relationship by continuously giving signs of a kind of openness, adventurousness, and curiosity as to both players in the process. I am thinking here of an old story told about Ernst Kris (few analysts, if any, were more knowledgeable than Kris in his time): Between appointments he would sometimes rush into the private rooms of the apartment in which he and his wife practiced, find her, and say in astonishment, "It's true! It's all true!" Frequently one can sense that very attitude in his stimulating writings. In a more measured way, Betty Joseph (1988) has emphasized that the analyst must always "rediscover" with each analysand the soundness of the principles guiding the treatment. This spontaneity in self-awareness shows in the analyst's voice, tempo of intervention, use of language, postural changes, and other nonverbal manifestations, as well as in the analyst's range in being both a reliable noninterventionist container and an animated participant in dialogue.

One can say that analysts establish their credentials by showing repeatedly and reliably that *they are better prepared than their analysands to be unprepared.* In effective analyses, the analysands, too, slowly begin to give signs of realizing and accepting that way to self-knowledge. These changes add to their willingness to trust the analysts as authorities on how to construct therapeutically useful evidence. They also add to analysands' desires to become genuine coauthorities and *to feel free to show it.* At this point the analysands give signs of knowing that, in the past, they were usually far too anxious, guilty, defensive, omnipotent in fantasy, and envious to have been qualified for this collaborative role. They also acknowledge their continuing, even if now more regulated, susceptibility to regression, and they are better observers of that susceptibility.

The end of it all is not idyllic. Not all conflicts have been fully resolved, not all hardships dissolved, not all mysteries solved, and not all disappointments and dissatisfactions done away with persuasively. The usual great pain involved in leaving a meaningful, beneficial analytic relationship testifies both to the gains that have been made, the continuing influence of conflict in the forever active unconscious mind, and the imperfectibility of any one analyst's analytic work. That the analyst can, in his or her own way, accept this ending without significant disappointment, resentment, shame, or guilt testifies to the kind of respect and individualization that I have emphasized as crucial to the analyst's knowledge of unconscious fantasy and her or his authority on evidence in the analytic process.

Last but not least, there is the analyst's capacity for containing whatever projections emanate from the analysand, whether they be persecutory fantasies, guilty suffering, or idealization. "Containing" implies being able to tolerate the analysand's use of the analyst as a repository of feelings that are too painful to bear, too fragile to sustain, or too precious to be kept within the turmoil of the analysand's inner life. That tolerance will be manifest in a capacity to listen empathically, explore patiently, and defer and dose interpretation until the analysand seems ready to take on the challenge of further understanding. Only then, after it has been gently modified by the analyst's understanding, will the analysand reexperience as his or her own what has been projected.

THE NARRATIVITY OF KNOWLEDGE

We are left finally with some large, basically epistemological questions concerning knowledge, authority, and evidence. These questions are brought out forcefully by the introduction into psychoanalysis of the narrational point of view—specifically, the narrativity of knowledge (Schafer, 1983, 1992). According to this point of view, the clinical psychoanalytic dialogue is best understood as a series of tellings and retellings by both parties to the dialogue. In addition, the interpretive lines followed by the analyst in his or her interventions and increasingly accepted, assimilated, and used by the analysand, may be understood as derived from master narratives. These master narratives make up the so-called general theory and major concepts of the analyst's school of psychoanalytic thought. The analyst's detailed interpretive efforts may then be regarded as story lines that are manifestations of these master narratives.

There are, of course, many different ways to talk about human development and suffering. That this is so within psychoanalysis itself is evidenced by the existence today of a number of different schools of thought (Kleinian, Freudian, Jungian, self psychological, etc.). Each of these schools may be characterized as operating within the horizons of its own master narratives: for example, for the Freudian, the instinctual and the tripartite mental organization, or structural theory, with object relatedness regarded as a developmental attainment; for the Kleinian, the primacy of the object relatedness within this Freudian scheme.

The narrativity of knowledge—its being subject to different tellings—is what is in question in the context of the general topic of authority, evidence, and knowledge. For this point of view has been misunderstood in two important ways, and each of these ways has been used to discredit the narrational conceptualization. The two ways spring, in my view, from a common source.

In one way, exemplified by Spence (1982), psychoanalysis is built on two kinds of truth: narrative truth and historical truth. Narrative truth is the explanatory life story worked out during treatment that has more or less beneficial results, but, owing to its having been arrived at by the extremely approximate and ambiguous method of present-day dialogue in the analyst's office, has no sure truth value. Historical truth is what truly happened, that is to say, the actual facts or events as they would have been recorded by objective observers present at the time of their happening or by mechanical devices. Historical truth is the only one with real truth value and is not necessarily congruent with the narrative truth of the treatment itself.

The misunderstanding exemplified by this way of handling the narrativity issue is this: that it assumes an ideal observer who adheres to no point of view at all, has no shaping and selective preconceptions, values, and methods of observation, and so is in a position of total disinterestedness and is invulnerable to critique from any other point of view. Implicitly, this hypothetical observer then speaks with the authority of God to all of us who are now cast in the role of firmly monotheistic believers. This figure is part of the scene even when mechanical recording is involved, because the recording itself has no relevance until examined by this hypothetical observer. The position described has been labeled variously as *objectivism*, *realism*, and *empiricism*. It is the position adopted by the school of logical positivism, a school that is just that—a school, a point of view—and one which, in its most dogmatic form, has lost most of its philosophical following in the present world of critical thought. In the world of psychoanalysis, however, which has in this respect lagged behind the times, the logical–positivist orientation still prevails, each psychoanalytic school claiming to be the only one that has got the facts "right."

The second way of misunderstanding the narrativity of knowledge has already been introduced in the immediately preceding remarks. In psychoanalysis, this view has been championed most recently by Hanly (1990). It is the direct assertion of the positivist view and does not posit narrative truth at all; at least it does not concern itself with that. Within this view, it is proposed that there is, finally, a knowable reality, an ascertainable truth that is our steady and only goal. This is a truth we can arrive at provided that we apply objective methods carefully and for long enough to eliminate uncertainties. Here again is the proposition of the godlike, totally disinterested observer, free of preconceptions and values. This would be the observer whose authority is such as to stifle critiques that are based on other epistemological assumptions. Presumably, this observer (or set of observers) is free of any constraints imposed by language, historical context, ideology, and so on.

As I understand them, both misunderstandings state or imply the idea, and may even be motivated by the fear, that without objective, nonnarrative truth there must result a chaos of unrestricted relativism or pluralism, in other words, a final babble of voices, a state in which "anything goes." To this idea or fear there are, however, several further narrativistic responses to be made. First, the narrativity of knowledge is not a cause or a prescription; it is an observation of what has always been the case and is obviously the case today in psychoanalysis; for there are and always have been more or less different versions of what psychoanalysis is (its principles, its methods, its findings), and there are and always have been different groups and interpretations at case conferences of the same material made even by analysts who belong to the same school of thought. Sometimes these variations come about because there are individual differences in comprehension, sometimes differences in scholarship or intelligence or experience, sometimes differences in sheer temperament.

To all of which the realist-objectivist-empiricist might respond: Yes, but all that variance can be reduced, if not eliminated, by careful control of criteria, method, language, and so on. To this, then, the narrativist would have to ask: But who adjudicates the instituting of such control when, inevitably, there would again be differences of opinion as to the best way of getting at and formulating "the real truth"? Would it be, as one critic has put it, "the voice from nowhere," which is to say, the voice of someone with total authority, power, and infallibility? Who else could it be?

If to this the answer were made that today there are ongoing objectivist research projects producing statistically reliable results, the narrativist could reply that not every analyst accepts the relevance of this research to the clinical process. These clinicians are particularly attentive to the researchers' necessary artificialities of method, the simplification of variables, the probabilistic nature of the findings as regards reliability and validity, and often the banality of the findings themselves. Nonacceptance of the clinical relevance of this research may be based also on its not having been demonstrated that all types of research can be integrated within one conceptual and methodological system. And finally, the narrative aspects of the data collection and reporting inevitably reintroduce the narrativity that presumably has been eliminated. Thus, the research findings may be regarded as of interest primarily to the research-minded and the very skeptical. It is, I believe, arbitrary and begs the question to impute naïveté or rigidity to clinicians who are not impressed by the research, for there do seem to be good grounds to question whether research of that kind is essential to clinical work and its betterment. For these clinicians, psychoanalytic objectivist research is best regarded as no more than another discipline, a neighboring field, perhaps even an interesting or suggestive stimulus to further thought. They rely instead on the time-honored methods of clinical work and reflective thought, these being the methods that have moved psychoanalysis forward since its inception.

To return now to the narrativist thesis, the point being made and defended here is that any concept of knowledge must imply its verbal formulation and its communicability. These implications necessarily open up an examination of how the knowledge is being told to oneself and to others, within which tradition, with which set of aims, to which audience, and much else besides. This point of view does not deny truth. There is plenty of truth. It is just that truth comes in different versions. It always has. In this regard, the entire matter may be formulated as one of giving up denials. There is a greater likelihood of chaos developing on the psychoanalytic information highway from denial than from some reflective thought.

The reason for remaining calm is that we analysts all live in one general culture with its limited supply of metanarrative possibilities or interpretive communities, as they have been called. We live with the ever-present experience that we can understand one another, even if not perfectly, if only we try. We need not agree. If pluralistic narrativity meant that we could not understand one another, there would be no point to meetings in which we discuss common problems, and there never would have existed the possibility of psychoanalytic debate or books and journals with their readership.

CONCLUSION

I have surveyed many of the issues raised by the complexities of authority, evidence, and knowledge in clinical psychoanalysis. I have pointed to the place of rhetorical manipulation, arbitrary claims of power and purity, the inevitability of a constructivist, pluralistic, and narrative understanding of the therapeutic process, and some common misunderstandings of these various aspects of the issues raised. If, at the end of my methodological and epistemological deliberations, nothing has been settled, I take satisfaction in that outcome because it is intrinsic to my point of view that, in the realm we are discussing, nothing can ever be settled. That unsettledness is in the nature of a science or, as I prefer in our present context, an exploratory discipline such as psychoanalysis is.

12

The Practice of Revisiting Classics: An Essay on Heinz Hartmann's *Psychoanalysis and Moral Values*

Customarily, psychoanalysts who intend to revisit a classic in public either write a paper on it or organize a panel discussion with participants who represent different points of view. In both cases, they aim to reappraise the classic in the light of theoretical and clinical developments since it first appeared. While some of these reappraisals may be critical, they are so in tribute to the importance of the contribution being discussed. In this essay I deviate from custom by paying two successive calls of my own on the same classic. These calls were made several months apart. I present both of them to avoid doing violence to the spontaneous development of my thesis in each of them. The alternative of condensing the two would, it seemed to me, read like a superficially integrated encyclopedia article: impersonal, preoccupied with the tension between conciseness and comprehensiveness, and lacking the spirit of its origins. I did not want to lose the meaning of revisiting, which is, as I view it, giving an account of a *fresh* rereading and rethinking. Hence, my constituting a panel of one.

Each of my readings of *Psychoanalysis and Moral Values* (1960) develops in its own way and, for the most part, covers different ground.

What overlap there is usually amounts to similar points being made in different contexts and so with different implications. Each reading should leave the reader with a somewhat different but not discordant sense of Hartmann's contribution.

Every panel discussion raises important questions about texts and their readers: What is a text? Can there be a single, definitive account of what the author of the text intended, meant, achieved? What is one to do upon encountering different authoritative and convincing truth-claims about one and the same text? How much does a "demonstration" of "truth" depend on its preconceptions, how much on the historical–cultural–professional context of its argument, and how much on rhetorical power plays? Continuing my efforts in chapters 2 and 12 especially, I reflect further on those questions during my development of this essay and again in its concluding Discussion section.

THE FIRST REVISIT

It was from within the context of adaptational propositions that he had built up as the proper framework for psychoanalytic theory, that Heinz Hartmann, in 1959, at the New York Psychoanalytic Society and Institute, presented his lucid, elegant, informative, and brave Freud lecture on moral values. I say "brave" because up till then moral values had been a neglected aspect of theoretical and technical discussion in psychoanalysis, owing I believe, to a forbidding bias. Although not institutionally explicit, that bias held that any analyst who showed interest in the topic of values could well be indicating a failure to recognize and uphold the objective, scientific, value-free posture so prized among psychoanalysts since the time of Freud. Or if not indicating that failure, endorsing one or another antianalytic position. That judgmental posture is prized even now, as we can see, for example, in the continuing paucity of psychoanalytic contributions to the important topic of moral values. It has been left to some postmodern theorists in the humanities to pick up this theoretical slack in psychoanalysis.

In his Freud lecture, Hartmann made it clear that he subscribed to the strong philosophical tradition of questioning whether any values are so absolutely grounded as to be universal and eternal. At the same time, and because he viewed structural development as an adaptational necessity, he argued that the production of more or less codified values is an adaptational necessity. A person's moral code is a substructure developed by his or her ego. The ego formalizes, generalizes, and integrates moral values to the extent that, far from being remaining superego derivatives, they become a set of moral principles that are attuned both to intersystemic necessities in the inner world and realistic relations with the external world. For this achievement, a special ego function of "value testing" is required. By enhancing the reality testing of inner as well as external reality, clinical analysis helps analysands to develop this function of value testing and thereby to organize moral codes insightfully. Thus organized, these codes feel authentic and appropriate to the analysands' lives. In this individualistic sense, values do get to be grounded after all, and this is Hartmann's pragmatic psychoanalytic response to the philosophical skepticism to which he subscribed.

In the course of attempting to find a place for moral values within structural theory or, in the more common usage, ego psychology, Hartmann realized that moral values do not fit neatly into the tripartite system of id, ego, and superego. They seem to belong to the superego system, though not to be compatible with its most primitive aspects. They seem to belong to the ego system, though not to fit easily into its pragmatism or utilitarianism. Nor can moral values be simply assigned to the ego ideal, because for Hartmann, as for Freud, the ego ideal is a function of the superego (Hartmann and Loewenstein, 1962) and also because the ego ideal represents *all* standards of excellence and perfection, not just the moral. Furthermore, the ego ideal is not usually regarded as an organizing agent on the order of the ego.

Thus, Hartmann realized that the theoretical problem of moral values required him to reconsider the sharp structural boundaries between ego and superego. He had to go beyond the direct implications of Robert Waelder's (1936) principle of multiple function; that principle retains sharp boundaries between psychic structures even though it gives much weight to intersystemic relations. It is also important that Hartmann, in line with his customary focus on adaptation, seems to have wanted to develop more fully the role in moral development of environmental influences and social contexts and traditions.

Inevitably, as Hartmann well knew, each advance brings one into new problem areas at the same time as it decreases the stability of existing modes of thought. Hartmann's important contribution in the area of moral values did lead into new problems. Specifically, it decreased the binding power of the formalism and closed-system model of structural theory. This is a change that some analysts, I among them, regard as beneficial to the further development of psychoanalytic thinking. Others, however, view it as leading toward unacceptable environmentalism and away from rigorous intrapsychic analysis focused on unconscious conflict. In my eyes, the change is liberating, and I do not see that it limits the clinical analysis of unconscious conflict in any way.

To recognize the liberating aspects of Hartmann's contribution, one need only turn back to the fine clinical studies and contributions of Edith Jacobson (1964, 1971), Annie Reich (1954) and the early Kohut (1971) on narcissism and self-esteem, and Ernst Kris on creativity and thinking (1952, 1975); for it will seem to the contemporary reader that these distinguished thinkers were spending an inordinate amount of time on psychoeconomic and structural formulations almost as though that aspect of formulating their clinical findings was their paramount obligation. Today, it is not these labored discussions for which these analysts are best remembered; rather it is their elucidation of relevant unconscious conflicts and other substantial issues. Contemporary writers, in contrast to them, are not so burdened with formalistic obligations, their attention having shifted significantly in the direction of the phenomenology of subjective experience and psychopathology, variations of technique, and the implications of this shift for the theory of the therapeutic process and analytic change. Many contemporary authors, even among the orthodox, are now more willing to let the metapsychological chips fall where they may while they get on with their work.

Hartmann's consistent regard for the environment and adaptive relations with external reality has come under attack not only for seeming to distract attention from the inner world but for other reasons, including I believe, widespread condescension toward the United States. Specifically, Hartmann's focus has continued to be misrepresented and underappreciated by many contemporary European critics and perhaps most of all by the French (see Green, 1991). These critics have taken Hartmann's emphasis on adaptation to imply the recommendation that superficial social adjustment and conformity be regarded as prerequisites of mental health. They overlook Hartmann's consistently careful avoidance of even giving the appearance of endorsing conformity to any one set of social pressures or advocating adjustment to any one set of values. For example, he emphasized that, in addition to autoplastic change, adaptation can take other forms: inducing change in one's social context or leaving that context for another. Recognizing, as Freud did, that throughout our lives we are subject to powerful pressures to conform and to comply, he viewed the development of all psychic structure as having major conformist features; however, he did also see the need to account for individual variation and for cultural change.

With respect to conformity, Hartmann was especially alert to the ways in which moral values are often inculcated in children's minds as facts, and he saw this as a significant source of influence on the ego's reality testing function. Taking all this into account, I find no merit in the common European criticisms of Hartmann's adaptational propositions and the derivations he made from them.

It is, however, now more than thirty years after Hartmann's Freud lecture. Since that time, ideas concerning the role played by moral values in human existence have come into serious question and in certain respects have changed radically. For example, today the distinction between fact and value is being severely questioned by numerous critical theorists. Philosophically, this questioning is not new, but it seems to me that it has become more intensive and urgent and to have taken new forms. Once the nature and function of facts have been problematized, Hartmann's reliance on the distinction between them and values has been radically destabilized. Now, every assembling of facts into a body of evidence is regarded as open to a critique of its assumptions regarding reference to a presupposed real world and discovered truth; a critique of its dependence on rhetorical style for its persuasiveness; a critique of those implied rules or narrative guidelines that control both its choice of facts and their arrangement into evidence; a critique of drawing binding moral conclusions from any body of "facts"; and a critique of the idea that there can be value-free facts. Thus, it is being argued now that "factual accounts" can always be viewed as being in the service of certain values of the thinker or investigator. Even work in the so-called hard sciences has not been exempt from this critical scrutiny.

This issue is perhaps clearest in the case of historical writing. Historians and philosophers of history have been arguing for some time that the facts—the bits and pieces of information they assemble into histories—become historical evidence only within the narratives developed by individual historians. Thus, a procolonialist can be shown to write a different history of colonization and colonies than an anticolonialist or one who claims absolute neutrality or objectivity in this area. Indeed, the last mentioned historian is likely to be roundly criticized by others for using language in such a way as to attempt to hide his or her values. In these critiques, each historian will be considered to be employing a limited range and sequence of contexts for the "facts" that have been chosen, possibly to be relying on different notions of evidence, and certainly trying to persuade readers to adopt a specific view of what is relevant to, and important to know about, the history of colonialism. And the historian's choice would be considered to express moral as well as aesthetic values. In this way, historical writing is characterized by many of its own practitioners and by other scholars as inherently ideological; in other words, they are value-laden narratives. For the most part, concern with arriving at some single, conclusive version of "how it really happened" has been left behind in modern thought.

Intellectual history in general supports the conclusion that, over time, many propositions that once were acceptable as statements of fact have come to be seen as statements of belief or superstition or submission to tradition. What is true of historical fact is true of some of the once secure facts of economics, anthropology, medicine, physics, and so on and so forth. Modern thinkers accept the idea that any argument must rely on factual assertions, but they recognize that the status of the facts being used must remain provisional, contingent, and contextual. To say anything at all, one is, of course, required to hold certain factual propositions unquestioned while developing the narrative or argument; however, one cannot exempt those start-up propositions from critical scrutiny by others. The arguments advanced in the present essay presuppose agreement, at least provisionally, with these contemporary developments in critical theory.

Psychoanalysts are among those concerned with histories, specifically life histories, and they too have their different points of view. Many of these differences have been organized into schools of psychoanalysis, and each school, like each historian, professes to base its truth-claims on hard clinical evidence. Each presents "the truth" not only of human psychic development but of its pathology and its appropriate therapy. For example, the ego psychological, the Kleinian, and the self psychological, each with roots in Freud, will use more or less different methods to create more or less different compelling evidence that will be compatible with more or less different truth-claims pertaining to the psychological aspects of human existence and their changes. And the facts which each school has chosen for its arguments and organized into narratives "based on evidence," already reflect the values implied in that school's outlook. In our discipline, as in the historical, there are no *absolute* grounds for deciding what is real or who is right or who is morally or ethically "good"; each well-developed school is sufficiently self-enclosed and self-validating to fend off the criticism of others to its own satisfaction. It is only within its own borders that it allows assessments of validity. Consequently, the so-called facts of psychoanalysis cannot be securely and convincingly distinguished from the values of the analyst. By "the values of the analyst" I refer to the personal values that enter into individual variability among analysts of any one school as well as to the group values implied in the point of view of each school considered in comparison to the others.

With this much in perspective, we may turn directly back to Hartmann to consider his determined effort to clarify and justify the special place of health values in the practice of psychoanalysis. Hartmann assumed that the analyst and the analysand agree on health values. That agreement makes analysis a joint enterprise, a voluntarily undertaken treatment. He made this assumption even while recognizing that there are moral aspects to valuing health and that, accordingly, there are historical and cultural variations in how and why health is valued. Hartmann also argued that the analyst should not generalize from the treatment situation to life as a whole, as in the instance of trying to derive a Weltanschauung from clinical psychoanalysis.

At the same time, however, it can be argued that he took too narrow a view of the matter. For example, there have always been questions about the practice of calling subjectively painful, disruptive forms of living in society "health problems" or more specifically "mental health problems." In this connection I have far more in mind than the clinical problems presented by those many analysands who, at one time or another, make defensive or self-flagellating use of this critical idea by questioning the morality of their being in analysis. They may, for instance, question their spending so much time and money and preoccupation on themselves when there are so many more serious problems in the world and when they are so unworthy. In these instances, *once the treatment is under way*, we analysts do try in a sustained though not totally reductionistic way to weave these moralistic self-criticisms into our interpretation of defense, guilt over self-interest, fear of the envy of others, and other such dynamic factors. Like Hartmann in this respect, our doing so takes for granted the appropriateness of our common endeavor, and we are supported in this belief when we observe that many of our analysands benefit in mood or function from our doing so.

Although these clinical problems may present formidable difficulties, there remain some basic issues in this realm which they do not confront. One such basic issue is this: Today especially we are obliged to question why we bring "health" into the discussion at all. This question is not new (see, for example, Jahoda, 1958; Szasz, 1961). Suppose an analysis is recommended and begun in response to a person's complaint of chronic low mood, painful anxiety, difficulties in social relationships, and failure to use personal assets fully in pursuit of a successful career. In this not unusual case, many of us have come to say all too casually that we are being confronted by "mental health problems." Accordingly, we recommend treatment in the interest of improved "mental health." In doing that, we are ignoring historical and cross-cultural perspectives that make it plain that there is no clear reason to invoke "health" at all.

Most immediately, in the example I mentioned, we are confronting dissatisfaction, unhappiness, or even misery over the quality of one's life. We do have grounds for saying that these phenomena probably have irrational roots and that our methods may modify or even extirpate these roots beneficially. But that contention alone does not adequately justify our speaking of "health." After all, as analysts we have just as good grounds for assuming that irrationality plays a part in our greatest happiness and our most sublime accomplishments, and from that we do not conclude that we are all ill. When analysands repeatedly insist that they are sick, we may well interpret the insistence as an attempt to deny responsibility and guilt, and to manipulate the analyst into making unanalytic countertransferential interventions, or if not that then to stop paying attention to acting out or exaggerated defensiveness.

Thus, it would not be arbitrary to argue that in calling *dis*ease "disease," analysts are asserting their own individualistic liberal values, and they are both misunderstanding and misrepresenting these values as fact. No matter, then, that an analysand coming from the same general cultural setting is ready to accept the designation of disease, for that acceptance merely shows that both parties to the analysis share these widely authorized moral values, the values that prescribe "mental health." At least consciously, both of them agree that it is right, even obligatory, to make a major investment in "mental health" through analysis; it is the mature, responsible, and socially desirable thing to do, something that one owes to oneself in order to reduce self-destructiveness and to get more out of life. This outlook can relieve one of much guilt for doing that much for oneself. But this outlook is by no means universal. In some of our subcultures and in some cultures in the world at large, attitudes of resignation, cynicism, or detachment are prized far more than the melioristic ideas of self-improvement implied or stated in "mental health" values. Time was that it was particularly the Americans who were criticized for this melioristic orientation, but now that psychoanalysis has been catching on worldwide, the issue has become somewhat freed of this nationalist bias.

Additionally, societal circumstances have now developed that highlight the ways in which and the extent to which health in general has always involved problems of value. In the present economic world, adequate health care for all cannot be afforded by most governments, or so it is claimed by those in power. What they do not always acknowledge is that what can be afforded is a matter of the priorities that are being set, and priorities certainly do express values. Perhaps particularly in the United States, the problems of autoimmune deficiency syndrome (AIDS) and health insurance in the context of huge military budgets have highlighted the moral value aspect of health care as well as health-related research. Not only has health been exploited for political advantage, but that exploitation has involved the expression of latent sexism, homophobia, racism, militarism, and varied forms of what I regard as tyrannical religiosity.

Although these social problems are not really new, it seems to me that they have become more dramatic, and this change has helped us see that Hartmann's world of the 1950s—a world of seemingly untroubled formalism and triumphant technology—is a world of the past and a world saturated with discredited idealizations. With the passing of these illusions, some of the strength of Hartmann's discussion has been sapped. In one way or another the truth about health and health values is recognized to be a function of its cultural–historical context as established by a particular methodology and enforced by a particular distribution of organizational and political power and the moral values that are both expressed and enforced by that distribution of power.

It remains to take up a particular aspect of the "health" problem. In the course of arguing that psychoanalysis is not a philosophy of life, Hartmann referred to clinical psychoanalysis as a technology. This statement sets forth an essential part of his thesis about health values in psychoanalysis and calls for extended comment in its own right. "Technology" is a trope with a set of mechanical connotations that, on the face of it, is chilling. By "technology," Hartmann almost certainly intended to refer only to the impersonal, neutral, value-free method of psychoanalysis that, like Freud, he thought possible and desirable. For him, analysis, like technology, should be a matter of knowledge, skill, and thoroughness; the individual analyst's personal feelings or prejudices should have nothing to do with it. Nevertheless, the trope of technology points to a serious flaw in Hartmann's argument.

First of all, it is now commonly recognized in our field that human beings, such as they are, and the requirements and exigencies of analytic therapy, such as they are, are simply misrepresented by a technological ideal. In this respect I venture to say that there was a flaw in Hartmann's testing of his own inner and outer reality. Calling psychoanalytic work a technology makes him sound today rather too much like Mr. Gradgrind of Dickens' *Hard Times* (1854): Gradgrind with his demonic version of utilitarianism. Where is there room in "technology" for recognizing nonverbal communication, rhetorical influences in the analytic dialogue, the role of the personal qualities of the analyst, the match of analyst to analysand, and the possibly productive interpretive use of countertransference?

Both Hartmann's technological ideal and his associated assumption that one can separate facts and values, encounter further problems in connection with the idea of evidence for interpretation and for the effects of interpretation. In critical theory today, the question of evidence for interpretation has often been discussed in terms of a distinction between facts and evidence. I already alluded to some aspects of this distinction in earlier chapters and in this one when I discussed the writing of history. It is generally assumed that facts can only become evidence in response to some particular question. Questions and evidence are regarded as correlatives rather than, as Freud and most analysts have assumed, independent variables. In addition to emphasizing the regulative effects of questions, critical theorists have been arguing that the questions one asks are a function of the context of aims, traditions, and values within which one is working.

Carrying this argument further, I would add that the assessment of psychoanalytic evidence must take into account that psychoanalysis is a process of dialogue. Consequently, even the facts of psychoanalysis must themselves be regarded as having been, to a significant though often indeterminate extent, elicited, shaped, and developed by the implied or stated questions that govern the analyst's interventions. In large measure, these questions will reflect the theoretical context within which the analyst is working. On this view, therefore, all the raw phenomena of psychoanalysis—those phenomena that appear to be its most basic, purely observational facts—are already products of multiple interactions: Questions and facts are thoroughly intertwined; reactions and facts are thoroughly intertwined; theories and facts are thoroughly intertwined. Even that arbitrary creature, the almost totally silent analyst, is to be viewed as being in a special kind of dialogue with the analysand; one may take this view because, in the analysand's psychic reality, the analyst is always bound to be making one or more points by his or her silent behavior.

In contending that psychoanalytic questions, facts, evidence, and conclusions are effectively inseparable, I continue to take a constructivist and hermeneutic position. I believe that position is the one that most aptly characterizes the day-to-day work of the psychoanalyst. Technology has no place in this conception. We must define our idea of expertise differently.

Why would Hartmann have developed his thesis about facts, health values, and clinical technology as he did? It may be useful to suggest that part of the explanation lies in his Classicist mentality. Classicism valorizes formalization, systemization, thorough-going rationalism, and rigorously enforced clarity and consistency. Ideally, classicistic work is so impersonal that contributions can be made with a minimum of individualistic coloring. The ideal does not tolerate self-expressiveness other than a minimum of personal style in the use of one's own reason. Further, one must always view one's subject matter in perspective and balance, with perhaps a touch of doubt. For the Classicist, theory is desirably gray and cool rather than colorful and volatile. I believe that

Hartmann took Classicism as his ideal for understanding, and most ego psychological writings have followed his example. Implicitly, striving to meet this ideal gives balance and moderation a distinctly moral tone.

Both the analyst and the historian of ideas would, I believe, agree that the tendency to revolt against the stringencies of Classicism never dies out. Sooner or later that tendency will reassert itself on behalf of the values of individualistic self-expression. Provisionally, we may designate this tendency the Romantic alternative. The terms *Classicism* and *Romanticism* only *seem* to say that we are merely contrasting two aesthetic positions, for in practice one cannot draw a sharp line between the aesthetic and the moral. Inevitably, Classicism's stance with respect to certain ideas about the good and the bad are often presented simply as the admissible and the inadmissible or the tasteful and the vulgar. In Hartmann's case, he seems to stand for balance, precision, impersonality, detachment, and the like. Thereby, it seems inescapable that he is endorsing or passing judgment on what is to be accounted "good" and what is not. It is consistent with this conclusion, I believe, that psychoanalysis in the United States, during the time when it was dominated by the values inherent in Hartmann's puristic work, which is the period mainly of the 1950s and 1960s, manifested a maximum of strictness, surveillance, and control. It was the technical consequences of this enforced ideal that seem to have sparked Leo Stone's courageous essay on the vicissitudes of relatedness in the psychoanalytic situation (1961). Hartmann's puristic influence does linger on, however.

Descriptively, the reaction against the classicistic technological emphasis features a shift in the direction of spontaneity, "presence," greater informality, and an experiential emphasis that includes the recognition and the use of countertransference in clinical work. Rather than scientist and specimen, the model is I-Thou. We have also been witnessing a growing preference for the analyst to focus on what may be construed as the most primitive, archaic, disordered aspects of the analysand's productions, this being done on the assumption that these aspects are the most individually authentic and problematic. The widening scope of analysis has come to refer not only to the attempted analysis of the more severely disturbed, such as the borderlines; it refers also to analysts being increasingly responsive to the preoedipal problems and conflicts of *all* analysands.

I realize that my classification of Classicism and Romanticism in psychoanalysis involves more than a little simplification and arbitrariness. Yet, I think it can be useful to emphasize that today, in contrast to the 1950s and 1960s, there exists a strong pressure toward a relatively Romantic position on values. As I indicated already, this position features concern with the self of both the analysand and the analyst, and thus on empathy, so-called holding, the experiential, the ineffable, the unverbalizable, the archaic, the so-called perverse, and so forth. The consequences for those who prefer Hartmann's kind of rigorous and thorough-going theorizing are of two kinds: On the one hand they are being left to shift for themselves, and on the other hand they are being confronted by theorizing that seems to them inadmissibly loose, eclectic, undeveloped, full of ambiguity, and idiosyncratic. In short they are confronted by "bad" theories that they can only deplore. And in relation to the newer developments in analytic technique, they can view these only with mistrust: mixed blessings at best, and at worst no longer truly psychoanalytic or responsible, and perhaps not even ethical. These changes and charges are symptomatic of a war of moral values.

The instance of moral codes presents this struggle clearly. As I noted, moral codes are structural developments in which Hartmann was particularly interested. To repeat: For him these codes represented the formalization, generalization, and systemization of moral values—those invaluable aspects of adaptation. But Hartmann did not consider the idea that strict codification, along with moderation and balance, are not the only modes of adaptation that one might prize. They, too, have their price. In current times, there are some analysts and many in the general population for whom that price is too high; their value priorities are not quite the same as those of a rigorous theorist of psychic structure. Thus, many analysts today would hold that the fullest attention to, and the densest account of, the pleasures and terrors of clinical work and of the flux of harmony and disharmony in the inner world and its relations with the environment, contain and convey all the theory that is needed. They regard anything more than that as too impersonal, detached, experience-distant, gray, and to be inappropriate to the inevitably highly individualized and shifting realities of analytic interaction. If there is in this position imbalance, inconsistency, and incompleteness, so be it; there are worse things in life, and anyway always occupying the safe middle ground is no guarantee of adaptation or therapeutic effectiveness. It may be better, they believe, not to take these Classicist ideals seriously.

My account of the problems associated with Hartmann's Classicist position is not to be taken as an endorsement of Romanticism as an unproblematical alternative. Because the Romantic emphasis falls on self-expression, subjectivity, individualism, intuition, and other such factors, Romanticism is closely linked to a certain kind of animistic and idealizing orientation to "nature" (whatever that is) and, in association with that, a merged conception of one's relation to other minds. These Romanticist features generate many problems in the realm of communication of ideas and the cultivation of skills. In clinical work, they make difficult any comparisons beyond simplistic judgments of emotional response. In other words, critical judgment too often tends to be replaced by "feel." Teaching becomes more difficult. Furthermore, there is always a tendency in all-out Romanticism toward cultism, heroism, rescue fantasies, and idealizations of the hero-leader. In the extreme, one encounters the Romantic abuses of the sadistic narcissist and the Romantic grandiosity of personal claims. Many moral values are rationalized as being inherent in "nature," and as being the only test of "authenticity," "spontaneity," and so on. What always threatens is a new kind of authoritarianism.

On the other hand, and with a regard now to those who would defend all-out Classicism with the argument that nothing else is true psychoanalysis, one must recognize the authoritarianism of that assertion; it adopts a conservative and controlling stance not only toward moral values but toward the entire history of ideas. A similar authoritarian foundation underlies what that classicistic tradition has represented as the truth about women, especially in relation to simplistic and phallocentric conceptions of penis envy, and also as the truth about narcissism, homosexuality, and perversion.

Inevitably, binary classifications such as Classicist and Romantic, do some violence to comprehensive and individualized gathering of reports of phenomena and the construction of evidence of any sort. The clinical world does not lend itself readily to this polarized description. It is my impression that the work of almost every analyst reflects an attempt to accommodate the tension between these more or less arbitrarily assembled extremes of the binary opposition. It is not usually a question of someone's making an absolute choice, even though "officially" he or she may take an extreme stand. For example, avowed Romantics work in relation to traditions even when manifestly they work against traditionalism; they need traditions to oppose in order to define themselves as Other. Also, they do develop their own standards and guidelines even if these are diffuse, and they do progressively make accommodations to the past, so that in time they usually come to be regarded as conservative or reactionary in their own way. Similarly, among themselves the Classicists value some individualization even though they strive for that impersonal mode of thought and exposition that should allow a high degree of substitutability of the work of one person for another. Thus, there is individual variation within their highly normative behavior. For instance, Ernst Kris among the Classicists seems to me to be considerably closer to Romanticism than Heinz Hartmann; similarly, among the Romantics, Hans Loewald seems considerably more of a Classicist than Heinz Kohut. It should be no surprise to psychoanalysts that value positions are never as fixed or one-dimensional as they might seem to be on the surface.

After these lengthy reappraisals of Hartmann's position on moral values, and before going further, it is time to remind ourselves of additional merits of his work in this difficult area. As always, Hartmann was not dogmatic. He was modest and circumspect in the claims he made. He said, for example, that we just do not know enough about pleasure possibilities to take an absolute stand on many points. He emphasized that the changes brought about by psychoanalysis will be valued differently within different value systems. He recognized that absolute value positions are necessarily arbitrary. He also strengthened the analyst's neutral stand by his approach to distinguishing facts from personal values, whatever the philosophical limits on this distinction might be. He also tried to preclude the use of his arguments to support any kind of unquestioning conformity: They may not be used on behalf of hedonism, utilitarianism, an overstrict moral code, or object-relatedness as against narcissism.

Also, Hartmann's essay contains passing statements, brief discussions, and many qualifications that taken together would seem adequately responsive to most of the problems I have been pointing out, if not to dispose of them altogether in the minds of some readers. There is, however, valorization implied in what he chose to put in the margins, so to say, and what he put at the center. I have questioned Hartmann at the center, because that is where he tried to be most influential and because in this way he set up a value hierarchy that includes unrecognized or underemphasized value judgments. Marginalizing is what is commonly done to the poor and oppressed, to those engaging in non-normative sexual practices, and all too often to women and "third world" populations. To get our bearings on moral values, we must therefore read Hartmann as we would wish to read our social problems, that is, to leave out as little as possible and remain constructively critical on every front.

To conclude this first revisit: The psychoanalytic study of moral values is not in hopeless disarray just because it is difficult to subscribe wholeheartedly to Hartmann's rigorously balanced, judicious approach. Since 1960, moral values have come to be seen as unimaginably complex and forever controversial. In the realm of moral values, there is no final resting place. Postmodern critiques and the rise of more or less Romantic alternatives to Hartmann's psychoanalytic Classicism now seem to have their own heuristic and clinical advantages. This, I say, is all to the good for psychoanalysis, because psychoanalysis has always thrived on flux and the vigorous debate that is stimulated by that flux.

THE SECOND REVISIT

Can we imagine a psychoanalysis that does not posit individualism as a primary or fundamental value? I think not, because each clinical analysis focuses on the makeup of one person's psychic reality and on the potential in that reality for beneficial change, where by "beneficial change" we mean change in mood and function that will benefit specifically that one person, there being no rules to cover all cases in detail.

Individualism need not entail total disregard of the needs and interests of others. It does not inevitably stand in opposition to interpersonal relatedness. Thus, social relatedness, too, will matter to the clinical analyst, though ideally, only when and to the extent that it matters to the individual analysand. There is, of course, a consensus among analysts that each analysand is bound to be in difficulty over his or her relatedness to others. In metapsychological terms, analysts expect that the adaptive functions of the ego and the ideal and moralistic functions of the ego ideal and superego respectively will be importantly involved in the interpersonal problems waiting to be analyzed. Again, however, much room is left for individual variation in the social aspects of the personal solutions finally arrived at. In these solutions, the inevitably abundant social input affecting the development and the themes of the analysand's ego, ego ideal, and superego functions will be worked *into* the best and most individualized integration possible or, if need be, worked *out of* that integration. Therefore, questions are bound to arise in every analysis concerning the vicissitudes of the analysand's individualized version of human relations. Thus, the individualistic perspective may still be said to be the dominant one.

Psychoanalysis and Moral Values (1960) is one of Heinz Hartmann's masterworks on psychoanalytic theory. It is an elegant and wide-ranging piece of work. In reviewing it within the framework of contemporary critical thought and social problems, however, one must be impressed by the fact that Hartmann did not take up the moral aspects of individualism. Possibly he did not classify individualism as one among the *moral* values; however, it is unlikely that for him the problem was simply one of classification. For one thing, Hartmann was aware that individualistic values are not universally shared or unambivalently held, and for another, he would have assumed that, inevitably, individualistic values would take on a more or less moral coloring—a "should" or "shouldn't" aspect—and also that these values would retain some moralistic residues of their partial origins in superego prohibitions and other commandments.

Analysts observe this moralization of individualism in those analysands for whom an open assertion of individuality is experienced as one of life's great dangers. Because we understand that morally deplored sexuality and aggression are bound to be linked unconsciously, if not consciously, to the assertion of individuality both as a right and as a vital need, analysts are not surprised that, on one level or another, this sense of danger is pandemic. Although in our clinical dialogues, we analysts may put these issues in terms of autonomy, independence, separateness, healthy narcissism, or self-assertion, we must still devote much of our effort to analyzing the extent to which these issues are rooted in fiercely asserted, deeply entrenched, and primitively conceived moral issues.

It is because psychoanalysis is allied with individualistic solutions to problems that it has been attacked again and again by old-line Marxists on the left and the Nazis and political reactionaries on the right. For, as Hartmann (1939) emphasized so thoughtfully, adaptation implies not conformity or blind faith in authority or in ideological slogans, but accurate and competent reality testing and a readiness to challenge and change the established or enforced order of things when accommodation no longer seems in the best interest of either one's own personality as a whole or the community as a whole.

Ever since the late 1960s, however, moral values in general have been problematized and politicized extensively and in new ways. Freud is reputed to have accepted the idea that, "What is moral is self-evident" (Jones, 1955, Vol. 2, p. 418). Today, however, nothing moral is self-evident except in the most homogenous and blindly conformist communities, and even then only on the level of consciousness or public conduct. In this new development of moral skepticism, many critical thinkers have been challenging the premises and the consequences of individualism. They have charged the entire social–political–ethical orientation of individualism with representing those fundamentally conservative bourgeois values that for centuries have justified the exploitation and oppression of the majority of the people of the world. They see this orientation as implicated in the perpetuation of poverty, hunger, addiction, racism, sexism, colonialism, and so on and so forth.

The arguments have been developed across many disciplines concerned with human beings, and I shall not review them here except to note that to a large extent they rest on the argument that individualism in Western culture can only be sustained by worldwide enslavement of the weak and the backward. I accept this critique, but I also emphasize that these critics have developed no consensus on a desirable alternative to the valorization and protection of individualism, and for my part I certainly have not encountered any alternatives that look like they could put an end to our present worldwide mess. As usual, effective criticism does not by itself establish absolute grounds for new and better moral values and practices. To this reservation, I might add the further reservation that postmodern criticism, by throwing all absolute value claims into question, seems inevitably to foster individualistic choices from among the many positions competing for one's loyalty. In this way the perspective that fosters critique of individualism seems inescapably to lend support to the object of its attack.

In any event, we can no longer be un-self-conscious about the individualistic values that prevailed unquestioned in the 1950s when Hartmann was formulating his thesis about moral values. These values are still very much with us, and for most contemporary analysts they have quite high priority. We see that this is so in our outrage at the way in which insurance companies and governmental policies have been invading and limiting the individualistic aspects of health care. Certainly, this is so in the United States. Our response is not simply an expression of economic self-interest, for basic assumptions of the analytic enterprise are being challenged. Indeed, most analysts proudly contend that amidst all other cultural pressures toward conformity, psychoanalysis still stands up for individuality.

If, however, every significant proposition concerning people can be seen to have a moral edge and so cannot be taken for granted, all aspects of the psychoanalytic point of view may be examined for their implicitly prescriptive aspects. For example, that psychoanalysis is a value-free science, that the practice of psychoanalysis is value-free except for the shared health values of analyst and analysand, and that the principles of psychoanalytic technique may be designated a technology—three essential building blocks of Hartmann's discussion—all are now open to review as hidden moral directives. Analysts must ask whether it is possible for them to do or say anything in their clinical work that is value-free. More broadly, they must ask, What are health values? And more narrowly, In what relationship to technology does psychoanalytic technique stand? I shall go on now to venture some brief, purely introductory remarks in response to each of these three large questions.

1. *Value-free?* In a way that is fully compatible with psychoanalytic understanding, more and more critical theorists have been accepting a constructivist view of the development of personal and societal perceptions, conceptualizations, and practices. The constructivist ascribes a central role to values in the way ideas of self and reality are developed by individuals in society. (We might recall here the proposals in the 1950s and 1960s by Erik Erikson [1950], Edward Bibring [1953], and Edith Jacobson [1964] on the ideals and values associated with the phases of psychosexual development.) One consequence of the rise of constructivism has been the increased difficulty of arguing

that there can be significant ideas that are value-free. Historical narratives, literary critiques, accounts of the family, accounts of gender, descriptions of bodies or of nature in general, and even such things as
greeting cards, advertising, jokes, and descriptions of psychoanalysis
itself—all are open to critical analysis as to the values built into their
stated or implied accounts of human relations. They have prescriptive
impact without our necessarily being aware that that is so.

On this basis, entire disciplines have come under the moral or ideological microscope, and enough persuasive arguments have been
advanced to legitimize ideological debate over much that was once assumed to be morally neutral. The idea that "the personal is political" is
gaining increasing credence within the humanities and social sciences.
Typically, analysts slough off these critiques; however, their doing so
does not invalidate the critiques. Indeed, this sloughing off should be
regarded as a manifestation of power. We analysts have the power in
our own domain to say that we need be concerned only with human
emotional suffering and the search for new knowledge of the mind. In
our role of helpers and healers as well as investigators, we are confident that we are justified in what we do. To critical thinkers, however,
far from justifying our individualistic enterprise, we are merely asserting an opinion and relying on the power of traditional humanism to
support us. Traditional humanism assures us that we are serving vital
human needs responsibly.

I have no quarrel with the established ethical requirement that, inevitably, it is an aspect of the responsibility assumed by analysts that,
so far as they can help it, they not impose their values on their analysands
in the course of trying to be analytically helpful. In the consulting room,
it is not expected that the individualism inherent in the enterprise will
be a problem. As a rule, it is taken for granted, in a way that is shared,
conscious, and ego syntonic, that relief from suffering and impaired functioning that express "poor health" is the guiding value. In this context,
the analyst is then free to regard unconscious repudiation of individualism not as valid ethical critique but as symptomatic of work to be done;
for example, work on pockets of guilt. For primarily, the analytic project
is dedicated to working on the self; it is expected that an individualistic
focus will achieve numerous secondary benefits in work, love, and play,
all of which will accrue from improvement in the self's "health." But
this responsible therapeutic attitude has no bearing on the problem with

which we are here concerned: analyzing the valorization of individualism in psychoanalysis. From individualism considered broadly and with no unproblematic conclusions, we may now move on to one of its particular manifestations, the valorization of, and confusion over, health values.

2. *What are health values?* Hartmann emphasized the essential clinical role of the sharing of health values by analyst and analysand. At the same time, he recognized that the importance of health values varies in different historical periods and cultural settings. What he did not take up, however, is the extent to which the moral implications of the definition of "health" are themselves open to critical scrutiny. "Health" may be regarded as an idea replete with moral values that control it both as an idea and a practice. Out of recognition of the constant play of power in human relations, one may therefore ask, Whose ideas of health are we talking about, and what are its assumptions? Whose health should matter? How much of what we call health is to be pursued, and what are the social consequences of that? There are many more questions of that sort.

To narrow the issue down to psychoanalysis, we may consider first the fact that analysts are not totally agreed among themselves on how to use the idea of mental health. For example, we see that this is so in case conferences and in discussions of adaptation, narcissism, and termination. As in our society at large, so in psychoanalysis, we encounter many varied presuppositions about what is health, who is healthy, whose health matters, and whose judgment counts. These variations imply variations in values. The problem is too vast to do more than illustrate a couple of specific instances in which the concept of shared health values is surrounded by ambiguity or confusion. My specific instances are informed consent, where the big factor is the power to decide matters of health, and discourse on gender, where phallocratic values among analysts have long been influential.

Informed consent is implied in the analyst's claim of shared health values. We are, however, already familiar with the question, What can informed consent mean in clinical psychoanalysis? Owing to the importance of unconsciously developed and maintained defense and transference, we cannot maintain that the analysand gives the analyst permission to treat the problems that will be encountered along the road toward relief from the severity of unconscious conflict. Not even the analyst knows, except perhaps in broadest outline, what lies in store for the two of them once they start out. Who can foresee exactly the resulting life changes, often of major proportions and therefore alarming as well as consequential not only to the analysand but to others in his or her life? Indeed, listing these problems in advance might well deter most people from beginning the analyses from which they will derive much benefit.

Also, in a high proportion of cases the initially *un*informed consent is withdrawn; then, analysands either bolt or consciously or unconsciously balk at going any further, instead taking power into their own hands and bringing their analyses to what their analysts regard as premature endings. Here too, however, critical questions can be raised: Premature according to whom? And premature for whom? Heinz Kohut (1977) raised these questions in his opening chapter on termination in *The Restoration of the Self*; in effect, he was challenging a moral bias in psychoanalysis against narcissistic solutions to problems. It is hard to deny that values are implied in the idea of a suitable termination. Although analysts may claim to be dealing only in facts provided by their analysands, what Hartmann wisely pointed out with respect to child-rearing may also apply here: Facts are often no more than moral judgments enforced by those who, like parents, are in power. Thus, power-backed morality shapes reality testing and self-perception from early on, and it plays its part both in psychoanalytic theorizing about therapeutic goals and in analysts' responsible use of their clinical authority.

In my view, informed consent can only be achieved bit by bit over the course of an entire analysis and is never fixed in place. It is not something to be given totally by analysand to analyst at the beginning, and it is not something the analyst can exact in any way that makes analytic sense. Informed consent is not like a nod or a handshake.

Discourse on gender has been heavily colored by unexamined health values, particularly those that invaded Freud's patriarchal ideas about heterosexual–genital–reproductive primacy. In my 1974 paper, "Problems in Freud's Psychology of Women," I argued that Freud imported into psychoanalysis an evolutionary ethic drawn from Darwinian thought: What underlay the heterosexual–genital–reproductive primacy of his developmental theory was the primacy of survival of the species. In asserting this primacy, however, Freud was in self-contradiction, because at the very same time he was also showing that the developmental route to heterosexual genitality is complex and uncertain, with many byways and fixation points. He was also showing that, at the least, that development requires much repression or strict subordination of alternative routes to pleasure and security. Freud's purely psychoanalytic account leaves the door open to detailed consideration of psychosexual ambivalence every step of the way; the door is also left open to environmental influences on choice through traumatization, seduction, oppression, identification, and forced idealization and moralization. There has always been this kind of object-relational and contingent aspect of Freud's psychosexual propositions.

In its own terms, Freud's psychoanalytic discourse on gender is coherent; strictly speaking, however, not all of his discussion is psychoanalytic (see Grossman, 1992; Grossman and Kaplan, 1988). In our time, recognizing that we need not follow Freud into self-contradiction, we have slowly, even if often reluctantly, half-heartedly, or faint-heartedly, changed our views of certain psychosexual matters. I mean such matters as automatically classifying homosexuality as a disease of nature that is to be cured if possible and also maintaining patriarchally that it is in women's essential nature to be passive-submissive-masochistic or to marry a man and be a mother who suspends or relinquishes her own vocation. In Hartmann's sense, these notions were being palmed off by psychoanalysts as facts of psychosexual development, this because moral values were being taken for granted and not critiqued for their controlling and judgmental aspects. Though diminished, this faulty practice has persisted.

Both of the progressive changes that I just mentioned have moved us away from Freud's unanalytic evolutionary ethic, and they illustrate how readily we moralize the idea of "the natural." Might we not, therefore, now extend our critique of what is psychosexually "natural" and declassify the so-called perversions as illnesses? I would make that extension. Why not maintain instead that it is more consistently psychoanalytic to regard perversions as nonnormative sexual preferences? This change does not compromise the clinical work of analysts. We remain free to go on trying to understand the origins and compositions of these nonnormative preferences. We may go on trying, if it seems appropriate to do so, to assist those analysands who wish to overcome these sexual preferences. We may go on showing analysands for whom these preferences are ego syntonic how, if that's what seems to be the case, such practices may be interfering with their reaching other goals which they claim to have set for themselves by undertaking an analysis, such as achieving a happy, contented, and stable sexual relationship with an intimate other, and how these costs are entailed by what they value in their nonnormative preferences.

In my view, the change that is required by this extension of the critique of the so-called natural is a self-critical reduction of the analyst's moral zeal. This is a zeal we analysts sometimes describe poorly as therapeutic zeal and often justify ethically as helpfully orientating the analysand toward maintaining an appropriate position in the "natural" life cycle. Would it not be more accurate, however, to view established practices along those lines as assertions of moral power and of a preference for conformity?

3. *Is psychoanalysis a technology?* My third question continues my critique of Hartmann's idea that the psychoanalytic method may be described as a technology. From one point of view, this seems to be an idea that has the stamp of the un-self-conscious, morally conformist 1950s all over it. Additionally, from the point of view of the psychoanalytic aspiration toward being a value-free science, the idea has the stamp of the idealized image of psychoanalytic treatment as a value-free, countertransference-free means to a desirable end. This idealization encourages us to think that analysis is no different from laying out the plans for a bridge or a coffee-bean grinder and then executing these plans efficiently. The analyst is expected to be a detached and completely objective observer and technician, thoroughly impersonal and purely rational.

We encounter here an instance of the ego psychological point of view shifting the characterization of events toward "the outside" and away from psychic reality. That is to say, we are encouraged to think about how things look to an independent observer of the situation and how analysts consciously represent their own intentions. The problem, however, is that neither of these emphases need have much to do with how the analytic procedure is experienced by the analysand. It is a mythic picture. It is a picture of analysis that rationalizes unrecognized exercises of power. This picture was frontally challenged in other terms by Leo Stone (1961) in his classic monograph *The Psychoanalytic Situation.* Stone persuasively developed a consistent regard for the psychic reality of the analysand's experience of the psychoanalytic situation, including the experience of the analyst's attempt to be this utterly detached and impersonal objective observer. Stone centered on the vicissitudes of relatedness in the analytic situation. And across the Atlantic, especially in London, the Kleinian object relations analysts had all along been developing to a high point their own understanding of relatedness in the analysand's psychic reality within the psychoanalytic situation (see, for example, Klein, Heimann, Isaacs, and Riviere, 1952).

Therefore, we may say that "technology" indicates a latently moral, self-justifying misapplication of the ego psychological approach. Intrinsically, it is an unanalytic idea in that it substitutes conventional reality for psychic reality as well as common sense for unconscious fantasy. In the guise of being value-free, it facilitates conformist consequences and contradicts even the individualistic moral values inherent in Freud's psychoanalysis. Technically, the idea of psychoanalysis as technology suggests that it is professionally and therefore morally irresponsible to draw un-self-consciously and unrestrainedly on one's own full humanity in doing analytic work. Leo Stone emphasized that, in fact, seasoned analysts were not working in this unreal "technological" way; as he saw it, the trouble was that, in their official and puristic teachings of technique, they were giving everybody in the profession a guilty conscience.

The official teachings implied the fear that nontechnological analysts would run wild with their countertransferences. Today, we are in a position to argue that that fear is based on a value-laden notion of the weakness of the ego in human relations. Specifically, it conveys mistrust of the possibilities of moral mutuality. It does not stand up for analysis as a special form of human relatedness and intense engagement. It depicts analysis as always running the risk of becoming simply a playground for instinctual forces. Much more is involved here than is suggested by frequent examples of truly bad practice and by too-ready explanations of overwhelming id impulses and impaired superegos. That "more" includes the values that are built into metapsychological theory and the principles of technique; these are the values that help shape the events of the analysis. I dare to say that Hartmann's word, *technology*, shows that, in his striving for theoretical purity, he could turn a blind eye to clinical phenomena he surely

knew intimately from first-hand experience and through his own subjective experience, and that consequently he lost his own way and ended
in self-contradiction. His approach has by no means eliminated instances
of serious countertransference transgressions from the practice of psychoanalysis.

To sum up this part of my argument, it no longer seems correct to
hope that psychoanalytic theory and technique can be exempted from
examination with respect to the moral assumptions on which they are
based. For, like every other undertaking, psychoanalysis cannot isolate
itself from the world of values in which it is embedded. It cannot set
itself above critical scrutiny. Its individualism opens it fully to that scrutiny. Although Hartmann did a superb job for his time—indeed, no one
else could have done it as well as he, and done it as conspicuously and
bravely as he did, in the Freud lecture at the New York Psychoanalytic
Society and Institute—it can nevertheless now be argued that he exempted too much from his account of the role of moral values in psychoanalysis. From a contemporary point of view it can be argued that in
his narrowing the discussion as he did, he was taking a stand with definite moral—in some ways even moralistic—implications. That was certainly not what he intended, but morality and moralism are inherent in
every person's construction of reality and cannot be eliminated even from
the most classically rigorous theorizing. It is not intentions that count in
the long run; it is ultimately the consequences of what is written and
enforced by those in power.

DISCUSSION

What is implied in the idea of revisiting a text? Certainly much more
than yet another close study to determine what it "really" says. We reread each text in the light of our contemporary understanding of the
issues with which it deals implicitly as well as explicitly. In this respect, it is not so much that we are going back to the classic; rather we
are bringing it forward. But, seeing that readings vary so much, one
must ask, forward to what? Can it be simply the case that what a text
"really" says can only be what it says to the present reader, that it has
no fixed or final meaning, that it changes with changing generations
of readers, and that what the author meant, intended, or achieved is

ultimately indeterminate? A strong case has been made for answering those questions with a yes. Therefore, it has been said that texts belong to their readers and to the conventions of an era and not to their authors.

There are, however, important considerations that lead to the conclusion that matters are more complex than that argument in its simplest form would allow. One such consideration is that there always exist powerful conventions that control author and reader alike. These conventions are based on cultural power that has been transformed into seemingly factual linguistic and logical givens. These conventions are practiced by what has been called interpretive communities and could also be called, as I have suggested elsewhere (1981, 1992), narrative communities. These communities share assumptions about life, communication, and modes of understanding. Consequently, there are only limited choices available to those engaged in writing and reading in any given cultural and historical setting. And so we do find much agreement within each of these communities on intentions, meanings, and consequences. In this way, we arrive at communal validation; at least we set limits on what may be accepted as strong or useful validations. For this reason, a relativistic chaos of interpretations is not implied by the idea that texts depend for their existence on individual readers. To paraphrase one of Hartmann's most popularized ideas, there are average expectable writings and readings of texts in any one culture at any one time in its history.

The conception of revisiting that I have just outlined conforms to one of the strongest ideas of texts in contemporary critical theory as set forth by philosophers and literary scholars (e.g., Culler, 1975; Fish, 1980; Ricoeur, 1977). It also conforms to the clinical analyst's orientation to the material that develops during analytic sessions. What counts in analytic sessions is not arriving at absolute certainty regarding "the facts" of an analysand's history or present life or of the analysand's "conscious intentions"; rather, what counts is entering as best one can into what gets to be defined jointly as the analysand's psychic reality or internal world, that is, into what he or she has made and is still making of the persons and events that matter to him or her, including everything pertaining to the analytic sessions themselves.

At the same time, however, we must allow that we cannot directly grasp or unambiguously define the analysand's psychic reality. Our understanding is always mediated by the analyst's allegiance to more or less established theoretical and technical guidelines—in other words, membership in one or another interpretive and narrative community. When an analyst retells an analysand's narratives (Schafer, 1983, 1992), that analyst will develop versions of the analysand's psychic reality that differ from those developed by members of other schools of thought and may even differ somewhat from those of other analysts within the same school. It is because there are interpretive and narrative communities of analysts that we observe large areas of overlap. It is universally accepted that each of the traditional analytical approaches implies a skeptical orientation toward "the facts" as they are being presented in the clinical sessions at one time or another; I mean skeptical, not dismissive, and I mean tentative or provisional, not downright suspicious. Analysts well know how often and how much these "facts" change: by reversal, by recontextualization, by being filled in to the point of leading toward a new understanding, and certainly by shifts in the transference.

Therefore, it should occasion no surprise to note the similarity between the postmodern conception of texts that I have been presenting and standard analytical attitudes toward the facticity of analysands' material. By extension, we may also say that readings of classic contributions of the psychoanalytic literature reflect this way of looking at things. Inevitably, even if unknowingly, revisiting a classic is acting on this contemporary understanding of the indissolubility of perception, interpretation, community, and history. And by further extension (so I hope to have demonstrated here), one analyst may produce varied, though still more or less similar and compatible readings of the same classic, even within a short space of time.

Obviously, the writings of leading contemporary critical theorists of psychoanalysis were not available to Hartmann in the years of his development as an intellectual and an analyst or at the time when he wrote his essay on moral values. Now, in the mid-1990s, I believe that I have benefited from these new developments, and have used them to construct a somewhat different picture of moral values in psychoanalysis. But that picture cannot be unique or idiosyncratic. It can only have developed out of the conventions of the narrative and interpretive communities to which I, along with many others, belong. Seen in that context, it is a version of the truth, and I hope I have made it a compelling version. In this version, it no longer seems correct to hope for a situation within psychoanalysis that can escape examination and critique of its moral assumptions and the moralization of its own practices. For, like every other undertaking, psychoanalysis cannot isolate itself from the world in which it is embedded and cannot exempt itself from ongoing critical analysis.

13

A Classic Revisited: Kurt Eissler's
"The Effect of the Structure of the
Ego on Psychoanalytic Technique"

At present, the student and practitioner of psychoanalysis confronts a wide array of recommended techniques and theoretical perspectives. Typically, technique and perspective are presented together as though they were thoroughly integrated and also as though, at least for one segment of those seeking analysis, they offered the best approach of all. On close examination, however, the integration is revealed to be not without flaws, the evidence limited and fundamentally impressionistic, and the authors' reliance on rhetorical persuasiveness plainly evident. Consequently, each analyst is in the position of being called upon to rethink her or his own approach. Those who ignore this call need not concern us here. Of greater interest is the question of how to go about this rethinking.

One way of rethinking analytic approaches that, increasingly, has been found useful is that of "revisiting" this or that classic in the literature. As I mentioned in chapter 12, the point of the revisit is not to get back to "the truth" as revealed in original source material, though it is often impressive how much wisdom these classics convey and how well they deserve to be considered classics. Rather, the point is to define our own position more clearly or fully by applying its principal ideas to a substantial construction of earlier times. Thereby we might hope to gain a better perspective on where we stand now, and why. In one way, these revisits are a form of applied analysis, and in another an analogue of clinical analysis, for in both types of work the analyst learns *through application* what is illuminating, important, unclear, or unsatisfactory in the approach being used.

In this essay I want to revisit a classic of psychoanalytic ego psychology. This classic played an important part in the history of Freudian analysis on the North American continent, most of all, I think, in the United States, and its consequences are still with us, even if only as a kind of unease over how far we have drifted from the concerns it embodies and partly formalized. The classic in question is Kurt Eissler's paper, "The Effect of the Structure of the Ego on Psychoanalytic Technique" (1953b). It is the paper in which the difficult idea of "parameters" of technique was introduced. I shall try to evaluate the epistemological, methodological, and ethical implications and consequences of Eissler's understanding and use of Freud's structural theory, or what is often loosely referred to as his "ego psychology."

By my reading of this classic paper, Eissler was attempting to establish what would, at that time (1953), have been a sound, contemporary, ego psychological Freudian theoretical base for those analysts engaged in therapeutic work with deeply traumatized or terrified analysands. These are analysands who, in order to salvage some psychic equilibrium, rely desperately on a pervasive and rigid network of defensive operations and transferences. For such analysands it is as though life itself, in every casual as well as significant aspect, had come to seem perilous.

Although analysts understand that the essential dangers to be analyzed are primarily intrapsychic, they also recognize that these terrified analysands are likely to project an enormous amount into the environment and, therefore, always to feel surrounded by great danger and to act accordingly. Usually, their networks of defenses and transferences originated so far back in their life histories that they seem virtually constitutional. Therefore, the ego of each of these analysands may be said to have been "modified," that is, to have departed from a hypothetical, normal, ego organization and mode of function.

Eissler's thinking on this subject was closely tied to Freud's "Analysis Terminable and Interminable" (1937a). In that paper, using his relatively new structural theory, Freud had proposed the idea of the modified or "altered" ego; he had also called it "deformed," "dislocated," and "restricted," thereby suggesting a crippled ego. An altered ego is not fully available to the analytic method; it cannot "guarantee unshakable loyalty to the work of analysis" (p. 239). Interpretation alone may culminate merely in a strengthening of defenses. In this context, Freud had also suggested that each person's ego can be placed in a continuum of increasing alteration that corresponds to the continuum from the fictional ideal of normality to unanalyzable psychosis, and it is probable that today many of the extreme analysands in question would be diagnosed as "borderline" at the least.

At the present time, psychoanalytic thought is more experience-centered than it was then. We might, therefore, favor expressing the matter of inaccessibility differently. To the extent that the ego is altered, it will experience interpretation as yet another version of old dangers; this is a version that threatens to bring about another traumatic overstimulation or deprivation, another seduction, punishment, exposure to guilt, humiliation, or collapse of self-esteem, if not annihilation of the self itself. A steady diet of interpretation—"interpretation only"—must therefore be experienced by the altered ego as one or another kind of tyranny.

Eissler's (1950b, 1953a) intrepid work with adolescent delinquents and schizophrenics seems to have kept much on his mind that analytic technique, in any of its then usual ego psychological forms, might not be suitable for them. Apparently, his clinical work with them led him to conclude that at times it is necessary to make major departures from interpretation only. He advised that, in the interest of their ultimate therapeutic goals, analysts should make sparing use of these departures, which he called "parameters," and only when they can anticipate analyzing their nonanalytic effects later on. Additionally, he seems to have believed that, in many of these cases, one cannot maintain a secure enough analytic base under these conditions to carry out that later analysis of parameters; therefore, when sufficient progress warrants it, each such analysand should be transferred to another analyst for a standard analysis. Apparently, Eissler saw that it is often necessary for the analyst to be unanalytically interventionist in order to bring certain analysands to the point where they are so much less terrified of facing their inner conflicts that, at least some of the time, they can understand and use interpretation for what it is, that is, as an aid to beneficial change.

In all of this reasoning, Eissler was, of course, ignoring the different approaches being developed abroad, especially those associated with the names of Melanie Klein, Fairbairn, and Winnicott. This narrowness of scope is still evident today in some (fortunately shrinking) guardians of ego psychological work in North America. I have reconstructed Eissler's line of reasoning from other papers of his, the classic paper on which we are now focused, and contemporary ways of addressing these difficulties. If my reconstruction is at all valid, Eissler was trying to do two things: on the one hand, to remain true to Freud, and on the other, to incorporate into his ideas on technique both Heinz Hartmann's (1939, 1964) subsequent contributions to Freud's structural theory, the work Kris and Loewenstein did in close alliance with Hartmann (see, for example, Hartmann, Kris, and Loewenstein, 1964), and the fruits of Eissler's own ventures into the widening scope of analytic work. At that time in psychoanalytic history, however, he could not avoid seeing that his adventurous work with these extreme cases was bringing him into proximity with the work of Franz Alexander (Alexander and French, 1946) and Frieda Fromm-Reichmann (1950). He nonetheless deplored their work, especially Alexander's emphasis on "corrective emotional experience" in the therapeutic relationship (see Eissler, 1950a).

Eissler attempted to discredit utterly the Alexandrian advice to manipulate the transference of difficult analysands in order better to confront them with the unreality of their resistant transference fantasies. He argued that that kind of manipulation, such as being unusually demonstrative to analysands with an unyielding, cold-father transference, introduces unanalyzable influences into the course of the therapy. He insisted that any improvements observed must be regarded as superficial, and he warned that they must involve a great cost to the analysand's ego as a whole. At best, he argued, they achieve a change of content that masquerades as structural change. A change of content of this sort would be, for example, the replacement of overt characterological sadism with overt excessive kindness when that change occurs in the absence of worked-through insight. This caution parallels Freud's (1937a) comment that analysis sometimes merely strengthens an analysand's defenses.

Eissler firmly believed that the taking of any position other than his would imply a rejection of the fundamental premises and findings of psychoanalysis. Hence his emphasis both on not encouraging pseudo-analytic changes by using parameters liberally, and on assessing in advance whether or not they will be analyzable in the future. He tried to show that the analytic curiosity, flexibility, and adventurousness that he, Eissler, stood for need not lead to Alexander's artificiality or Fromm-Reichmann's interpersonalism, nor perhaps ultimately to Ferenczi's earlier deviations. There is much to recommend this stand against deliberately manipulative enactments with analysands; play-acting of that sort is unanalyzable by definition.

Eissler also followed Freud in noting that, even under ideal conditions, the analytic process is influenced by noninterpretive factors. He mentioned specifically the personality of the analyst, the necessary use of questions and nonverbal communication. He recognized that each analyst is a specific human being, who will be responded to as such by the analysand and, further, be responded to in ways that may lead to beneficial change in behavior that has not yet been analyzed or may not even be analyzable. In trying to avoid idealizing the analytic method, Eissler included unavoidable parameters in his model of the standard analysis. There were, he implied, quite enough of these without deliberately or carelessly piling on more of them out of unanalytic and misguided therapeutic zeal.

Eissler's paper prepares us to anticipate the possibility of contributing to unanalytic consequences at those choice points during the analytic process when we select from among a number of possible overt interventions or decide not to intervene (interfere). In particular, we are alerted to the ways in which we may muddy or limit the analysis of transference when, through unanalytic therapeutic zeal buttressed by rationalization, we introduce serious parameters and when, out of our recognition that some flexibility or inventiveness is called for, we depart from our customary interpretive modes. He also alerted us to the need to sort out the different types of improvement that follow upon our interventions. Therapeutic zeal should never substitute for reflective analytic work. In today's terms, he was cautioning against entering into enactments and, on top of that, disregarding the necessity to try to analyze them when they do take place.

Along with these virtues, however, this classic paper includes some notable problems. It is, after all, to be expected that later generations will define some inconsistencies, overreachings, blind spots, contradictions, and exaggerations in the creative efforts of every imaginative contributor to our field, such as Eissler has been. Some of the problems I shall go on to note in Eissler's paper are, I think, serious but not hopeless, and one at least is hopeless but not serious. I shall get the hopeless one out of the way before moving on to more weighty matters.

In his treatment of the ego's defenses, Eissler developed what is perhaps the outstanding Gothic tale in the ego psychological literature. In this tale, the defenses that modify the ego are always threatening to engulf it. Eissler called the defenses "cancerous" threats to the ego, implying that one cannot fear them too much. It is a horror story of the defenses as live, idlike entities with evil aims of their own. In this, Eissler was not treating defenses as components of the ego. His is not a narrative of the ego pursuing incompatible goals owing to its being both split and organized on several levels that cover a range of primitivity and unconsciousness; that is, an ego oriented toward a number of psychically real, but disparate, dangers simultaneously. That way of putting the matter would fall within the realm of ordinary, acceptable, structural discourse.

Eissler's animistic way of putting it would seem to correspond to the unconscious paranoidlike fantasies about the workings of one's mind that we actually do encounter in our clinical work and that the Kleinian object relations analysts have always highlighted usefully in their clinical approach to the analysis of defense (see, for example, Schafer [1968], on the theory of defense). In terms of Eissler's own commitments and project, however, he was contaminating metaphor, the interpretation of unconscious fantasy, and the metapsychological formalization of mental processes. True, if one goes back to Freud's 1937(a) text on termination (see pp. 236–237), one occasionally finds him, in his customary way, metaphorically enlivening his discussion of the ego in conflict by introducing some anthropomorphic formulations concerning the dangerousness of defenses. Conceivably, it was from these rhetorical excursions that Eissler took off and began treating several discrete discourses as one. Indeed, structural theory has never been well fortified against invasion by the primitive language of unconscious fantasy. In this respect, Eissler's story is not at all the same as that told by the Kleinian analysts when they interpret the unconscious fantasy content of the so-called mechanisms of defense (Schafer, 1968), in this following Freud's own example (1926). So much for the hopeless problem.

Turning now to the serious problems, the first one to consider arises from Eissler's having relied heavily on Freud's idea of a continuum ranging from normality to psychosis. Perhaps he did so in order to pave the way for his extensive comments on schizophrenia later in this essay, comments with which I shall not concern myself here. Be that as it may, I believe that our contemporary understanding requires us to regard the idea of a continuum as a problematic metaphorical preconception rather than as a conclusion compelled by hard evidence. One could just as well use the metaphor of a wheel, a set of coordinates or, as in Kleinian theory, positions that may be or become flagrantly or subtly psychotic.

The idea of a linear diagnostic continuum is a cousin of the developmental proposition that there exists a simple continuum extending from an initial autistic or totally narcissistic and primitive state to an ideally normal, object related and conventionally rational state. That proposition fits poorly with our clinical work, which would far more readily support formulations of complex contexts and subtle layerings of variables, pertaining to both adaptation and illness. Yet another cousin of this continuum ranges, according to Freud (1912c), from the animistic thinking of so-called "primitive peoples" to scientific thinking.

Neither does modern developmental research support any simple conception of a purely autistic or narcissistic starting point. Further, the phenomenological resemblance of dream-thinking to psychosis is no sure guide to developmental theory or stages in the workings of the mind and of civilization. And Freud's anthropological idealization of the scientific has not withstood the critical thought of modern times, especially so in relation to moral and material values. My point here is that no single organizing metaphor—be it continuum wheel, or whatever—should control our thinking entirely. In elaborating any general hypothesis we always have options, and we are only required to remember that, like any clinical "parameter," each metaphoric aid has its built-in problems; none of them can be all-encompassing, and each will remain vulnerable to criticism from other points of view.

We encounter other problems when we try to correlate diagnosis and accessibility with treatability by interpretation alone. For example, on the contemporary scene we find differences of opinion about accessibility in relation to diagnosis. These differences are embodied in varied conceptions of what needs to be interpreted, and how and when. We also find varied conceptions of what constitutes an interpretable response to an interpretation. Furthermore, these varied conceptions seem to apply in some measure to all analysands, not just to the seemingly remote ones.

Thus, there are analysts who are working interpretively, and at least to some extent effectively, with psychotics and other analysands who initially seem to be altogether inaccessible, and who are working not so differently with less extreme analysands, too. Foremost among these analysts are those who think in object relational terms. Their ideas about communication, interpretation, and response to interpretation, which include many elements specific to their school of thought (those of Klein and Winnicott in particular), allow them to adhere closely to a purely interpretive, inner world directed, clinical approach, even in work with the most extreme of cases. These analysts are doing basic research in psychoanalysis, working well past the narrow boundaries established by research of the rating scale or word-counting types.

Freud's and Eissler's ideas about diagnosis and the reduced effectiveness of interpretation when psychosis is in question now seem limited. The what, when, and how of interpretation of the clinical dialogue are more complex than they understood them to be, and the degree of object relatedness in functional psychosis seems to be greater than they imagined. In their eyes, some contemporary approaches to interpretation might therefore seem to be overrun with unassimilable parameters and mistaken, if not grandiose, therapeutic zeal, while many of us today would not think so.

I have already emphasized more than once that one of the momentous changes in interpretation that has been spreading throughout contemporary analytic work is the recognition that countertransference response is part of the analytic dialogue and an essential constituent of useful interpretation. This is all the more the case in work with the difficult, basically desperate, analysands we now accept for analytic treatment. Even the act of interpreting may get to be too much in the service of disruptive countertransference. For interpretation, however insightful, may be used to subdue, seduce, mislead or hurt analysands. Although Eissler was probably aware of this hazardous aspect of interpretation, he did put it in parentheses in this paper, and by doing so failed to give a true picture of the complexity of careful, ego psychological analytic work—even of his own, I suspect.

If we remain aware of these limitations of Freud's and Eissler's model, we are less likely to succumb to inappropriate technical constraints, and more likely to assess open-mindedly novel interpretive approaches to difficult or seemingly immovable analysands. Also, we are less likely to draw premature or mistaken theoretical conclusions about malignant disorder and the limits of analyzability when all that we might have established is that the unique combination of analysand, analyst, therapeutic approach and life circumstances have combined to render one analytic undertaking ineffective or even deleterious. In these analytic situations, there are simply too many uncontrolled variables for us to be licensed to draw the kind of definitive conclusions that Eissler's argument tends to encourage.

Viewed in a still broader perspective, it can be said that Freud and Eissler presented their case as though by 1937 or 1953 analysts already knew all there was to know about technical consistency and sound interpretation. They wrote as if we had already come to the end of the history of analytic understanding and the interpretations that that history made possible. This static and monolithic picture of psychoanalysis tends to support exaggerated conformity, excessive rationalism, increased rigidity of judgment and serious stifling of curiosity and inventiveness. In this respect, Eissler in particular seems to have juxtaposed, rather than integrated, his noteworthy adventurousness and some continuing strict conservatism. Freud had done the same prior to Eissler. He, too, had always been trying to strike a balance between the freedom of his interpretive genius and his excessive concern with conventional, now-dated, ideas about scientific rigor and professional acceptability.

The underpinnings of Freud's excessive concern are set in the ungiving concrete of naive realism and empiricism. The realist–empiricist commitment entails consequences that allow and support claims to absolute or final knowledge that stands outside of time and methodological controversy. Eissler joined Freud in making this excessive claim, if only implicitly.

The implied omniscient claim to which I am referring was made manifest in Eissler's recommendation that the analyst use only analyzable parameters, for this idea puts analysts in the position of arrogating to themselves supreme powers. Although Eissler explicitly warned against an omniscient posture, in effect, his recommendation tends to reinforce the opposite tendency, that is, a disruptive grandiose countertransference: the analysand can be known definitively and in one way only. It is generally accepted today that a sound analytic attitude should include not only elements of uncertainty, suspense and the potential for surprise, which, it should be emphasized, implies a potential for regret, too, but also a recognition that the world of psychoanalysis is pluralistic. With that recognition truly integrated, analysts will carefully avoid making hidden claims that in their work they always know exactly what's what. It is hard enough to maintain an approximate sense of what is going on moment by moment and to be able to convince colleagues that you have even that much just right.

One must agree with Eissler that it does make good sense to be circumspect when we deliberately introduce parameters, for we cannot count on the consequences of these moves being detectable, let alone analyzable or sufficiently analyzable. Furthermore, as Eissler emphasized, what we gain in one respect we may lose in another, more important, and perhaps hidden, respect. On the other hand, the modern temper in the conduct of analytic work and the modern understanding of theory in relation to practice would support an analytic attitude that avoids excessively meticulous circumspection, for that mode introduces its own disruptive artifacts. For example, it may occasion mutual anxiety and guilt in the transference and countertransference over apparent departures from "true and exact analytic procedure."

Another seriously excessive claim is involved in the way Eissler, still following Freud's 1937 discussion, implies that one can establish an operational psychoanalytic definition of normality. Both of them were arguing that the "normal" ego may be defined as one that can be worked with in analysis by interpretation only; consequently, the more that parameters seem to be required, the less normal the ego. As I indicated earlier, this operational definition seems to work well provided that, as Eissler suggested, one puts in parentheses all the other, uncontrolled, variables in the analytic situation. But the extensive use of these parentheses does too much violence to what, in any form, can be stated about the everyday vicissitudes of practice. Is it even appropriate to bring such operational definitions into psychoanalytic discussion, seeing that analysis is so complex a process of dialogue and other interaction and that it encounters so much variation in external life circumstances of both analysts and analysands? Further, decisions concerning tact, timing, and dosage, as well as potentially useful lines of interpretation, are in many ways matters of personal style as well as school of affiliation. A high degree of selectivity in technique and in interpretation cannot really be avoided.

If, in addition, we take into account what the history of ideas plainly shows, namely, that, inevitably, value judgments will be hidden in our ideas of normality, then any striving toward operationalism must introduce into our discipline a false note of neutrality and scientific rigor. When we, in turn, idealize that neutrality and rigor, we subtly imbue our work with an inappropriate, conformist, authoritarian ethic (see also chapters 11 and 12). With authoritarianism now on the table, we have arrived at my final point.

Eissler has often been faulted unfairly. It has been charged that by introducing the concept of parameter, he established a damaging technical conscience for Freudian ego psychological analysts. Certainly, the term *Parameters!* has been used to disparage or discredit work without what we could call due analytic process. However, *this* problem was not of Eissler's making—that we can see when we consider the long-lasting effects of his ideas. Eissler's tone is not that of the harsh superego of the sort we encounter in such overused, derivative pronouncements as "I wouldn't call that analysis!" Eissler was introducing a concept in order to help therapeutically minded analysts keep their analytic bearings in the difficult, ambiguous, and varied world of clinical work. He was trying to clarify further the principal baseline of psychoanalytic work: interpretation.

The problem is, however, that baselines for psychoanalytic work can never be drawn precisely. Mostly, our rules are cautions. Furthermore, they stand at some remove from any specific psychoanalytic situation, and they are not rigorously linked to utterly systematized theory. None of our theories are *that* well worked out, and, no doubt, in the future these rules will change with the analytic times. But when the rules are applied in threatening and discrediting ways, we may say that they have been moralized. I suspect this moralistic consequence reflects the steady pressure of anxiety aroused by doing analytic work and the inadequately analyzed, though not altogether eliminable, superego pressures involved in our efforts to be healers.

To conclude this revisit, I will simply express my hope that my attempt at developing a reappraisal of this classic ego psychological essay has shown that keeping one's eyes fully open when we reread can benefit our present grasp of psychoanalysis in all its complexity. Eissler was taking stock of where things stood then, in 1953; it is our turn now. I have been taking my turn in this collection of essays.

14

The Evolution of My Views on Nonnormative Sexual Practices

I

It is particularly in connection with the psychology of women that the problems in Freud's theory of psychosexual development have been identified, articulated, and explained in detail and with much sophistication. A large part of this development may be attributed directly and indirectly to the efforts of feminist thinkers. Starting from this advance, it requires no great leap in reasoning to conclude that, if the psychoanalytic psychology of women is problematic, then that of men, from which it purports to be derived, must be equally problematic. Expectedly, therefore, strong arguments have been advanced to show that this is so, too, and on this expanded critical basis, one readily sees that there is much to question about Freud's views on gay and lesbian sexuality for, at bottom, these views have been derived from his phallocentric approach to the psychosexual development of both sexes.

First presented as a keynote address at a meeting organized by the Gay and Lesbian Candidates Association of the New York University Postdoctoral Program in Psychoanalysis and Psychotherapy, 1994.

237

There is no uniformity to be found in these many critiques. Inevitably, they have varied with the critic's school of psychoanalytic thought, personal predilections, and continuing access to new ideas and information from other fields of humanistic study. Also, they build on one another and become ever more compelling. Beyond that, many feminist critiques have themselves been criticized as too narrowly focused on gender relations and thus neglectful of large issues in the theories of sexuality in general (Rubin, 1984).

To a modest extent I have participated in some aspects of these critical developments. Drawing in part on the work of fine thinkers in many fields of study and in part on my own observations and reflections as an analyst, I have in the past attempted to contribute something of my own (1974, 1978, 1992, 1994a). In this essay I want to explore some further aspects of the problems with which all of us have been concerned.

My account will not abide by the conventions of chronological time. That kind of linear chronology might seem to be the basis for the truest version, but it is not so at all. Insights and criticisms develop in bits and pieces that are packed with multiple implications, only some of which can be realized at the moment of conception. Like interpretations as described by Heinz Hartmann (1951), insights and criticisms have "multiple appeal"; that is, all kinds of surprising consequences elsewhere in the mind than at the point of initial focus. The evolution of my ideas has been like that, as is no doubt the case with many others who work in psychoanalysis. Additionally, if I give some idea of what I have evolved *to* before going too far back in my history, I may make my retrospective account more accessible. Consequently, the early part of this essay will cover more of the present phase of my evolution: where I have arrived rather than where I started from.

I am not going to refer to the vicissitudes of my personal development or the dynamic factors influencing me at present. These necessarily have contributed to the evolution of my views on psychosexuality, both normative and nonnormative. In this respect, my silence expresses my agreement with Freud and many others: bringing intimate personal considerations to bear in expounding and assessing theoretical ideas is a two-edged sword; it settles nothing about lines of argument and the conclusions reached. We all have personal reasons for those aspects of reality that we see clearly and emphasize as well as for those we remain

blind to or deplore out of bias. In self-contradiction, Freud fell victim
to the two-edged sword, as have many analysts after him, for he and the
others have tended to brush off feminist and other critics of the psychoanalytic bias against nonnormative sexual orientations and practices as
expressions of penis envy or other problems with sexuality. By "double-
edged sword" is meant, for instance, that to countercritical cries of
"penis envy," one can always and easily reply "castration anxiety" or
"repressed mother envy." And in the present context, one must finally
say to all of this only, "So what?!"

The term *phallocentric*, however, is not party to these arguments,
because, when this term is properly used, it refers to faulty and biased
methodology and reasoning and not to personal intention specifically;
it refers to viewing the world from the standpoint of the phallic male.
As a metaphor, however, "double-edged sword" itself conveys a phallocentric orientation in that it symbolically links reasoned argument to the
phallus.

II

I want next to take up directly the different sexual practices, both the
normative or publicly conformist and the nonnormative or publicly individualized. It has come to seem to me worthwhile to structure my
thinking about sexual practices around the antithesis of curiosity versus rushing to moral judgment, both positive and negative. Presumably,
analysts are thoroughly committed to curiosity, including curiosity about
the evolution of moral judgments and the way these are made and conveyed implicitly as well as explicitly. And yet, if you read between the
lines, and as I have argued in earlier chapters, you soon realize that, in
traditional Freudian psychoanalysis, many moral judgments have been
taken for granted as factual statements, while many other moral judgments have been presented as reasoned conclusions based on careful
exercises of curiosity in the form of purportedly scientific investigation
or, even more simply, uncontroversial reality testing.

Earlier I pointed out that Heinz Hartmann emphasized this point
among others in his 1959 Freud Lecture *Psychoanalysis and Moral
Values* (1960), at the New York Psychoanalytic Society and Institute.
There, he pointed out how, in child rearing, parents and educators use

words like *good* and *bad* and many ordinarily descriptive words as though they are simply conveying facts about things and practices, when in effect, if not in intention, they are expressing moral preferences or imperatives. It is that way in the case of gender development; specifically, when the boy is told, "Boys and men do this, not that; they are this way, not that way; they aspire to this, not that; they look good this way, not that way," and so on, he is being indoctrinated with moral prescriptions masquerading as factual descriptions. The indoctrination proceeds similarly in the case of girls.

What Hartmann did not go into, however, are the observations that show that children are pretty smart about these so-called realistic lessons. Children are not just great fabricators in fantasy; often, they do correctly take communication of facts as more than mere information. Consequently, they realize that what is being conveyed along with these "facts" is the warning that in the future they will be judged—loved and admired or scorned, punished, and emotionally abandoned—if they either do or do not conform to the norm without question or protest. Additionally, children do go further in fantasy to envision extreme rewards and dire consequences if they get the so-called facts right or wrong. The rationalist parents who say later on, "But we never threatened; we only informed and explained," are naive about their own inner lives and the inner lives of their children.

I am emphasizing that we must remain aware how readily so-called normative facts are already infused with musts or ought to's and that they thereby serve to perpetuate the moral import and impact of the norms they embody. Emphasis on normative facts amounts to a two-sided attack: it both encourages identification with unconsciously held parental superego pressures, and at the same time it encourages projection of one's repressed nonconformist tendencies. Both of these developments then lead to persecutory attitudes toward that which, in others, is not normative. As I understand it, that's how it has played itself out with regard to gay and lesbian sexual orientations and practices, those much persecuted manifestations of the forbidden, the condemned, the unnameable, and therefore the unthinkable. And that is also how it has played itself out between men and women, organizing intergender relations around sadism and masochism.

It was Freud who prepared us to understand these developments: how, through superego identification and projection, we persecute in

others what we come to condemn and repress in ourselves. We persecute by abuse, derogation, ostracism, neglect, discrimination, and so on,
sometimes grossly and sometimes subtly. Freud showed that what we
do condemn is heavily conditioned by overt and implicit pressures; that
it is not natural, not an inbuilt part of human nature to show sexual bias;
in other words, that kind of discrimination thrives through nurture, not
nature; history, not biology.

More is involved, however, than direct or disguised moral pressure.
We have to take into account the coercive force of language. I touch here
on a very large area of study and will single out for mention only one
aspect of it that has already received much attention, fruitfully so. I refer
to the organization of language and therefore of thinking in binary terms
which pervade identity formation and human relations. It is not just a
matter of good and bad but also, and with special relevance to this essay, masculine and feminine, heterosexual and homosexual, oedipal and
preoedipal, genital and pregenital, paternal and maternal, active and
passive, and so on and so forth. Contemporary critical theory has brought
out how these binary arrangements set up implicit hierarchies of value
in favor of the first term of the two. They also dichotomize much too
much, and they introduce arbitrary assumptions about symmetry.

Much of Freud's formal theorizing was cast in binary and symmetrical terms, even though, clinically, his basic interpretations often did not
observe the constraints imposed by his formal conceptualizations. In
most of his clinical works he gave us mixed and asymmetrical cases,
often called overdetermined, and that is just what we all usually claim
to encounter in clinical work: mixed cases and asymmetries. These cases
replace the balanced black and white contrasts. But nothing really
changes then, for there is still the assumption that what is mixed are
hierarchically valorized and symmetrical opposites. And here we see how
basic constituents of language control our thinking, just as they controlled much of Freud's thinking. We learn from the first to think of
paternal-maternal or masculine-feminine as hierarchically valorized and
symmetrical opposites. Even male and female bodies or genitals are
divided up that way, as in the case of the erect penis and the vagina as a
hole to receive it, as though a "hole" is all there is to it, as though the
vagina is only a "hole" and that that's all it's good for, and as though it's
the only receptive body opening. Before modern anatomy took over,
anatomists considered this vaginal "hole" the penis turned inside out;

in effect, it was another form of setting up ranked opposites even while seeking to deny a fundamental difference between the sexes (Laquer, 1990). The idea of "the opposite sex" epitomizes this way of constructing nature.

Much of my evolution as clinician and theorist has consisted in divesting myself more and more of the idea of opposites, seeing how much mischief has been sponsored by that way of thinking. And I have paid increasing attention to the binding and disruptive power of so-called symmetrical opposites in the thinking of my analysands. So often it turns out that, for them, what seems a simple linguistic convention represents, unconsciously, a powerful and simplistic moral bias, an overwhelming idealization, as well as persecutory or guilty orientations.

Psychoanalytically, the word *opposite* is usually inappropriate and misleading. The better word for it is "difference." The analyst's curiosity should be dedicated to defining and understanding differences. That kind of curiosity is individualizing; it downplays classifying and diagnosing. Thinking along these lines, the noted methodologist of anthropology, Clifford Geertz, recommended "thick description" of the single scene or event or person (1973).

What has evolved in me along with this divestiture of binaries is a tentative, if not suspicious, attitude toward all universalizing propositions about men, women, fathers, mothers, children, child-rearing practices, psychosexual development, and so on. To my mind, all the key issues of psychoanalysis are too saddled with these overambitious generalizations that push us toward classification and diagnosis, and that too often are based on questionable dichotomizations. They get in the way of empathic listening, curiosity, or graphic description. Also they affect adversely appraisals of need for treatment, therapeutic change, and termination. Reductionism replaces good phenomenology and good practice.

To return now to the different sexual practices: It is just these nonconformist practices that threaten particularly those who are polarized by binary thinking and on this basis have become fiercely normative. Polarized men need to buttress their own identities by surrounding themselves in fact or fiction with "dumb cunts" and deriding, ignoring, or defeating other sorts of women, that is, if they even can get past using "dumb cunt" to cover all women. In an equivalent way, many polarized women hope, in *their* binary terms, to develop a solid feminine identity by making sure to marry a man and have children at no matter what psychic cost to them and to scorn those women who don't share these goals; at the same time, they may reduce all men to "brutes." For both types of threatened people, to be normative or conformist is to be worth something, to be justified, to be safe from persecution in the inner world and the outer world.

We are dealing here with what has been called the process of naturalizing, that is, making it seem simply factual that people follow natural norms and defend them vigorously, if not brutally, perhaps even murderously. It was one of Freud's great contributions to denaturalize prevailing convictions about the sexual innocence of children and related convictions about the affects of disgust, shame, guilt, and fear. At the same time, however, and going in the opposite direction in his mode of theorizing and generalizing, he appears now to have been further naturalizing the idea of a heterosexual, genital, reproductive culmination of development. Thus, he could not go all the way with the curiosity that led to his being able to denaturalize as much as he did, which was plenty. When it came to gay and lesbian sexuality, he stopped short. He viewed these sexualities as manifestations of arrested development. For him they were, by implication, forms of pathological development. Ostensibly a nonjudgmental conclusion, implicitly it did reaffirm in a pseudoscientific way the normative morality of his time. For there is no impermeable line between the idea that there is something different about you and something wrong with you, and as a next step, between the idea that something is wrong with you psychologically and something is wrong with you morally. That's why, for instance, children and grownups feel humiliated and vulnerable by admitting publicly that they need psychological treatment, and are, of course, far more vulnerable in the case of acknowledging gay and lesbian proclivities.

What Freud did in the realm of sexual orientation and practices was to mistake a norm as a fact of nature. How he came to do so and what that acceptance entailed I took up in my first large contribution to this topic in the early 1970s. Having noted what I have evolved to as well as developing a broad intellectual context for my ideas about sexual differences, I shall review a few of the main theses in that article, "Problems in Freud's Psychology of Women" (1974). Not only do I still stand by these theses; I now believe that already then I was involved in an historical trend that, in one form or another, has been achieving ever wider acceptance among analysts and at least some segments of the general population. Or, if not acceptance, then at least recognition as a point to be debated. In recounting these earlier theses, however, I won't avoid filling them in further with considerations that date from later years, including the present time. As I said to begin with, I do not see a linear rendition as necessarily the most valid or informative telling of history.

III

A central part of my argument then (and now) is that Freud's Darwinism led him to adopt what I called an evolutionary ethic. Specifically, he viewed the individual as the carrier of the reproductive organs and substances designed to guarantee the survival of the species. Above all, there was to be the successful transmission of the germ plasm from generation to generation. From this point of view, it seemed to him to follow that psychosexual development should culminate in genital, heterosexual, reproductive orientations. Anything else would go against the plan of nature. Whatever its vicissitudes on the way to that endpoint—and, as he showed, there are various phases, modes, zones, pleasures, and pains to encounter along the way—it is only the endpoint that is to be considered natural.

It was in this way that Freud naturalized and moralized normative sexual practices. He did not see that he was making an unwarranted leap from biological theory to moral judgment when he assumed that development *ought to* culminate in reproductivity. Also, he did not see that he was making a moral judgment when he reasoned that, because development *can* proceed to reproductivity, it is *only* the reproductive heterosexual who is the mature, normal, healthy, fully developed person, the better off person, and so, by implication (which he would have consciously repudiated), the person who is a better sort of person than others who have developed differently. Once Freud idealized this form of development, other forms had to be seen as immature, unfortunately arrested, perhaps irremediably so, although under ideal circumstances they might be amenable to the growth-enhancing method of psychoanalysis. Just as in his phallocentric way he regarded the clitoris as a stunted organ, he regarded those who diverged from the norm as stunted people. In his personal stance, he was tolerant; in his analytic formulations, he was not.

Freud was not lacking in what he took to be sound empirical evidence to support his position. He did always aim to be dispassionately objective, and, to be accurate about it, he did a lot better in this emotionally highly charged realm than the bulk of his contemporaries. What I believe happened is that when he looked in depth at his sample of homosexually inclined analysands, he saw much unconscious sexual conflict involving fear, envy, rivalry, resentment over feelings of damagedness, narcissistic excesses, and so on and so forth. This seemed to be the evidence that clinched his point—as though it was not already in his mind as a preconception and a value judgment (Freud, 1887–1904). In fact, however, nothing conclusive follows from Freud's observations of homosexually inclined analysands, for every heterosexual analysand in analysis shows the same or similar conflicts, and it was Freud himself who introduced us to this perception.

There is more behind Freud's conclusions. There is the further observation that, for many heterosexually active analysands, curative effects seemed to derive from the analysis of these unconscious complications of gender identity and predilection. Again, however, nothing conclusive follows from this observation either. Of the various reasons why this is so, I want to emphasize one in particular: Freud's Darwinian ideology committed him to bringing his "immature" analysands to heterosexual reproductive positions, and for their part almost all of his analysands, too, were committed to this goal. Insofar as they were motivated in their analytic work, they wanted to get rid of their unconscious "perverse" and "inverse" tendencies, for that's what their pathogenic repressions seemed now to be about. Freed from these repressions, and helped toward a mixture of renunciation, sublimation, and continued repression, they could hope to succeed in achieving genital heterosexual love, reproductivity, and pleasure instead of suffering. They and Freud were together in this.

I believe that, by and large, it is still that way in the analytic treatment of the great majority of analysands. Heterosexual tendencies are taken for granted; it is conflict over them that is to be examined, understood, and reduced. In contrast, homosexual tendencies are considered central to psychological problems, and it is the temptation to act on them in fact or fantasy that is to be examined, understood, and reduced. Strong cross-gender identifications must be modified, pregenital fixations loosened so far as possible, and the troublesome homosexual tendencies finally subordinated to heterosexual genital primacy. Ideally, the analysand will accept a degree of latent homosexual leaning as natural but idealize its expression through aim-inhibited friendships, empathy, creativity, and so on. Renunciation is the goal. Nowhere in evidence is recognition of the line of argument developed, for example, by Judith Butler (1990): her using Freud's own explanation of the passing of the Oedipus complex, in his monograph *The Ego and the Id* (1923a), to draw other conclusions. Specifically, she read Freud to be showing that identification with the lost oedipal object—the parent of the opposite sex—should favor homosexual resolutions of that complex. Freud mentioned this problem but did not deal with it effectively.

With these points, we have entered the thickets of Freud's idealizing of compulsory heterosexuality and his characterization of the young child as polymorphously perverse. Polymorphous, yes, but why perverse? "Perverse" was meant to include the homoerotic, too. Here, we must confront the general idea of perversion. Listen now to the *Shorter O.E.D.* on Perversion: "turning aside from truth or right; perversion to an improper use; corruption, distortion . . ." (1973). We should not overlook the fact that the history of the word *perversion* includes major legal and religious ideas of impropriety. On that account, "perversion" and "perverse" can be seen to be all the more loaded with moral connotations. Significantly, the illustrative quotation given in the *O.E.D.*, from Bacon, is "Women to govern men . . . slaves (to govern) freeman . . . (are) total violations and perversions of the laws of nature and nations." The *O.E.D.*'s choice of example naturalizes moral condemnation of feminists as well as nonnormative psychosexuality. Remaining for a moment in this etymological context, we can recognize the same bias in the use of the word *straight* for normative sexuality: straight as opposed to what?—crooked, twisted, off the mark?

What, then, might we assume was between the lines of Freud's use of the word *perverse* when he spoke of pregenital sexuality as being polymorphously perverse? I would say that in his theorizing Freud was looking backward from the teleologically prescribed endpoint of Darwinian sexual development. We can anticipate this conclusion from the word *pregenital*, for that word implies that one is speaking of matters that the individual ought to get beyond. It is implied that it is not enough to stay with the words *oral, anal,* or *phallic-exhibitionistic*; it is required to abide by the prescriptive use of the prefix *pre.*

In addition to moralizing genitality as the allegedly natural endpoint, I think an esthetic value judgment is also implied in the idea of genital primacy. Freud argued that oral, anal, and phallic are all well and good as subordinate features of adult sexual life, but that it would go against the ideas of integration and maturity if, instead of sublimating them, one were to linger too long over, or be altogether gratified by, their sensuous potential. Here, the specific forms of integration and maturity that Freud was idealizing derived from his teleology of reproductive sexuality. His idealization includes implications of being decorously pleasing as well as being stable and efficient, or perhaps more exactly being decorously pleasing just because one is stable and efficient. In addition to Freud's era being the era of Darwin in metaphors of reality, it was also the era of the idealized powerful machine. Many concepts of beauty and art smack of that unexamined esthetic value judgment, that is, the judgment that normative moral correctness is essential to beauty. Esthetics serves as a vehicle for moral prescription—among many other uses, of course.

It seems to me, therefore, that in this respect Freud was working in conformity with the moral and esthetic dictates of his culture, and so he was effectively using the language of that culture in a way that tended to fence us all in further. Today, we realize more than ever that language is not just a tool of thought or a vehicle. Words teach us what to think as well as how to think and how not to think. The power is in the word, and parents and educators may themselves be regarded as the vehicles for the words of history, culture, material necessity, and distributions of power. Thus, for example, in the case of the United States military, the effort to combine the words *gay* and *hero* or *gay* and *fighter* fails; it falls on deaf ears in the chambers of Congress, too, as well as of the largely unthinking public that elects so biased a Congress. The combinations are unthinkable. Heroes have to be heterosexual men—by definition—and women, whether lesbian or not, couldn't possibly, really, reliably fight well; at least natural women couldn't. Ask U.S. Senator Sam Nunn. This is not a digression. We are not that far from the thinking of the average traditional analyst or at least from what is prescribed for his or her thinking by much of the analytic literature and the teaching in many training institutes. We tend to be indoctrinated by the extreme naturalization not only of normative sexual practices but of prevailing gender differences—oppositeness of the sexes, so-called.

To begin with, I mentioned curiosity as being the antithesis of rushing to moral judgment. Assuming that psychoanalysis is defined by its particular form of curiosity about the human mind in human relationships, let me now frame this question: How would the consistently curious analyst think and speak about these matters? I've been trying to illustrate some aspects of this way of thinking in what I have presented in my critique thus far. I will be doing more of the same in the remainder of this essay. Obviously, there can be no one way. We are dealing with individual differences in both parties to an analysis.

To continue the argument, I want to return to the prefix *pre*. The word pregenital, on which I have already commented, is closely allied to the word *preoedipal*, even though it does establish a somewhat different center of interest. I maintain that *preoedipal* is also a teleological, implicitly moralistic term. It naturalizes a normative development that has been, from Freud on, usually understood in the sense of the positive oedipal, the crystallization though not the culmination of heterosexual development. The negative oedipal Freud identified and emphasized especially in *The Ego and the Id* (1923a) and he regarded it as the seat of crystallized homosexual love as well as the capacity to identify with the opposite sex. Nevertheless, the negative oedipal remains pretty much neglected in most of his formal theoretical writings as does the mother in his case histories. Further, in his theories this neglected woman remains pretty much the unarticulated sex object of the oedipal boy and rival of the oedipal girl. Therefore, preoedipal refers to what is pre*heterosexual* as well as pre*genital*.

In my 1974 article, I argued, and I am not claiming priority here for every detail of this argument, the arbitrariness of Freud's attributing to penis envy specifically so dominant a role in the lives of all women. He attributed this envy directly to the shock of discovering, at the phase-appropriate moment, the anatomical difference between the sexes (1925). He asserted that the shock is instantly mortifying to the girl, so much so that then and later there remains imprinted on her mind a lasting sense of inferiority that serves as the basis for penis envy. Back then, I argued that Freud had stopped short of asking what he might have been expected to ask if he had continued to exercise his enormous curiosity. Specifically, he didn't ask, "What would there have to be about the girl's development prior to this moment that would make her that vulnerable and would lead her to that position?" But to ask this question is to acknowledge the central role of the child–mother relationship in all psychic development of both sexes. Freud did acknowledge that role somewhat a little later on, but it is apparent that he did so with some uncertainty or ambivalence, for in his concluding *Outline* (1940) he backtracked from this acknowledgment.

Looked at in this light, the prefix *pre* seems to me out of place when discussing the gratifications, frustrations, attachments, and fears during the very first years of development. All of these have to be taken up first on their own terms; their subsequent transformations, if any, should not intrude at the very beginning. At each point, they should be approached with unhampered curiosity. There should be no implication that they are not yet the real thing. Certainly, they usually undergo important transformations during the remainder of development, and Freud did pay much fruitful attention to these developments in the case of both boys and girls. Nevertheless, my entire argument suggests to me that, if anything, the most fitting alternative term for the oedipal is *postdyadic*.

Postdyadic preserves the sense of continuity and transformation in development that is so essential in psychoanalytic thinking. *Postdyadic* has greater heuristic potential. The oedipal triangle is, then, *postdyadic*; the dyadic is not *preoedipal*. Today, many analysts are working on this assumption even though they may not always realize it or say so publicly. To put the matter most conservatively, however, I would assert that, in psychoanalysis, the words *pregenital, preoedipal, perverse,* and *inverse* are disorienting as well as judgmental, and so they tend to limit curiosity about the individual case.

IV

When I began to read the psychoanalytic literature as a sophomore in college, at which time I began my passionate and faithful adherence to it, I had already been thoroughly indoctrinated with all the conventional sexual biases in and by the world in which I grew up. This indoctrination had the forceful assistance of my unconscious infantile fantasy life, itself a variable that was not by any means independent of my upbringing and general cultural–linguistic conditioning. Consequently, Freud's point of view seemed to me inexorably logical, realistic, and scientifically secure. When, some fifteen years later, I began my psychoanalytic training in seminars at the Western New England Psychoanalytic Institute, it all still seemed that way to me. Everything I read and everything I was taught reinforced this point of view. Certainly, tolerance and curiosity were strongly supported, but unconsciously one was discouraged from questioning the established psychosexual order, the presumably natural order of things in the psychosexual realm. Compliance was richly rewarded. Mine was. And, to be sure, the tolerance and curiosity were those of the superior other.

Once I began to teach Freud in my institute, however, some five years after that, I began to formulate, fleetingly, inadmissible questions about Freud's point of view. Briefly, I became aware that Freud's position did not hang together and that it included bias. Nevertheless, it took some more years before I paid sustained attention to these questions. It became harder and harder to teach Freud's psychosexual theory with conviction. Partly, this was because candidates, too, had begun to raise hard questions.

By then, we were all in the protest period of the late 1960s and early 1970s when almost anything previously taken for granted as natural or right or as part of nature was being thrown into question. At that time, saying "the Establishment" was also a way of saying (to paraphrase the Clinton campaign), "It's history, stupid, not biology." Intellectually at least, sexual mores were being challenged, reexamined, and revised. At that time I was working therapeutically with undergraduate students at Yale University. Expectably, they were into all kinds of sexual experimentation and question-raising, too. Further, it was the time of the dropout, the pill, the mind-altering substance, and newly begun coeducation, each of which raised further difficult questions. It was a time when therapy itself came to be widely regarded as part of the problem rather than part of the answer. All this questioning reached the point where many of those in clinical training regarded it as a matter of principle never to come to seminars. In retrospect, I would say that as a result of all these social changes and pedagogical experiences I was prodded to pay more and more attention to my half-repressed questions.

During this time I was studying closely ego psychology and its psychosocial ramifications. Outside of psychoanalysis, I was reading about interpretation in many fields: the humanities and social sciences, especially in literary criticism, cultural and intellectual history, the philosophy of history and other branches of philosophy, anthropology, and feminist papers of that period and earlier. I was becoming more and more sensitized to how culture-bound, time-bound, and gender-bound perspectives establish what we're supposed to take for granted about gender roles, sexual orientations, and distributions of power in general, and equally sensitized to the rhetoric of dominant perspectives. I began to see more clearly that we are limited in what we look for, in what we can see when we do look, the vocabulary available to us to conceive it and tell it, and what we use as the criteria of solid evidence; also that there are many presuppositions we must remain blind to, and so on and so forth. If I had read only psychoanalysis, I would never have gotten as far as I did in being alert to how far ideology extends into what is circulated in psychoanalysis as established fact.

In psychoanalysis, for example, it seems like a straightforward technical principle that in doing character analysis one must render what is ego syntonic, ego alien, thereby making it possible to analyze pathological character traits. That's the way one develops in the analysand motivation for therapeutic change. Taking a second look, however, one realizes how much space this technical principle leaves for the analyst's personal values to be imposed on the analysand. Here we need think only of the ego syntonic homosexual orientation in whatever way that is structured in character, and of how so many analysts tried to make these orientations ego alien or else resignedly thought it was hopeless even to try. It was much the same with those women who had developed in an assertive, competitive way and were not committed to, or even oriented toward, settling down at home as wife and mother.

Another example of much broader scope was the valorization of universalized theory, the kind of theory that Freud was overeager to develop. This valorization continues to burden us in today's plethora of all-encompassing theories of personality development, gender definition, and much more. This theorizing tries to explain too much too fast. Freud's (1887–1904) letters show that he couldn't wait to universalize his formulation of his own Oedipus complex or his interpretation of castration anxiety and penis envy. Today, we realize that, with all the gains that accrue to understanding and therapeutic efficacy from his rapid generalizations, there also accrued built-in negative valuations of women, femininity, and all unconventional sexual orientations and practices. Today, there are more analytic child development theories than one can count, and none of them is based on absolute, incontrovertible, value-free factual findings. They can't be. I believe that this valorization has not yet been sufficiently studied.

In any case, as, back then, I read more, thought more, brought my wider reading and critical theory to bear, I began to teach more effectively and challengingly, and from that change came my 1974 essay on the questions I have been discussing here. I have been at it ever since and not only in the area of sexuality. I have been trying to show in all my writings that all aspects of psychoanalytic theory need to be constantly reexamined with sustained curiosity and with references to newer developments in critical thinking. I keep on finding more and more to challenge, more and more that doesn't hang together, and more and more stimulation of curiosity. Being curious is what goes best with being consistently analytic, especially when it is curiosity about the structure of thought and the entailments of presuppositions, and of course, about moral judgments hidden in the language we use when speaking of individual differences, sexual and otherwise. This book testifies to my commitment to the ideal of sustained analytic curiosity.

References

Abel, E., Ed. (1982), *Writing and Sexual Difference.* Chicago: University of Chicago Press.

Ablon, S. L. (1990), Developmental aspects of self-esteem. *The Psychoanalytic Study of the Child,* 45:337–365. New Haven, CT: Yale University Press.

Abraham, K. (1916), The first pregenital stage of the libido. In: *Selected Papers on Psychoanalysis.* New York: Basic Books, 1954, pp. 248–279.

———— (1921), Contributions to the theory of the anal character. In: *Selected Papers of Karl Abraham.* New York: Basic Books, 1953, pp. 337–392.

———— (1924), A short history of the development of the libido, viewed in the light of mental disorders. In: *Selected Papers on Psychoanalysis.* New York: Basic Books, 1954, pp. 418–501.

Abrams, S. (1990), Orienting perspective on shame and self-esteem. *The Psychoanalytic Study of the Child,* 45:411–416. New Haven, CT: Yale University Press.

Alexander, F., & French, T. M. (1946), *Psychoanalytic Therapy: Principles and Applications.* New York: Ronald Press.

Belsey, C., & Moore, J., Eds. (1989), *The Feminist Reader: Essays in Gender and the Politics of Literary Criticism.* London: Blackwell.

Bernheimer, C. & Kahane, C., Eds. (1985), *In Dora's Case: Freud-Hysteria-Feminism.* New York: Columbia University Press.

Bibring, E. (1953), The mechanism of depression. In: *Drives, Affects, Behavior,* ed. P. Greenacre. New York: International Universities Press, pp. 13–48.

Bion, W. R. (1962), *Learning from Experience.* London: Maresfield Reprints/H. Karnac, 1984.

———— (1967), Notes on memory and desires. *Psychoanal. Forum,* 3:272–273, 279–280.

Blum, H. (1980), The borderline childhood of the Wolf Man. In: *Freud and His Patients*, Vol. 2, ed. M. Kanzer & J. Glenn. New York: Jason Aronson, pp. 341–358.

Breuer, J., & Freud, S. (1893–1895), Studies on Hysteria. *Standard Edition*, 2. London: Hogarth Press, 1955.

Butler, J. (1990), *Gender Trouble: Feminism and the Subversion of Identity.* New York and London: Routledge.

Culler, J. (1975), *Structural Poetics: Structuralism, Linguistics, and the Study of Literature.* Ithaca, NY: Cornell University Press.

——— (1982), Reading as a woman. In: *On Deconstruction: Theory and Criticism after Structuralism.* Ithaca, NY: Cornell University Press, pp. 43–83.

de Lauretis, T. (1984), *Alice Doesn't: Feminism, Semiotics, Cinema.* Bloomington: Indiana University Press.

——— (1986), *Feminist Studies/Critical Studies.* Bloomington: Indiana University Press.

Dickens, C. (1854), *Hard Times.* London: Penguin Classics, 1985.

Eissler, K. R. (1950a), The Chicago Institute of Psychoanalysis and the sixth period of development of psychoanalysis. *J. Gen. Psychiatry*, 42:103–157.

——— (1950b), Ego-psychological implications of the psychoanalytic treatment of delinquents. *The Psychoanalytic Study of the Child*, 5:97–121. New York: International Universities Press.

——— (1953a), Notes upon the emotionality of a schizophrenic patient and its relation to problems of technique. *The Psychoanalytic Study of the Child*, 8:199–251. New York: International Universities Press.

——— (1953b), The effect of the structure of the ego on psychoanalytic technique. *J. Amer. Psychoanal. Assn.*, 1:104–143.

Ellman, M. (1968), *Thinking about Women.* New York: Harcourt, Brace & World.

Erikson, E. H. (1950), *Childhood and Society.* New York: W. W. Norton.

——— (1959), Identity and the life cycle. *Psychological Issues*, Monogr. 1. New York: International Universities Press.

Fairbairn, W. R. D. (1954), *An Object-Relations Theory of the Personality.* New York: Basic Books.

Feldman, M. (1990), Common ground: The centrality of the Oedipus complex. *Internat. J. Psycho-Anal.*, 71:37–48.

Felman, S. (1981), Rereading feminity. *Yale French Studies*, 62:19–44.

Fenichel, O. (1941), Problems of psychoanalytic technique. *Psychoanal. Quart.*

Fish, S. (1980), *Is There a Text in This Class? The Authority of Interpretive Communities.* Cambridge, MA: Harvard University Press.

Fiumara, G. C. (1992), *The Symbolic Function: Psychoanalysis and the Philosophy of Language.* Oxford & Cambridge, MA: Blackwell.

Flax, J. (1990), *Thinking Fragments: Psychoanalysis, Feminism, and Postmodernism in the Contemporary West.* Berkeley: University of California Press.

Frankiel, R. V. (1992), Analyzed and unanalyzed themes in the treatment of Little Hans. *Internat. Rev. Psycho-Anal.*, 19:323–333.

Freud, A. (1936), *The Ego and the Mechanisms of Defense.* New York: International Universities Press, 1946.

Freud, S. (1887–1904), *The Origins of Psychoanalysis: Letters to Wilhelm Fliess,* tr. E. Mosbacher & J. Strachey. New York: Basic Books, 1954.

———— (1900), The Interpretation of Dreams. *Standard Edition,* 4 & 5. London: Hogarth Press, 1953.

———— (1905a), Fragment of an analysis of a case of hysteria. *Standard Edition,* 7:1–122. London: Hogarth Press, 1953.

———— (1905b), Three essays on the theory of sexuality. *Standard Edition,* 7:123–243. London: Hogarth Press, 1953.

———— (1908), Hysterical phantasies and their relation to bisexuality. *Standard Edition,* 9:155–166. London: Hogarth Press, 1959.

———— (1909a), Analysis of a phobia in a five-year-old boy. *Standard Edition,* 10:1–167. London: Hogarth Press, 1955.

———— (1909b), Notes upon a case of obsessional neurosis. *Standard Edition,* 10:151–249. London: Hogarth Press, 1955.

———— (1911), Formulations on the two principles of mental functioning. *Standard Edition,* 12:213–226. London: Hogarth Press, 1958.

———— (1912a), The dynamics of transference. *Standard Edition,* 12:97–108. London: Hogarth Press, 1958.

———— (1912b), Recommendations to physicians practising psycho-analysis. *Standard Edition,* 12:109–120. London: Hogarth Press, 1958.

———— (1912c), Totem and Taboo. *Standard Edition,* 13:1–161. London: Hogarth Press, 1955.

———— (1914a), Remembering, repeating, and working through. (Further recommendations of the technique of psycho-analysis, II). *Standard Edition,* 12:145–156. London: Hogarth Press, 1958.

———— (1914b), On narcissism: An introduction. *Standard Edition,* 14:67–102. London: Hogarth Press, 1957.

———— (1915a), Observations on transference-love (Further recommendations on the technique of psycho-analysis, III). *Standard Edition,* 12:157–171. London: Hogarth Press, 1958.

———— (1915b), Instincts and their vicissitudes. *Standard Edition,* 14:109–140. London: Hogarth Press, 1957.

———— (1916), Some character-types met with in psycho-analytic work. *Standard Edition,* 14:309–333. London: Hogarth Press, 1957.

———— (1917a), Mourning and melancholia. *Standard Edition,* 14:237–258. London: Hogarth Press, 1957.

———— (1917b), On transformations of instinct as exemplified in anal erotism. *Standard Edition,* 17:125–134. London: Hogarth Press, 1955.

———— (1918), From the history of an infantile neurosis. *Standard Edition,* 17:1–122. London: Hogarth Press, 1955.

———— (1920a), Beyond the Pleasure Principle. *Standard Edition,* 18:1–64. London: Hogarth Press, 1955.

———— (1920b), The psychogenesis of a case of homosexuality in a woman. *Standard Edition,* 18:145–172. London: Hogarth Press, 1955.

——— (1921), Group Psychology and the Analysis of the Ego. *Standard Edition*, 18:65–143. London: Hogarth Press, 1955.

——— (1923a), The Ego and the Id. *Standard Edition*, 19:1–59. London: Hogarth Press, 1961.

——— (1923b), The infantile genital organization: An interpolation into the theory of sexuality. *Standard Edition*, 19:139–145. London: Hogarth Press, 1961.

——— (1925), Some psychical consequences of the anatomical distinction between the sexes. *Standard Edition*, 19:241–258. London: Hogarth Press, 1961.

——— (1926), Inhibitions, Symptoms and Anxiety. *Standard Edition*, 20:75–172. London: Hogarth Press, 1959.

——— (1931), Female sexuality. *Standard Edition*, 21:221–243. London: Hogarth Press, 1961.

——— (1933), New introductory lectures on psycho-analysis. *Standard Edition* 22:1–182. London: Hogarth Press, 1964.

——— (1937a), Analysis terminable and interminable. *Standard Edition*, 23:209–253. London: Hogarth Press, 1964.

——— (1937b), Constructions in analysis. *Standard Edition*, 23:255–269. London: Hogarth Press, 1964.

——— (1940), An outline of psychoanalysis. *Standard Edition*, 23:139–207. London: Hogarth Press, 1964.

Fromm-Reichmann, F. (1950), *Principles of Intensive Psychotherapy.* Chicago: University of Chicago Press.

Geertz, C. (1973), *The Interpretation of Cultures: Selected Essays.* New York: Basic Books.

Gilligan, C. (1986), *In a Different Voice: Psychological Theory and Women's Development.* Cambridge, MA: Harvard University Press.

Gillman, R. D. (1990), The oedipal origin of shame: The analysis of a phobia. *The Psychoanalytic Study of the Child*, 45:357–375. New Haven, CT: Yale University Press.

Goldberger, M. & Evans, D. (1985), On transference manifestations in male patients with female analysts. *Internat. J. Psycho-Anal.*, 66:295–310.

Green, A. (1991), Interview with André Green. *Psychologist Psychoanalyst*, 11(4):10–18.

——— (1992), History of psychoanalysis. *Psychologist Psychoanalyst*, 12(2):7–8.

Grossman, W. I. (1992), Hierarchies, boundaries, and representation in the Freudian model of mental organization. *J. Amer. Psychoanal. Assn.*, 40:27–62.

——— Kaplan, D. M. (1988), Three commentaries on gender in Freud's thought: A prologue to the psychoanalytic theory of sexuality. In: *Fantasy, Myth, and Reality: Essays in Honor of Jacob A. Arlow*, ed. H. Blum, Y. Kramer, A. K. Richards, & A. D. Richards. Madison, CT: International Universities Press, pp. 339–370.

Hanly, C. (1990), The concept of truth in psychoanalysis. *Internat. J. Psycho-Anal.*, 71:375–383.

Hartmann, H. (1939), *Ego Psychology and the Problem of Adaptation,* tr. D. Rapaport. New York: International Universities Press, 1958.

——— (1951), Technical implications of ego psychology. *Psychoanal. Quart.*, 20:31–43.

———— (1960), *Psychoanalysis and Moral Values*. New York: International Universities Press.

———— (1964), *Essays on Ego Psychology: Selected Problems in Psychoanalytic Theory*. New York: International Universities Press.

———— Kris, E., & Loewenstein, R. M. (1964), Papers on Psychoanalytic Psychology. *Psychological Issues*, Monogr. 14. New York: International Universities Press.

———— Loewenstein, R. M. (1962), Notes on the superego. *The Psychoanalytic Study of the Child,* 17:42–81. New York: International Universities Press.

Heimann, P. (1950), On counter-transference. *Internat. J. Psycho-Anal.*, 31:81–84.

Horney, K. (1967), *Feminine Psychology*. New York: W. W. Norton.

Jacobson, E. (1964), *The Self and the Object World*. New York; International Universities Press.

———— (1971), *Depression: Comparative Studies of Normal, Neurotic, and Psychotic Conditions*. New York: International Universities Press.

Jacobus, M. (1986), *Reading Woman: Essays in Feminist Criticism*. New York: Columbia University Press.

Jahoda, M. (1958), *Current Concepts of Positive Mental Health: A Report to the Staff Director, Jack R. Ewalt*. New York: Basic Books.

Jones, E. (1955), *The Life and Work of Sigmund Freud*, Vol. 2. New York: Basic Books.

Joseph, B. (1985), Transference: The total situation. *Internat. J. Psycho-Anal.*, 66:447–454.

———— (1988), Object relations in clinical practice. *Psychoanal. Quart.*, 57:626–642.

———— (1989), *Psychic Equilibrium and Psychic Change: Selected Papers on Betty Joseph*, ed. E. G. Spillius & M. Feldman. London: Tavistock/Routledge.

———— (1993), A factor militating against psychic change: non-resonance. In: *Psychic Structure and Psychic Change: Essays in Honor of Robert S. Wallerstein, M.D.,* ed M. J. Horowitz, O. F. Kernberg, & E. M. Weinshel. Madison, CT: International Universities Press, pp. 311–325.

Kalinich, L. J. (1993), On the sense of absence: a perspective on womanly issues. *Psychoanal. Quart.*, 62:206–228.

Kernberg, O. F. (1975), *Borderline Conditions and Pathological Narcissism*. New York: Jason Aronson.

Klein, M. (1940), Mourning and its relation to manic-depressive states. In: *The Writings*, Vol. 3. London: Hogarth Press, pp. 344–369.

———— (1946), Notes on some schizoid mechanisms. In: *The Writings*, Vol. 3. London: Hogarth Press, pp. 1–24.

———— (1957), Envy and gratitude. In: *The Writings*, Vol. 3. London: Hogarth Press, pp. 176–235.

———— Heimann, P., Isaacs, S., & Riviere, J. (1952), *Developments in Psycho-Analysis*. London: Hogarth Press.

Kohut, H. (1971), *The Psychoanalysis of the Self: A Systematic Approach to the Psychoanalytic Treatment of Narcissistic Personality Disorders*. New York: International Universities Press.

———— (1977), *The Restoration of the Self*. New York: International Universities Press.

Kris, E. (1939), On inspiration. In: *Psychoanalytic Explorations in Art.* New York: International Universities Press, 1952, pp. 291–302.

——— (1952), *Psychoanalytic Explorations in Art.* New York: International Universities Press.

——— (1956), The recovery of childhood memories in psychoanalysis. *The Psychoanalytic Study of the Child,* 11:54–88. New York: International Universities Press.

——— (1975), *The Selected Papers of Ernst Kris.* New Haven, CT: Yale University Press.

Laquer, T. (1990), *Making Sex: Body and Gender from the Greeks to Freud.* Cambridge, MA: Harvard University Press.

Lewontin, R. C. (1991), Facts and the factitious in natural sciences. *Criti. Inqu.,* 18(1):140–153.

Loewald, H. (1960), On the therapeutic action of psychoanalysis. *Internat. J. Psycho-Anal.,* 41:16–33.

Loewenstein, R. M. (1975), A contribution to the psychoanalytic theory of masochism. *J. Amer. Psychoanal. Assn.,* 5:197–234.

——— (1982), *Practice and Precept in Psychoanalytic Technique: Selected Papers of Rudolph M. Loewenstein.* New Haven, CT: Yale University Press.

Mahony, P. (1986), *Freud and the Rat Man.* New Haven, CT: Yale University Press.

Miller, N. K., Ed. (1986), *The Poetics of Gender.* New York: Columbia University Press.

Moi, T. (1985), *Sexual/Textual Politics: Feminist Critical Theory.* London: Methuen.

——— (1987), *French Feminist Thought: A Reader.* London: Blackwell.

Orgel, S. (1995), A classic revisited: K. R. Eissler's "The Effect of the Structure of the Ego on Psychoanalytic Technique." *Psychoanal. Quart.,* 64:551–570.

Racker, H. (1968), *Transference and Countertransference.* New York: International Universities Press.

Reich, A. (1951), On counter-transference. *Internat. J. Psycho-Anal.,* 32:25–31.

——— (1953), Narcissistic object choice in women. *J. Amer. Psychoanal. Assn.,* 1:22–44.

——— (1954), Early identifications as archaic elements in the superego. *J. Amer. Psychoanal. Assn.,* 2:218–238.

——— (1960), Pathological forms of self-esteem regulation. *The Psychoanalytic Study of the Child,* 15:215–232. New York: International Universities Press.

——— (1973), *Psychoanalytic Contributions.* New York: International Universities Press.

Ricoeur, P. (1977), The question of proof in psychoanalysis. *J. Amer. Psychoanal. Assn.,* 23:835–872.

Rizzuto, A. M. (1991), Shame in psychoanalysis: The function of unconscious fantasies. *Internat. J. Psycho-Anal.,* 72:297–302.

Rothstein, A. M. (1994), Shame and the superego: Clinical and theoretical considerations. *The Psychoanalytic Study of the Child,* 49:263–277. New Haven, CT: Yale University Press.

Rubin, G. (1984), Thinking sex: Notes for a radical theory of politics. In: *The Lesbian and Gay Studies Reader*, ed. H. Abelove, M. A. Barale, & D. M. Halperin. New York and London: Routledge, 1992, pp. 3–44.

Rukeyser, M. (1978), *The Collected Poems*. New York: McGraw-Hill.

Sandler, J. (1976), Countertransference and role-responsiveness. *Internat. Rev. Psycho-Anal.*, 3:43–48.

———— Ed. (1987), *Projection, Identification, Projective Identification*. Madison, CT: International Universities Press.

———— Rosenblatt, B. (1962), The concept of the representational world. *The Psychoanalytic Study of the Child*, 17:128–145. New York: International Universities Press.

Sartre, J. P. (1938), *Nausea*, tr. L. Alexander. New York: New Directions, 1949.

Schafer, R. (1968), *Aspects of Internalization*. New York: International Universities Press.

———— (1968), The mechanisms of defence. *Internat. J. Psycho-Anal.*, 49:49–62.

———— (1970), An overview of Heinz Hartmann's contributions to psychoanalysis. *Internat. J. Psycho-Anal.*, 51:425–446.

———— (1972), Internalization: Process or fantasy? *The Psychoanalytic Study of the Child*, 51:265–268. New Haven, CT: Yale University Press.

———— (1974), Problems in Freud's psychology of women. *J. Amer. Psychoanal. Assn.*, 22:454–485.

———— (1976), *A New Language for Psychoanalysis*. New Haven & London: Yale University Press.

———— (1978), *Language and Insight: The Sigmund Freud Memorial Lectures, 1975–1976, University College, London*. New Haven, CT: Yale University Press.

———— (1981), *Narrative Actions in Psychoanalysis: Narratives of Space and Narratives of Time*. Worcester, MA: Clark University Press.

———— (1983), *The Analytic Attitude*. New York: Basic Books.

———— (1984), The pursuit of failure and the idealization of unhappiness. *Amer. Psychol.*, 39:398–405.

———— (1990), The search for common ground. *Internat. J. Psycho-Anal.*, 71:49–52.

———— (1992), *Retelling a Life: Narration and Dialogue in Psychoanalysis*. New York: Basic Books.

———— (1992a), Men who struggle against sentimentality. In: *Retelling a Life: Narration and Dialogue in Psychoanalysis*. New York: Basic Books, pp. 116–127.

———— (1992b), Response to André Green. *Psychologist Psychoanalyst*, 12(1):7.

———— (1992c), Response to André Green. *Psychologist Psychoanalyst*, 12(1):8.

———— (1993), On gendered discourse, and discourse on gender. *Psychiatry and the Humanities*, 14:1–21.

———— (1994a), Gendered discourse and discourse on gender. *Psychiatry and the Humanities*, 11:1–21.

———— (1994b), Commentary. *Psychoanalytic Inquiry*, 14:462–475.

———— (1995), Blocked incorporation. Typescript.

———— (1997), *The Contemporary Kleinians of London*, Madison, CT: International Universities Press.

Scott, J. (1988), *Gender and the Politics of History.* New York: Columbia University Press.

Segal, H. (1964), *Introduction to the Work of Melanie Klein.* New York: Basic Books.

———— (1986), *The Work of Hanna Segal: A Kleinian Approach to Clinical Practice.* London: Free Association.

Shorter Oxford English Dictionary on Historical Principles, The, 2 vols., rev. ed. C. T. Onions. Oxford: Clarendon Press, 1973.

Showalter, E., Ed. (1985), *The New Feminist Criticism: Essays on Women, Literature, and Theory.* New York: Pantheon.

Silverman, M. (1980), A fresh look at the case of little Hans. In: *Freud and His Patients,* Vol. 1, ed. M. Kanzer & J. Glenn. New York: Jason Aronson, pp. 95–120.

Spence, D. P. (1982), *Narrative Truth and Historical Truth: Meaning and Interpretation in Psychoanalysis.* New York: W. W. Norton.

Spero, M. H. (1984), Shame: An object-relational formulation. *The Psychoanalytic Study of the Child,* 39:259–282. New Haven, CT: Yale University Press.

Steiner, J. (1993), *Psychic Retreats: Pathological Organizations in Psychotic, Neurotic, and Borderline Patients.* London & New York: Routledge.

Stone, L. (1961), *The Psychoanalytic Situation.* New York: International Universities Press.

Szasz, T. (1961), *The Myth of Mental Illness: Foundations of a Theory of Personal Conduct.* New York: Hoeber-Harper.

Thelma & Louise (1991), Produced by R. Scott and M. Polk, directed by R. Scott, starring S. Sarandon and G. Davis, Percy Main Productions, MGM.

Waelder, R. (1936), The principle of multiple function: Observations on overdetermination. *Psychoanal. Quart.,* 15:45–62.

Winnicott, D. W. (1958), *Collected Papers: Through Pediatrics to Psycho-Analysis.* New York: Basic Books.

Yorke, C., and collaborators (1990), The development and functioning of the sense of shame. *The Psychoanalytic Study of the Child,* 45:377–409. New Haven, CT: Yale University Press.

Name Index

261

Subject Index

Author's note: Because this is a psychoanalytic book, certain concepts (e.g., anxiety, guilt, fantasy, conflict, aggression, and sex) are used or implied so frequently that indexing each one of these would be of no use to the reader.